# Genghis Khan

**British Library Cataloguing in Publication Data**
Hoang, Michel
  Genghis Khan.
  1. Mongol Empire. Genghis Khan. Great Khan of the Mongols
  I. Title
  950.2092

    ISBN 0-86356-293-0
    ISBN 0-86356-288-4 pbk

First published as
*Gengis-khan*
by Librairie Arthème Fayard, Paris 1988
© Librairie Arthème Fayard 1988

English translation copyright © 1990 by
Saqi Books and New Amsterdam Books

This edition first published 1990
Saqi Books, 26 Westbourne Grove,
London W2 5RH

Typeset by AKM Associates (UK) Ltd, Southall, London
Printed and bound in Great Britain
at The Camelot Press, Trowbridge, Wiltshire.

# Genghis Khan

Michel Hoang

Translated from the French
by Ingrid Cranfield

**Saqi Books**

*The publishers and the translator wish to acknowledge the invaluable help of Emeritus Prof. Charles R. Bawden, F.B.A., and of Dr David Morgan and Prof. Tim H. Barrett of the School of Oriental and African Studies, University of London, in advising on the translation of certain names and terms.*

# Contents

# Maps

# Chronology, 1155–1227

## Central Asia

1155  Birth of Temüjin

1177  Alliance with Jamuγa
c. 1182  Marriage to Börte
1185  Temüjin forms alliance with the Kereyid
1187  Temüjin elected Khan
1194  Temüjin deteats Tatars

1205  Death of Jamuγa
1206  Temüjin proclaimed Genghis Khan
1207  Tibet becomes vassal state to Genghis Khan
1209  Invasion of the Minyak lands

1218  Proclamation of the *jasaγ*. Occupation of the Qara-Khitai

1222  Temüjin meets Chang Chun

## China

1164  Peace initiatives between Song (southern China) and Jin (northern China)

1194/5  Emperor Ning Zong (13th emperor of Song dynasty, ruled 1194/5–1224/5)

1211  Beginning of Genghis Khan's Chinese campaign
1215  The Mongols occupy Beijing

1220  Seizure of Jinan
1221  Alliance between Mongols and Song against Jin

*Chronology*

1223 Return of Genghis Khan
to Mongolia

                                   1224 Peace between Song and
                                         Jin

1227 Death of Genghis Khan.     1227 Destruction of Xixia
Empire divided up among        empire
his descendants

| Near East | | Europe | |
|---|---|---|---|
| | | 1165 | Philip Augustus |
| 1171 | Saladin, master of Egypt | | |
| | | 1189 | Third Crusade |
| | | 1190 | Death of Frederick Barbarossa |
| | | 1192 | Enrico Dandolo, doge of Venice |
| 1193 | Death of Saladin | | |
| | | 1202 | Fourth Crusade |
| 1204 | Crusaders occupy Constantinople | | |
| | | 1209 | Albigensian Crusade |
| | | 1214 | Battle of Bouvines |
| 1218 | Crusader invasion of Egypt | | |
| 1218 | Mongol conquest of Khwārezm | | |
| 1220 | Genghis Khan takes Samarkand and Bukhara | | |
| 1221 | Genghis Khan takes Merv (Mary) | 1221 | Fifth Crusade. Mongol victory over Russians and Kipchak |
| | | 1226 | St Louis (Louis IX) becomes King of France |

# A Note on Names

Pinyin has been used for Chinese names.

Modern Mongol has been used for terms and modern names. For historical names and terms, the English edition of *The Secret History of the Mongols*, edited by Francis Cleaves (Harvard University Press, Boston, Mass., 1983), has been followed. Some of the terms and names include the Greek letter *gamma* ($\Gamma$, $\gamma$), which in pronunciation is something between a *g* and a *k*.

Place names follow *The Times Atlas of the World* (Times Books, London, 1987), although some traditional or historical names are given supplementarily for ease of recognition (e.g. Yellow River for Huang He).

The names of Genghis Khan and of Kublai Khan are so well known in English that to alter them would be pedantic. However, the designation *khan* is properly spelt *qan* and this is the spelling that has been adopted in other names (e.g. Qabul Qan).

# Introduction

The story of Genghis Khan cannot be told in the same way as can that of his contemporary, King Philip Augustus of France. In the middle of the twelfth century, when the future conqueror of Asia was born, the Mongols constituted neither a true nation nor a kingdom or empire in the Western sense of the terms. Living in groups of tribes each under the authority of a khan, they formed and broke alliances from time to time with the passing of the years. They lived nomadic lives in a region that had no frontiers defined either by geography or history and no fixed capital. It was not until 1220, several years before his death, that Genghis Khan set himself up in a military camp at Karakorum. In 1235, Ögödei, his successor, made this site, meeting place of the caravanserai routes, into a 'town'. Even then, it was only in 1264 that Kublai Khan, grandson of the conqueror, mounted the throne in Beijing — then named Khanbaliq, the khan's town — from then on, the seat of government of the khanate.

As late as the mid-thirteenth century, the Mongols remained ignorant of writing, a fact which makes it difficult to gain access to their history. The obscurity which clouds this period also cloaks in uncertainty Genghis Khan's first 30 years, or nearly half his life: details on this are scanty and not very reliable. The historian must therefore have recourse to foreign sources or the Mongol chronicles written after the conqueror's death.

The life of Genghis Khan has been the subject of two Mongol chronicles, of which there are two versions, probably written shortly after the death of the great khan. The first chronicle, *Altan debter* (*The Book* [of the dynasty] *of Gold*), traces the history of the line of Genghis Khan. The original has been lost, but a Chinese version of 1263 is extant, *Shengwu qinzhenglu* (*Account of the Campaigns of the Warrior Emperor Saint*), and there is also a Persian version, dating from 1303, *Jāmi at-tawārīkh* (*Collected Annals*), further edited by Rashīd al-Dīn, who himself noted that the original was only fragmentary.

The second chronicle, *Mongqol-un niucha tobcha'an* (*Secret History of the Mongols*), includes a mythical genealogy of Genghis Khan, an epic account of his reign and part of that of Ögödei, his son and successor. The original of this too has been lost, and it is not known in what language it was written (vertical Uighur-Mongolian, Sino-Mongolian, or another language altogether?). Nor is it known when it was written: René Grousset inclines towards 1252; Uemura Seiji, towards 1228; but a passage in the chronicle suggests that it was completed in July of the Year of the Rat, which would be 1240. Like *The Book of Gold*, the text of *The Secret History* was intended for the eyes of Genghis Khan's family only, a fact which explains the title.

This chronicle has more than once been imperfectly copied by Chinese scribes, who kept only its essence in a book they entitled *Yuanchao bishi* (*Secret History of the Yuan Dynasty*), after the dynastic name Genghis's descendants adopted when they enthroned themselves at Beijing after conquering China in 1279. Apparently working from several versions of the manuscript, the scribes transcribed the original in ideograms, in accordance with an interlinear translation, and then translated it into the vernacular. Not until the nineteenth century did the Russian Sinologue Kafarov (better known by the name Palladius) translate this text into his language. His work of erudition cleared the way for new translations by Western specialists, notably that of Paul Pelliot, begun around 1920 and unfinished at the time of his death, then those, respectively, of Haenisch, in German; Kozin, in Russian; and, more recently, Cleaves, in English; in the Far East, several Chinese and Japanese Mongolists (including Li Wentian, Chen Yuan and Kanai Yasuzo) have made studies of *The Secret History*.

Because of the poverty of its sources, *The Secret History* has assumed a singular place in Mongol studies. The Sinologue Arthur Waley called it a 'pseudo-historical novel' because, as he demonstrated, it was difficult to prove or disprove the facts related in it. None the less the historian who compares translations of *The Book of Gold* and *The Secret History* will find that, although the works were written quite independently, the accounts related in them are almost identical. It is therefore possible to distinguish the true historical thread in these books from the episodes that are based on legend, although deciding which is which is of course not always easy. These chronicles, especially *The Secret History*, allot generous space to epic flights: the bards used an oratorical idiom that remained undimmed right up until the beginning of the twentieth century and whose heritage still pervades the epic poetry of Mongolia today: the chanting of this poetry by the indigenous people has been the subject of study and collection by philologists and musicologists.

On Genghis Khan himself there are other Mongolian, Chinese or Persian texts, written long after the events they relate and drawing heavily on older works: *Yuan Shi, The Precious History*, or the *Chronicle* of Sayang Sechen. The Chinese texts generally conform to the official historiography of the imperial court. Accordingly, they attach considerable importance to Chinese affairs proper and show very little interest in what was happening in the world of the 'barbarians'.

We have also the accounts of several medieval travellers — William of Rubrouck, Giovanni da Pian del Carpini, Odoric of Pordenone, Marco Polo — who have left us colourful descriptions of daily life among the Mongols, as well as those of the Taoist sage Chang Chun and of some Chinese ambassadors, whose evidence was often very subjective. Middle Eastern sources, equally, are partial in both senses of the word, since their authors — Rashīd al-Dīn, Ibn al-Athir, Juwaynī, Nasawī — suffered from nomadic invasions, but they contain valuable historical and ethnographical information.

It is worth adding that the history of the Mongols in the thirteenth century was almost exclusively recounted by foreigners: Chinese, Persians and Arabs, as well as Armenians, Georgians, Russians and Westerners. It is history by proxy, and therefore biased; sometimes it is conventional; sometimes it is false; often it is doubtful. While the world awaited the discovery of these later works, *The Secret History of the Mongols* remained a fundamental reference, since it was the first and virtually the only written source of information on the relevant period.

Since the Lamaist Buddhist temples, which might have provided safe repositories for documents relating to Mongolia in the thirteenth century, were destroyed, it is archaeology that has shed most light on Genghis Khan. For many years Soviet researchers studied the steppe civilizations (at the Andreyevo and Minusinsk sites), but most attention has been attracted by excavations in Mongolia itself. At the beginning of the century, the Russian archaeologist Kozlov discovered the old Xixia city of Kara Khoto, destroyed by the Mongols at the time of Genghis Khan. Digs have taken place here since, and one might have thought that documents in the Xixia language — a script that has still not been fully deciphered today — would yield information not only on the Xixia empire but also on the Mongol empire under Genghis Khan. In the course of excavations in the far north of Mongolia, along the Siberian borders (Noin Ula), archaeologists have uncovered sepulchres of Xiongnu chiefs (first millennium BC), which contained objects that, without significant alteration, must have been familiar to the Mongols of the thirteenth century: hangings, tent panels decorated with animal or anthropomorphic motifs, felt mosaics mounted on canvas, etc. Soviet (Kiselev), Mongolian (Perlée), and Japanese (Mori Masao) researchers have made studies of these epochs. Moreover, Chinese archaeologists have excavated several ancient sites in eastern Inner Mongolia (Tsagaan Suburga, Boroqoto), including imperial residences from the Khitan dynasty of the Liao (eleventh and twelfth centuries). Mongolist scholars have moreover studied and compared at least twenty important archaeological sites which contain ancient cities and fortifications attributed by some to Genghis Khan. Lastly, finds at Karakorum, the capital city of the Mongols after the death of the great khan, have included utensils, weapons and Chinese ceramics dating from the thirteenth century, but the excavations have not brought to light any written documents. In many respects, Mongolia is still virgin territory.

The discovery in 1974 of the huge terracotta army in the tomb (not yet fully excavated) of the Qin Chinese emperor Shi Huangdi (221–206 BC), followed in 1987 by the digging up of another army of bronze soldiers in the Chinese province of Sichuan (*c.* 1000 BC), would lead one to believe that Far Eastern archaeology is destined to make a great and swift contribution to our knowledge of vanished civilizations. Perhaps the sepulchre of Genghis Khan himself will also one day come to light. The hope of Mongolists rests on archaeology. Does not a Mongol proverb, almost as old as time itself, remind us that 'to build high, one must dig deep'?

# 1
# The Funeral Cortège

*Let me tell you a strange thing too. When they are carrying the body of any Emperor to be buried with the others, the convoy that goes with the body doth put to the sword all whom they fall in with on the road, saying: 'Go and wait upon your Lord in the other world!' For they do in sooth believe that all such as they slay in this manner do go to serve their Lord in the other world.*

**Marco Polo,**
**The Book of Ser Marco Polo, the Venetian,**
**Concerning the Kingdoms and Marvels of the East**

At the end of August 1227, just as the then undisputed overlord of the greatest empire in the universe was breathing his last, one word, one single word counted for more than any other in the world: the secret.

Chroniclers have claimed that the great khan had taken a bad fall from his horse, a fall from which he never recovered. The legate of Pope Innocent IV, Giovanni da Pian del Carpini, returning from Mongolia in 1247, reported that he had been struck by lightning. Still others have maintained that he drank a poisoned beverage served to him by a concubine. But no one can be certain of the exact cause of his death.

After months of weakness, and sensing that he was very close to death, Genghis Khan Temüjin had summoned to his bedside his two sons and his most trusted lieutenants to dictate his will and give them his final words of advice. For several days, the khan conducted lengthy discussions with his most intimate circle of followers. His principal preoccupation was the war and the state of the empire. Above all he wanted to ensure that the succession would proceed smoothly so that the power of the khanate would remain unbroken. Everyone agreed that the news of the imminent demise of the great khan must not be allowed to slip out. Concealment was a requirement that was not only absolute but also more pressing than

*19*

any other. Even at this early stage, politics demanded that facts be falsified.

In front of the imperial tent, a long spear decorated with black felt was staked into the ground, its head in the earth, as a sign that the sovereign had been taken ill. An armed guard was deployed all around the tent. No one, on pain of instant death, was allowed to enter within except with explicit permission. The great conspiracy of silence had begun. It was to last three months.

Temüjin was about 66 years old. His hair and beard had long since turned white. He had come to lay siege to Ningxia (now called Yinchuan), the fortified capital of the Minyak empire of the Xixia, against whom he had been waging war for over a year, and he had retreated to the other side of the Yellow River (Huang He), not far from the Great Wall, on high ground, a place where he could find some refreshment, for he was already aware that it would not be long before he entered the realm of his brave ancestors.

The great khan was unable to summon up enough strength to leave his bed. There was a proverb from the mists of time: 'When a Mongol is separated from his horse, what is there left for him to do but die?' So it was that, in spite of the care and the invocations of the shamans, Temüjin began to see the shadows of death closing in on him. And the end came to the 'conqueror of the world by virtue of the Eternal Blue Heaven', the man who was known as Genghis Khan, 'oceanic khan', 'universal khan', because his empire stretched almost from one side of the earth to the other and, the chroniclers said, 'it took a whole year to travel from one end of it to the other'.

For the first time, after a dark age that had lasted centuries, 'all who lived under felt tents', that is, the entire Mongol people, were reunited under the same banner. From the shores of the Pacific Ocean to the banks of the Caspian Sea, from the deep and sombre ravines of the Siberian taiga to the granite foothills of the Himalaya, the vast shield of central Asia bowed to the wish of Temüjin, Genghis Khan. By the sword or by diplomacy, through terror or persuasion, Temüjin had subdued or enslaved a hundred peoples. Merkid, Xixia, Naiman, Kirghiz, Tatar, Georgian, Chinese, Khitan, Uighur, Bulgar, Persian — all, shamanist, Moslem, Buddhist or Nestorian Christian, all trembled at the mere mention of his name.

The kingdoms conquered by the great Mongol khan no longer exist. In some cases the names of the people have changed, but on a modern atlas

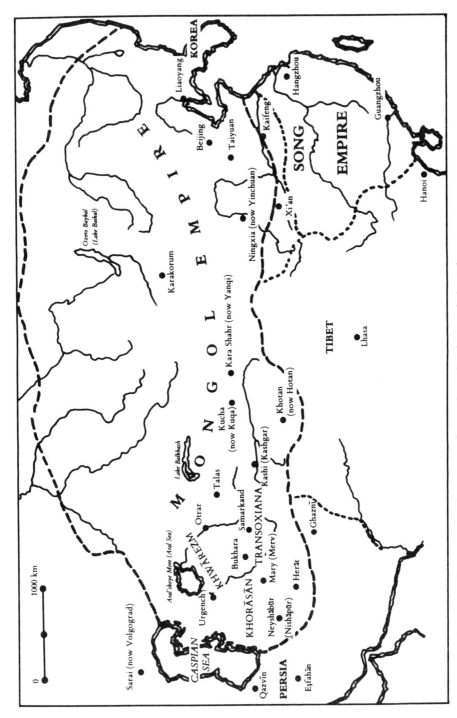

Map 1.  The Mongol Empire at the Time of Genghis Khan's Death (1227)

21

one can identify the approximate limits of that colossal empire: it comprised the region of present-day Mongolia; Manchuria; the easternmost part of the Soviet Union; North Korea; the northern Chinese provinces of Hubei, Shandong, Shanxi, and part of Henan; the autonomous regions of Ningxia and Inner Mongolia; the vast zones of western China — Xinjiang and most of Qinghai — the Soviet republics of Kirgiziya, Tadzikistan, Turkmeniya, Kazakhstan, and Uzbekistan; all of western Iran and three-quarters of Afghanistan; and lastly the fringes of central Siberia as far as the western shore of Lake Baikal (Ozero Baykal). Various military expeditions also ravaged Iraq, the Indus valley in western Pakistan, Genoese territories on the Black Sea, and Russian principalities situated between the Dneper and Volga rivers. These raids, some of them victorious, served as armed reconnaissances, paving the way for later conquests. One by one, cities of opulence — Beijing, Samarkand, Bukhara, Kabul, Herāt — fell before the assault of the Mongol armies. Nothing could stem their relentless and devastating tide.

This formidable empire, this immense bloc, had been forged by Temüjin at the point of the sword in the course of the last 20 years of his life. Prior to this, he had struggled for another 20 years to unite the entire nomadic Mongol people. And this empire must not only survive but be consolidated and expanded still further. So had Genghis Khan resolved.

Above all, the demise of the great khan must do nothing to slow down the military operations that were already in progress. The war against the Xixia of the Minyak had been going on too long already. Not far from the Yellow River, the massive fortifications of the city of Ningxia protected it from a frontal assault and it had been necessary to surround it to reduce it to a state of complete isolation. Failing the remotest hope of being rescued by reinforcements, its defenders had at last yielded: at the close of negotiations with the Mongols, Li Yan, sovereign of the Minyak empire, had taken the painful decision to offer Temüjin his surrender within one month. If the death of the khan could be kept secret, the Xixia ruler would capitulate according to plan. If, on the other hand, the embattled Xixia learned of the death of Temüjin, there was a risk that they might postpone their surrender or even renege altogether.

Li Yan was therefore left in ignorance of the fatal turn of events. When he presented himself, together with his escort, before the Mongol lines, he was seized and promptly executed according to the posthumous instructions of Genghis Khan. Then the Mongols entered the besieged city and put almost the entire population of Ningxia to the sword.

War and politics were not the only matters at issue. The death of the khan caused a power vacuum. Temüjin had indeed divided up his vast empire between his sons: Jochi, the eldest, had received the steppes of western Siberia and Turkestan and had been promised the territories which it was anticipated would be conquered in the west. But he died in February 1227, just a few months before his father, and his inheritance was passed to his sons, of whom Batu is now the best known. To Chagatai was allotted the ancient kingdom of Qara-Khitai, eastern and western Turkestan. Ögödei, the third son, was to be formally invested with the office of the great khanate; he was Genghis Khan's designated successor and the whole immense region on both sides of Lake Balkhash (Ozero Balkhash) was bequeathed to him. Finally, as was the custom, the youngest, Tolui, was to be endowed with the original inheritance, cradle of the Mongol people, the territory at whose heart lay the sources of the three great rivers of Mongolia: Orhon Gol, Tuul Gol and Kerulen (Herlen Gol). In addition, he was to be given command of 100,000 of the 130,000 warriors who then comprised the Mongolian army. Thanks to this superbly trained cavalry, Tolui was able to fix his hopes of conquest on a very specific goal: south China.

Carving the empire up in this way into huge continental principalities was not by any means a prelude to its disintegration. Quite the contrary. Temüjin had made very plain what the scheme of his conquests was. Chroniclers claim that on his deathbed he gave an arrow to each of his sons and grandsons and asked them to break it, which they did with ease. Then, taking an equal number of arrows, the khan gathered them together in a bundle and again asked his descendants to break them. When they had tried and failed, Temüjin spoke these words of advice: 'Stay united like this bundle of five arrows, so that you will not be broken individually.' When the bequests had been shared out, each of the beneficiaries was to vow strict obedience to Ögödei, who was given the mission of realizing Genghis Khan's great imperialist dream in the Orient, the Occident, and the South. The Korean peninsula, south China and the Turkish and Arab-Persian Middle East were to be the next objectives for the conquerors of central Asia. The empire was to march on.

Messengers were despatched to ride at full speed to all points of the compass to announce the death of the supreme sovereign to the princes and tribal chiefs, and to summon them to the *quriltai* — the tribal council of apanaged·princes and nobles — where their successors would be designated and the provisions of the deceased's will made known regarding the transition of power.

Certain expeditionary corps were camped at the foot of the Caucasus, others along the Indian borders of Kashmir, but each commander involved in the supreme council had received the order to abandon all current operations, to leave conquered cities in the charge of a garrison and to hasten to the great *ordo*, the travelling court of the khan, which was at that time in the area of Karakorum. Although horses were provided at stages all along the way, some travellers took three months to reach the heart of Mongolia. Meanwhile, the general staff had prepared to thwart any possible attempts at rebellion by vassal tribes, who were always quick to rise up whenever political trouble erupted or the central grip on the reins of power slackened.

Leaving behind it the bulk of the army engaged in sacking the Minyak capital and sorting out the captives, the armed guard of Temüjin threw itself into the final preparations for accompanying the sovereign's body back to the land of his birth. Political exigencies made this a double mission: once again, internal stability as well as diplomacy necessitated the conspiracy of silence that surrounded the fate of the master of the world.

In those last days of August 1227, abandoning the Great Wall, that interminable stone caterpillar, to the first squalls of autumn, an astonishing procession left the loop of the Yellow River (Huang He) bound for the north across the vastness of the Gobi desert. The caravan comprised a thousand warriors of Temüjin's Imperial Guard. This was the élite of the troops of Genghis Khan, the guard of honour recruited from the bravest swordsmen and mounted bowmen. Frequently marked by ugly scars, they had fought on the battlefields of Transoxiana or Khwārezm, serving their leader with loyalty of the highest order and with total disregard for their own lives. Behind them rolled the army, encumbered by heavy waggons filled with loot, and hundreds of animals: fresh horses, yoked oxen, mules and saddled camels. The vehicle which carried the mortal remains of the great khan was drawn by about fifteen oxen, and a heavy escort surrounded the hearse, which was adorned by banners streaming in the wind like long horses' tails. Behind them again came straggling little groups of sheep, which mounted shepherds ceaselessly headed back towards the main flock.

The long caravan advanced as rapidly as the terrain permitted: sometimes this consisted of endless stretches of broken stones which hindered the animals' progress, sometimes it was a flat, monotonous expanse of hardened earth, the surface crumbly after recent storms. Here and there this desert landscape was interspersed with bald patches of thin yellowed grass or with muddy depressions. From the tops of the knolls that receded into the distance beside the depressions, it would have been difficult to discern the slow cortège snaking its way across this stony wilderness: they looked, man and beast, like moving islets tossed on a dead sea.

Wearing on their heads bright turbans or felt caps, and clad in filthy pelisses glistening with grease, most of those in the caravan were armed. Indifferent to the clamour of the herd and to the pervasive odour of sweat emanating from the sheep, some of the men dozed as they rode. For days on end, the long procession made its way from one oasis to another, aided by ghostly landmarks which only a few of the horsemen were able to discern and interpret. At night, men and animals huddled together for protection from the icy north wind which swept down over the fires of branches and dry grass. But by day the heat rose fiercely, bringing myriads of horseflies which, swarming in voracious but elusive clouds, tormented man and beast alike. The halts at the often evil-smelling reed-beds barely quenched the cattle's thirst. There were few springs and it was often necessary to get what they could from a thin layer of muddy water covering the earth: the animals eagerly scrabbled at the mire. In arid regions, clumps of camel grass and black saxaul were the only nourishment the caravaneers had, and many animals had to be sacrificed.

Other rigours were added to the scarcity of water and vegetation. Sometimes, with the suddenness of lightning, the wind would spring up. Bitter and blinding, gravel laden with ochre dust would begin to swirl with ferocious force, smothering every living thing in its suffocating shroud. The raucous cries of the cameleers would make the terrified beasts quickly lie down. But very soon the sandstorm would muffle the din. Every trace of life seemed suddenly to shrink, dissolve and become buried in the turbulence of the atmosphere. Wind, sand and stone remained the sole masters of this space, in which neither men nor animals had any significance. And then the discordant howling of the tornado ceased. As suddenly as the storm had arrived, the sky became calm and, within an instant, only silence seemed to reign over the infinite void.

The caravaneers were used to the roughness of the terrain, to the caprices of the climate and to the difficulties of these long journeys. Each man knew he must stay alert and brace himself with all his strength to resist the hostility of nature. Each knew he must control his mount, unsaddle frightened animals in a single deft movement, reassure them and be friend and colleague to them in adversity. Temüjin's thousand warriors did not deviate a foot from their mission: faithfully to conduct their deceased leader to the land of his birth and to his eternal home which awaited beyond the chaos. Those who, for years, had had no other clothes than hides, no shelter but felt and no weapons other than bronze ones had returned from their distant conquests with their waggons full of shimmering silk stuffs, voluminous sacks of fine flour, brightly-coloured ceramics and precious stones. Those who had never been anything but simple shepherds and skilful horsemen, never certain of getting enough to eat, had, thanks to the master, the great khan, become invincible warriors, conquerors of unlimited pastures, lords of the entire world.

The caravan marched on for some weeks, passing through the semidesert of the Gobi to the steppes of Mongolia, and everywhere it spread death. If a herd of dziggetai (wild asses) or some frightened ibex appeared on the horizon, a swarm of horsemen would immediately break away from the troop, followed by a pack of hounds, and round them up with deadly efficiency. When, after a frantic gallop, they had captured the wild beasts, the horsemen would kill them outright with sword thrusts or a volley of arrows. Animals taken thus were, according to the requirements of ancient rituals, offered as a funerary sacrifice. Doubtless, flights of wild geese, jerboas which quickly dived into the safety of their burrows and numerous other animals slipped through the net of this pitiless slaughter. If they did manage to escape it was only because an arrow shot by an archer is less swift than the flight of a bird, and a spearhead cannot match the massive strength of the boulder behind which the rodent cowers.

There was no vengeance in these brutal killings. It was simply that received orders had the force of law: until a new order was issued, nobody must either learn of or disclose the death of the khan. Every hunter who crossed the caravan's path, every shepherd guarding a flock, every encampment where people might see and recognize the hearse with its funereal markings, all had to die instantly. Only the elimination of witnesses guaranteed the secret of the state. Thus was put to death every human being — man, woman or child — who had the misfortune to encounter the thousand-strong caravan of guardsmen of the dead Temüjin. From the Great Wall to the heart of Mongolia, long after the funeral cortège had passed by, the bodies of the anonymous victims remained set in their absurd configurations of surprise and horror until wild animals came to scent and then devour their remains. These scattered corpses were merely the dross of the history of the Mongol power over the universe.

This macabre episode surrounding the end of Temüjin has been recounted only by the Persian chroniclers and by Marco Polo. Chinese chronicles are silent on the subject. Nevertheless most historians have accepted the fairly reliable testimony of the Persian authors because the barbaric practices of which they tell seem to correspond with Genghis Khan's mode of rule.

The cavalcade halted when the scouts reported that the imperial camp was only two days' ride away. They had already made contact with advance sentinels who were keeping watch in the area surrounding the *ordo* of Karakorum. An escort of warriors was thus despatched, and soon there appeared, from all points of the horizon, horsemen who had come to receive their dead leader in his movable ancient capital.

Even before the banner-bearing heralds had betrayed the truth that the khan was dead, the news had spread with astonishing speed through the *ulus* — the Mongol people and nation. When, on the approaches to Karakorum, the cortège at last passed through the first circle of chariots that ringed the city, a silent crowd was already gathered there. Men had stepped out of countless scores of felt tents: driven by curiosity, every officer and groom, every freedman and slave had hastened to be present when the funeral procession passed. No doubt there were many whose faces registered deep shock. Even those among the conquered, captives reduced to slavery or pressed into service, stared unblinkingly, and many of the fierce warriors of the *ordo* seemed transfixed by the force of their emotion. For the death of a god carves a deep rift in people's habits and certainties. Gradually consternation gave way to hysteria. Holding their children up high so that they might see the hearse, women shrieked and wailed and sometimes burst into fits of sobbing. Genuine grief was to be followed by the ritual grief of the great 'heartbroken lament' which opened the imperial funeral ceremony.

The waggon that bore the mortal remains of Temüjin was rolled up to the enclosure reserved for sons of the khan, chiefs of clans, the *noyans*, and high-ranking army officers. Then the crowd parted to allow the shamans, *beki* and *emchi*, to pass. All wore long kaftans covered with esoteric motifs — coloured plaits, arrowheads, animal tails. On their heads they wore strange caps of bear, wolf or marmot skins, sometimes decorated with coloured pearls. Some carried large flat drums which they beat slowly with bent mallets; others droned out weird, unearthly-sounding chants, whose tones were now extremely deep and low, now shrill and plaintive. Entering into a trance, the shamans executed expressive motions to the accompaniment of shouts and harsh cries that grated on the ear. Then leather bottles of *airag*, fermented mare's milk, were brought in and the high priests poured it into cups and sprinkled the contents towards all four horizons, up towards the sun, and finally over the funeral waggon. These were the ritual offerings to Tenggeri, the Supreme Blue Sky, who, it was believed, would, from his unfathomable vastness, partake of the libations.

The chants and libations went on for days. Then the *noyans*, clan chiefs, and members of Genghis Khan's extended family gathered before old Börte, widow and first wife of Temüjin, who had borne him several sons, and paid her the customary respects. Several more days were to pass before all the clan chiefs had arrived to join the *ordo* of Karakorum.

At last the shamans deemed the moment propitious to conduct the body of the khan to the mountain which was to be his place of everlasting repose. Dressed in robes of state and a cloak of precious silk, Temüjin was placed within a nest of five coffins. His body was lifted onto a heavy waggon draped with imperial banners and, amid the lamentations of the Mongol people, Temüjin embarked on his last journey. Not long since, on the slopes of one of the wooded hills which the Mongols considered sacred places, in the heart of the Burqan Qaldun massif, now known as the Hentiyn Nuruu (Hentiy chain), he had miraculously found refuge when he had come up against his enemies insufficiently armed. It was there too that he had invoked Tenggeri, the Eternal Blue Sky, supreme deity of the Mongols, at a fateful turning-point in his life. And lastly it was there that the three great rivers, Orhon Gol, Tuul Gol and Kerulen (Herlen Gol), which brought their life-giving waters to the meadows of his ancestors, had their source.

Tradition has it that Temüjin was buried at the foot of a great tree up in the mist-swathed hills. An enormous ditch was dug and the great khan's fully erected felt tent was lowered in prior to the burial there of his mortal remains. Jewels, arms and receptacles filled with food were placed beside jars of milk and *airag*. Whether it was customary at that time to kill slaves destined to serve their master in the hereafter is not known; perhaps a simulated burial occurred instead, recalling the earlier practice. Nor is it known whether horses were interred with their saddles, bits and bridles, but several authors have referred to the sacrifice of disjointed horses set up on supports close to the tomb. Thanks to these accumulated offerings, the great khan was able to cross into the next world provisioned with foodstuffs to fortify the body and milk spirits to warm his heart, and accompanied by a herd of mares and stallions on which to ride into eternity.

Once the funeral ceremonies were over, the location of the sepulchre became a secret, and a guard fiercely prevented anyone from approaching. Moss, grass, and shrubs were allowed to grow and slowly take possession of the burial mound. As the seasons went by, the vegetation grew denser, until at last the slopes of the Hentiy mountains were entirely covered by forest.

Today no one can recall which mountain bore the name Burqan Qaldun. Some claim that the Mongols know and have kept the secret to themselves for nearly eight centuries. To the south of the Huang He (Yellow River), in the Ordos region, some of the original inhabitants point out to curious travellers sites that they say house objects belonging to the great khan: a sword, a saddle, a bow or a horn. A tumulus conceals the remains of his courser. Legends are still related of a curse that afflicts those who seek to profane the sepulchre: a khan suddenly went blind when he tried to disinter some relic; Moslems who had broken the taboo lost the use of their limbs. It has even been suggested that a phantom town, the 'city of Genghis Khan', exists somewhere on the steppe.

Nevertheless, to this day no one has succeeded in discovering the sepulchre of Genghis Khan Temüjin, one of those rare conquerors who might well have earned the title 'cosmocrat'.

# 2
# Son of the Steppe

*His father Yesügei the Hardy was very valiant, and his clan,
known as the Kiyad Borjigin, are renowned for their valour. But
the courage and bravery of Temüjin surpass those of all other
men.*

**Léon Cahun, *La Bannière bleue***

## The Emperor with Cat-like Eyes

The only contemporary portrait that is a likeness of Genghis Khan is now
in the Historical Museum of Beijing, in a collection of ancient paintings
representing the Yuan emperors, the Mongol dynasty which dominated
the 'Middle Empire' (China) between 1279 and 1368, and whose founder,
Kublai Khan, received at his court the famous Venetian merchants of the
Polo family. Prominent in this gallery of official portraits is that of
Kublai's grandfather, Temüjin, who united the steppe nomads and whom
the Mongol sovereigns considered the 'Great Patriarch' (*Taizu*) of the
Yuan dynasty. Executed by a Chinese artist following the conquests of
the great khan, this portrait of the man who forged a mighty empire
doubtless bears a close resemblance to the historical model, even if it has
been stylized like almost all the Chinese paintings of this genre. All other
later portraits — Persian miniatures from Tabrīz, Chinese paintings or
European illustrations — are merely interpretations that owe much to
the imagination of the artists, some representing the Mongol khan in the
guise of a Persian prince, or even in Western dress and with the features
of a European monarch.

Let us pause before this square of stretched silk, on which we see the portrait, outlined in ink, of the Mongol conqueror, his head turned slightly to the left. His massive bulk corresponds closely with the thickset type common amongst Mongols today. Is it his age that has given weight to the sovereign's silhouette? The face is full, fairly strong; the nose rather long and unremarkable; the mouth finely drawn. His hair is greying, as are the straightish eyebrows, the moustache which droops down over the corners of his mouth and the Chinese-style beard. From the lines etched across his rather high forehead it would seem that the man was well into his fifties, but the artist may have tried to lend majesty to his subject by making him appear older, perhaps even endowing him with the long beard worn by ancient sages, for it is well known that the Chinese accord respect to people of advanced years, age being equated with knowledge and experience. His cap clears the ear, which is rather long-lobed, a sure sign of great wisdom, since that, according to tradition, was the shape of the Buddha's ear.

Temüjin wears a cap of light fur which covers the back of his neck, such as was worn at that time by nomads, and his robes are crossed over to the right, in Chinese fashion. This detail is important: like the Europeans who believed that only the 'noble savages' wore feathers on their heads, so the Chinese for long considered that men who fastened their robes on the left — that is, on the other side — could not lay claim to 'civilized' status. In their eyes, the fact that the nomads living beyond the Great Wall fastened their garments as Chinese women did was yet another indication of their barbaric customs. It is quite possible that the court painter, as an afterthought, to please the patron who commissioned the portrait, may have felt it desirable to flatter his subject by correcting the manner of his dress. But it is equally likely that the khan, who was familiar with Chinese customs and in constant contact with military advisers and technicians who were either Chinese or had adopted Chinese customs, chose to dress in Chinese fashion towards the end of his life.

According to rare eye-witness accounts, the Mongol conqueror was tall and robust, with sparse grey hair and 'cat-like' eyes. These descriptions, which date from 1222, that is, just five years before the sovereign's death, accord quite well with the portrait kept in the Beijing Museum, except for the inexplicable 'cats' eyes'. Did this mean that the khan had clear, round feline eyes, or that he seldom blinked? Obviously there is no way of knowing. Whatever the explanation, the artist indicated no peculiarity in his subject's gaze, though he did give the emperor the characteristic eyes of the people of the Far East, and they are divided vertically by a bar like those of typical Mongols.

This painting is one of a series of official portraits of sovereigns. It was formally commissioned and, like portraits today, gave nothing away to fantasy: the image of Genghis Khan is set, uncompromising and true-to-life, like an identity photo in a police file. At first glance, the face seems almost expressionless. However, on closer examination one can discern in his look an unquestionable expression of gravity, authority and even severity; of great forcefulness, but tempered by an obvious tranquillity. The simplicity of his dress and the absence of ornaments or honorific signs add to the dignity of the man. Here we almost have the portrait of a Confucian man of letters on a silk background. In fact, the portrait of the khan tells us more about certain things peculiar to Chinese society in that era than about the subject himself.

## The Central Asian Void

An enormous sphere, often hidden behind a mass of thick cloud. A ball on which one can make out, more or less clearly, vast blotches marking the extent of the seas and oceans. Slabs, some light, some dark, which are the continents, lapped, in this strange sculpture, by these waters. And then, here and there, often indistinct, the folded wads of mountain chains and the sinuous threads of the longest rivers: this is the vision of planet Earth one might see from the moon. Of humanity there is no trace, nor any sign of the hand of man on the landscape.

And yet, if by chance some astronauts were to look more carefully at our planet, they could, without the aid of optical instruments, make out the Great Wall of China: flowing from the Yellow Sea on the Pacific coastline to the borders of the Gobi in the heart of central Asia, the gigantic wall is the only work springing from the spirit and hand of man that is visible to the naked eye at that distance. Like a stone dragon snaking its powerful coils around a large part of the Chinese earth which fed it, this immense work of military architecture has defied the elements for 2,000 years. Historians say that it took only twelve years, some two centuries before the Christian era, for it to be built, on the orders of the sovereign who founded the Qin dynasty. During the course of the building, which in its magnitude matches the works ordered by the pharaohs, hundreds of thousands of peasants forcibly uprooted from their land perished at the foot of 'the world's longest cemetery'.

If the illustrious tyrant played a decisive role in the construction of the

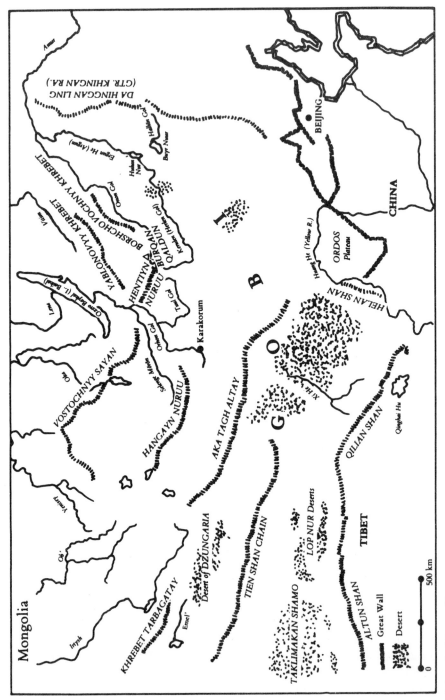

Map 2. Mongolia

Great Wall, as he doubtless did, it would seem certain that this consisted merely of connecting several fortification systems that had been built one or two centuries previously in the time of the Warring States. Indeed the *Zhou Li* (*Ritual of the Zhou*) reports that towards the fourth or third century BC a specification had already been drawn up for an 'officer for fortifications, charged with the repair of defences and walls, such as interior and exterior walls, and interior and exterior ditches'. Another chronicle, the *Shu Jing* (*Classic of History*), mentions a prince of Lu who, in the eleventh century BC, exhorted his troops thus: 'On the eleventh day of the cycle, I shall march against the barbarians of Xiu . . . Prepare your stakes and your planks because, on the eleventh day of the cycle, we shall erect our earthworks.' Several centuries before Christ, Chinese strategists had therefore built ramparts of beaten earth, encased in shuttering, defensive works that were gradually consolidated with stones and bricks, until the Qin emperor, founder of imperial China, had recourse to improved techniques of masonry.

The Great Wall, which is so vast that no photograph could begin to represent the totality of it, extends for nearly 6,000 kilometres, counting a number of secondary structures. For want of repairs — the imperial treasury was empty more often than not — many sections of the ramparts have fallen into ruin, battered more severely by the elements than by the ravages of man. Until the Ming dynasty, which died out in 1664, the Chinese made great efforts to ensure the wall's upkeep. During these centuries, the Great Wall marked both the physical and the geographical boundary between the Chinese empire and the barbarian world of the steppes.

The fact that one of the most advanced nations of the time conceived, constructed and maintained such a system of fortifications says a great deal about the threat that it was seeking to dam up: the nomads. And the fact that generations of Chinese emperors, strategists and engineers, at ruinous cost and with the forced labour of hundreds of thousands of men, tried to cut themselves off behind the ditches, the *chevaux de frise*, the watchtowers and the battlements of the Great Wall raises questions about the origin and power of these despised but feared barbarians who were the ancestors of Genghis Khan.

People have long liked to imagine the ancient nomads of central Asia — Huns, Tatars, Mongols, Tungus and others, all somehow connected and indistinguishable from one another in one amorphous human mass — rising up in sudden surges from the vast windswept steppes. Their sole language would have been the sword, their sole activity plunder. They would have come in savage hordes, pounding down in waves, as brutal as they were unexpected, to raid the fertile lands of the civilized world and immediately lay them waste. The womb from which these Asiatic nomads sprang lay somewhere else, vague, unnamed, unnameable; a huge limitless void without culture, temples or cities, without states or laws; a hellish region of death and desolation. The reality, altogether more complex, deserves that we pause for a moment to survey the expanses that gave birth to the Mongol conquerors.

Ignored for centuries not only by Europeans but also by Chinese, Indians, Persians, and Arabs, central Asia remains one of the least known parts of the globe. The ancient Western world was mute on the subject of this region, treated by historians and geographers alike as *terra incognita*, while the annalists of ancient China for the most part pass over it, a place of profound barbarity best left alone. Between the seventh and the eighth century, some information begins to emerge about this area, thanks to the accounts of Chinese Buddhist pilgrims and, a little later, of Moslem travellers. In the Middle Ages, under the sovereigns of Genghis Khan's dynasty, the *pax mongolica* imposed by Genghis and his successors facilitated the movement of people from place to place. Various explorers crossed central Asia, and some have left us remarkable descriptions, notably the Flemish William of Rubrouck, the official envoy of St Louis (King Louis IX); the Italians Marignolli, Odoric of Pordenone, and Giovanni da Pian del Carpini; and best known of them all, the Venetian trader Marco Polo. Chroniclers from the Middle East, such as Rashīd al-Dīn or Juwaynī, also wrote valuable accounts of the Mongol invasions and their consequences.

It was as much due to physical as to political barriers that the continent for so long resisted the advance of Western man. After the empire of Genghis Khan was painfully split up, central Asia turned in on itself and the Far East was to be reached, not any longer by the caravan route, but only by the caravel route. A great darkness that was to last almost four centuries fell on this huge region. It continued until Jesuit missions to Mongolia and the Capuchins began to make occasional incursions. It was not until the nineteenth and twentieth centuries that genuinely scientific expeditions finally opened up the heart of Asia. It is to the curiosity and obstinacy of these explorers, as well as to expansionism — the Russian Academy of Sciences played an important role in these explorations — that we owe the gradual dispersal of the last blanks on the map.

Tibet, in particular, was for a long time forbidden to *piling* (strangers). In 1740, the few Capuchins living there had to return to China after their expulsion by the authorities in Lhasa. Even in the nineteenth and twentieth centuries, at a time when the last shadows on the planet were retreating before the advance of exploration, Tibet, locked from within against Westerners, defended itself from the gaze of the curious. Like so many others, the Russians Przhevalsky, Pievtsov and Grumm-Grzhimaylo; the Swede Sven Hedin; Carey from Britain; the Frenchmen Bonvalot, Henri-Philippe d'Orléans and Grenard; and, closer to our time, other less well-known travellers, notably Mme Lafugie, from France, all found their access barred to the holy city. To enter it, a very few travellers, disguised as pilgrims and knowing a smattering of Tibetan, had to muster extraordinary resources of stubbornness: such was the case with Fathers Gabet and Huc, in 1846; then of Harrer and the 'Parisian' Alexandra David-Neel. London managed to plant some observers — half explorers, half secret agents — amongst the merchants and Indian pilgrims travelling in caravans: in 1904, Colonel Younghusband succeeded in entering Lhasa, though at the head of an armed column. Others, such as Dutreuil de Rhins or the missionary Rijnhard, paid the ultimate price for attempting to penetrate these inviolate regions.

**A Harsh Environment**

Formed of mountain massifs and high plateaux extending from Siberia in the north to India in the south, and from China in the east to the present-day Moslem Soviet republics in the west, high Asia is a gigantic geological complex, and source of some mighty rivers — Huang He (Yellow), Jinsha Jiang (Yangtze Kiang), Lancang Jiang (Mekong), Nu Jiang (Salween), Ganga (Ganges), Indus, Syr-Dar'ya and Amudar'ya — which permitted the development along their courses of old sedentary Eastern civilizations. The mountain chains which make up the region — Altay, Altun Shan, Karakoram, Tien Shan, Aka Tagh, Himalaya, etc. — have, by and large, an east–west orientation; there the highest peaks on earth are to be found, the result of geological folding in which the great continental plates of Siberian Angara in the north and Indian Gondwana in the south collided with ancient land projections, while the Tien Shan and Altun Shan massifs were shaped by Alpine-type folding. Erosion, accelerated by extremes of the continental climate, carved out deep valleys. Along the Tibetan border, the Tien Shan and Altay are regions of rather sharp relief, while in central Tibet, western Turkestan and

Mongolia there are vast plateaux, punctured by great closed basins such as the Qaidam Pendi and the largest part of Mongolia.

The roughness of the terrain is matched by empty and monotonous landscapes. Millennia of frost, rain, and wind have eroded the flanks of the rocky massifs, causing the basin floors to collect considerable quantities of geological detritus. In certain regions, in times of storm, the soil turns to powder and swirls about, and the air is darkened by clouds of dust particles. This is the loess, well known to geologists and geographers, and called *toprak* by the Turks and *huang tu* (yellow earth) by the Chinese. Precipitation turns it into a muddy paste, but subjected to the fierce heat of the sun it becomes rock-hard. Ochre-yellow or brownish, this dust retains very little moisture. In northern China it can attain a thickness of anything from 15 to 100 metres. When the water table rises in the piedmont regions the earth becomes very fertile: grain-bearing soils in northern China, grasslands in Mongolia and oases on the edge of the Tarim. But this fertility disappears on the plateau, where the soils, thin and unstable, are constantly swept by the wind. In Turkestan there are therefore zones of shifting dunes transforming the landscape into a strange, surreal scene which has astonished many a traveller in a caravan. In other areas, the waters that run off high ground may evaporate in the space of a few hours, leaving behind the occasional bit of sterile crust.

So Mongolia may properly be described as a region of imprecise extent and without natural frontiers. In the north are the upper basins of the great Siberian rivers: the Irtysh, the Yenisey and the Amur. In the north and west, mountain chains: the Altay, which culminates in a peak of 4,600 metres; the Govĭaltay and the Gurvan Sayhan Uul, somewhat lower. In the centre, chains of forested hills, the Hangayn Nuruu in the west and the Hentiy, which are connected with the Yablonovyy Khrebet mountains of eastern Siberia. The territory is high (on average over 1,500 metres above sea level) and never descends below 500 metres. The entire southern fringe looks like a sterile steppe broken by desert zones: the *gov* (from which we have the name Gobi). The Chinese call it Han-hai, the dried-up sea, since for hundreds of kilometres there is nothing to be found there but sand and pebble.

These arid desert landscapes, these endless stretches of pebble, over which loom sometimes snowcapped peaks, have been described by travellers, often using the same terms. Marco Polo in his *The Description of the World* (*The Book of Ser Marco Polo*) wrote, on entering Mongolia:

Lop is a large town at the edge of the Desert which is called the Desert of Lop . . . The length of this Desert is so great that 'tis said it would take a year and more to ride from one end of it to the other. And here, where its breadth is least, it takes a month to cross it. 'Tis all composed of hills and valleys of sand, and not a thing to eat is to be found on it.

Doubtless the Venetian exaggerated the dimensions of the Gobi somewhat, but the Swede Sven Hedin, in 1900, gave an almost identical account:

A solitude of poignant sadness. In the north of the Lop Nur, the dunes lend a certain variety to the landscape, and the sparse dead trees in the desert recall the life that formerly animated what is now dead earth. Here, on the other hand, the monotony is absolute; in these parts sterility has reigned at all times. No movement on the ground, and nowhere any trace of vegetation. The soil is smooth as a floor; everywhere there is a compact sheet of tough clay which, in an earlier epoch, was covered by the waters of the lake.

The climate reflects the landscape: harsh and brutal. The Asian monsoon, which brings a refreshing seasonal rainfall, does not penetrate as far as the heart of central Asia. Ulan Bator, today's Mongolian capital, which is at about the same latitude as Paris, undergoes, in summer, the heat of the Sahara and, in winter, polar temperatures. The temperature range is considerable: in June the mercury may climb to 45°C while in January it falls to around –30°C, with sudden dips as low as –50°C. The last snowfalls have been known to occur in May, even in the very first days of June, and the season of bad weather sometimes begins suddenly in June. After leaving Lyons in April 1245, the Italian Franciscan Giovanni da Pian del Carpini found this climate 'strangely irregular': 'In high summer, when other countries are experiencing spells of great heat, lightning strikes with a frightening crash and creates mass terror and destruction among the people. In the same season, the country is subjected to plentiful falls of snow. The wind whips up icy storms to the point where it is difficult to ride a horse.'

At the turn of the twentieth century, Sven Hedin described it in similar terms:

The sun rises, the heat becomes terrible in the eddying clouds of gad-flies. The sufferings which these flies cause us are, at times, quite intolerable . . . After the last night's march, we are exhausted, man and beast. I throw myself down into the shade of the first tamarisk I come to and fall into a deep sleep until the sun starts to burn my head. In the daytime, the thermometer has sometimes risen to 40°C in the shade.

It is June 1900. Two months later, the Swedish explorer notes: '14th August. During the night the temperature fell to –3.2°C. The ground, hardened by frost, offers some resistance as we begin the day's journey, but gradually it softens and by afternoon it has become a frightful sea of mud.'

It is a climate marked by extremely violent contrasts, with considerable temperature variations: the sun shines intensely for a good part of the year, but the wintry spells are interminable. The weather is at its most clement in the autumn: the sky is clear, the winds light, the cold at night fairly mild, while the warmth of the sun's rays is generous. Very quickly, however, the harshness of winter returns in force and the gusts of wind, as though seized by destructive frenzy, lay flat the sparse vegetation of the steppe.

## The Living World
Nevertheless, these vast steppes, which extend almost uninterruptedly from the borders of Manchuria to the gates of Europe, are not entirely sterile. Where the dry subtropical climate — as in Iran — does not make a desert of the land, the steppes are carpeted with a complexity of vegetation. Wherever humidity sets in, life begins to blossom forth. Vegetation grows along the banks of great stretches of water, such as the Onon Gol, the Kerulen (Herlen Gol) or the Orhon Gol rivers; near the small lakes and ponds that appear infrequently in the tundra and run away into the sands; and on the shaded upland slopes, while the sunny slopes begin to resemble tundra that has been afflicted by baldness.

The forested zones which extend beyond the great Siberian taiga, making the landscape gloomy, comprise quite a number of varieties of tree: pine, fir, larch, black and silver birch, aspen and willow. In the pleasant season of the year, on the wooded uplands which the Mongols call *qang yai*, there appear in brazen profusion vast numbers of wild plants: forget-me-not, mallow, columbine, clematis, iris, gentian, rhubarb, peony and rhododendron. Wild animals feed on these: massive elk, bear, lynx, roebuck, and the maral or Siberian stag celebrated in Mongolian mythology. It is also fur country: squirrel, wolverine, marten and sable, much sought after by trappers, and even snow leopard. On more open ground, where grass alternates with stones, wild roses and honeysuckle are still to be found growing, and, as in all cold areas, shrubs with edible berries. Where the land becomes semidesert the vegetation thins out, but wild plants send up the occasional shoot: blood-coloured panic-grass and tufted sheep's fescue.

On the high plateaux that signal the nearness of Tibet the vegetation is sparser: here one may meet dziggetai, the timid wild donkey; hare; and pika, which look like prairie dogs. This is also the domain of the yak, an enormous, long-haired variety of cattle with an outstanding capacity to withstand cold. Aquatic birds gather around swamps, favourite prey for the raptors which they attract to those areas.

It is the steppe that constitutes the true face of Mongolia. Where aridity does not itself cause sterility, the development of grassland is subject only to the constraints of the climate. Here grow pasture grasses: hair-grass, orache, tufted stipa grass and artemisia. On rockier ground there is the tenacious couch grass, caragana and bulb plants such as onion, wild garlic, and tulip. In summer, for some weeks, the steppe is covered with a shock of colour of every imaginable kind. There live herds of timid dzehyran (Persian gazelle) and saiga, along with strange wild sheep with curved horns, which, according to the Franciscan William of Rubrouck, were used to make large drinking cups. This is also the home of the wild Bactrian camel, small in stature, unpredictable in nature; the wild ass; and also the famous small Mongol horses resembling tarpans, described by Przhevalsky, which were directly descended from a prehistoric race and which the Mongols had hunted for meat before they took to using them as mounts.

Great flocks of birds inhabit these regions: common partridges and larks, jackdaws and crows. There are also many birds of prey, which the Mongols used to train for falconry. Marco Polo speaks of tame lions, leopards, wolves and eagles, but there is no real evidence that the Mongols used these animals, except to employ falcons and eagles for hunting:

> The Emperor hath numbers of leopards trained to the chase, and hath also a great many lynxes taught in like manner to catch game, and which afford excellent sport. He hath also several great Lions, bigger than those of Babylonia, beasts whose skins are coloured in the most

beautiful way, being striped all along the sides with black, red, and white. These are trained to catch boars and wild cattle, bears, wild asses, stags, and other great or fierce beasts. . . . When they are to be so employed the Lions are taken out in a covered cart, and every Lion has a little doggie with him. There are also a great number of eagles, all broken to catch wolves, foxes, deer, and wild goats, and they do catch them in great numbers. But those especially that are trained to wolf-catching are very large and powerful birds, and no wolf is able to get away from them.

The 'lions' are evidently tigers and the wolves trained to hunt seem to be a figment of Messere Polo's imagination; he is confusing them with the dogs that were used in the great *battues*.

The fact is that these regions, so lacking in beauty or appeal, are far from being uninhabited. Ever since prehistoric times, stoneworking cultures have put in an appearance here, notably around the shores of Baykal Ozero (Lake Baikal), from where they swarmed towards Mongolia and various parts of Siberia. In these inhospitable-looking places, men create small tribal societies. As time goes by, they organize themselves into principalities and then, in due course, they build a vast empire.

## Son of the Speckled Wolf and the Tawny Doe

It was into this austere, if not hostile, world that was born the child who was to become Genghis Khan.

> The origin of Genghis Khan is Börte-chino [the Blue Wolf], born from Heaven which is above, by celestial order; whose wife is Qo'ai Maral [the Tawny Doe]. He crossed the sea to arrive at this place. When he had established his camp at the source of the river Onon, at [Mount] Burqan Qaldun, there was born [to them] Batachiqan. The son of Batachiqan [was] Tamacha; the son of Tamacha [was] Qorichar Mergen. The son of Qorichar Mergen [was] A'ujam-Boro'ul.

Thus begins *The Secret History of the Mongols*, the more or less epic chronicle of the founder of the Mongol empire and of his dynasty.

According to the bards of the Mongolian steppe, a wolf and a doe were the first progenitors of the princely clans before Genghis Khan. These are emblematic animals often to be found, cast in bronze, at numerous Siberian sites. The wolf is a totemic animal from the great myths about

origins current among the Turco-Mongol people. It may seem surprising
to see the doe coupled with the wolf, the carnivore for whom she is
generally likely to be the prey, but here it is obviously a matter of a
symbolic union of the male qualities of the wolf — strength and daring —
with the female qualities of the doe — agility and grace.

Just as there is a symbolic link between the carnivore and the
herbivore, as discussed in depth by the Turcologist Jean-Paul Roux in *La
Religion des Turcs et des Mongols*, so one can see here a reference to animal
totemism. Among the other myths concerning the origin of the forebears
of Genghis Khan one notes a legend which has a connection both with the
animal and with the sun: in this, the union between wolf and doe
produced a woman named Alan Qo'a. She was said to have been fertilized
by a ray of sun passing through the chimney of the tent and touching her
belly, from which emerged the ancestors of the great khan.

The future Genghis Khan was born under a very modest felt tent.
Mongol chronicles say that the newborn child came into the world
clutching a clot of blood in his right hand. According to Turco-Mongol
tradition, this promised a glorious future in warfare. It seems that the
baby's father, Yesügei, gave his first-born the name Temüjin in
remembrance of a Tatar warrior whom he had overcome some time
before and who bore that name. That Yesügei should give his son the
name of a defeated enemy may strike one as odd, but in the warrior
tradition of the steppe a person who had been defeated was supposed, in
giving up his life forces, to transmit the energy to his victor. Besides,
there may have been in Yesügei some vainglory in thus recalling a feat of
arms from the past. The word Temüjin has been traced to the Turco-
Mongol root *temur* (iron), so that the name of the future founder of the
Mongol empire can appropriately be rendered as 'Blacksmith'. There are
some tales on the subject, but no firm evidence that Temüjin was ever a
blacksmith in his youth. Possibly, however, the designation corresponds
to some shamanist symbol: the Mongols, as Jean-Paul Roux has shown,
certainly established a link between metallurgy and the shaman,
'manipulator of fire and of iron'.

Temüjin was born one Year of the Pig on the slopes of an isolated hill,
on the right bank of the Onon Gol river (east of Lake Baikal, and north of
the northeast frontier of present-day Mongolia, now in Soviet territory),
where his people had erected their camp. This particular Year of the Pig
has not been identified with any accuracy. We know that, as in the
Chinese calendar, the Mongol year was divided into twelve lunar months,

each under the sign of a zodiacal animal. But unravelling these calendrical systems and the contradictions between Chinese and modern chronology is hardly an exact science. The birth of Genghis Khan can therefore be placed somewhere between 1150 and 1167. Paul Pelliot inclined towards 1167. René Grousset finally opted for 1155, as did the German Mongolist Walther Heissig and the Russian Munkuev. It seems not unreasonable to accept the last-named date. There is, on the other hand, agreement about the date of Genghis's passing: the Chinese annalists in the *Yuan Shi* (*History of the Yuan Dynasty*) pinpointed the date of the khan's death as August 1227.

The baby's father was the chief of a subclan or *kiyad*, a branch of the Borjigin *oboγ* (clan). According to some chroniclers, he was descended from some sovereigns of an earlier era and was thus of royal blood, but this is not an established fact. He took part in various battles against neighbouring tribes, some genuinely Mongol, others Tatar or Ruzhen. It seems certain that it was following one of these battles that he was given the surname Baγatur, the Valiant. Being the head of a rather insignificant clan, Yesügei-Baγatur joined forces with a certain To'oril, who had taken the title of king of the Kereyid tribe (Ong Qan). The latter, wanting to seal the alliance of armed fraternity, had made Yesügei the Valiant his *anda* or sworn brother. The ritual involved each drinking a few drops of the other's blood poured into curdled milk: this pact of friendship was to play a decisive role in the destiny of Temüjin.

Despite his links with the Kereyid khan, Yesügei seems to have exerted hardly any influence on the neighbouring clans. His wife Hö'elün, also of noble origin, belonged to the Onggirad tribe. With an entourage of servants and a small circle of people who were linked to them by family ties or by loyalty, Yesügei and his wife lived a nomadic life around the upper reaches of the rivers Onon Gol, Kerulen (Herlen Gol) and Tuul Gol.

According to *The Secret History*, Yesügei met his wife in most romantic circumstances: while out on a hunt with his falcon he crossed the path of a horseman from the Merkid tribe taking back to his camp a young woman perched on a waggon. It was a fateful meeting, for in a flash Yesügei was stung with desire for the young beauty. Instantly abandoning the hunt, he galloped to the family yurt, rousing his brothers, Nekün Taisi and Daritai, and together they raced off in pursuit of the couple he had seen on the steppe. Very soon the object of the chase came in sight. The young woman, realizing that the battle was lost before it began, dissuaded her fiancé from putting up any defence and told him to make his escape. The Merkid man disappeared over the horizon. The three men were hard put to stop the waggon and capture the lovely Hö'elün. The latter surrendered and eventually became — whether with resignation or consent we do not know — the bride of Yesügei the Valiant.

Customs were harsh, and the vendettas caused by the abduction of women or the stealing of cattle could leave a bloody legacy that ran through generations of pastoral nomads. Apparently, Hö'elün was a faithful and beloved wife to Yesügei. Besides Temüjin, she gave him three sons, Jochi Qasar (the Tiger), Qachi'un, and Temüge, as well as a daughter, Temülün. By another woman Yesügei had two additional sons, Bekter and Belgütei.

How did Yesügei's offspring live? The family's resources were modest. Stock farming, which provided their subsistence, occupied the whole clan: the children began at an early age to help tend the animals and gather vegetables and wild berries. The great hunting expeditions organized by the nomads demanded considerable physical resilience and very skilled horsemanship. When they were still young, Temüjin and his brothers learned to recognize the edible plants that grow in the forest margins, to watch over the cattle as they grazed around the tents on the yurt (pasture land accorded to each tribe by custom), to milk the mares, and to churn the milk which, along with meat, was the staple food in the nomad diet.

Temüjin was, by all accounts, very robust and much given to rough and violent exercise, particularly riding, this being the only method the nomads had of moving from place to place. When he reached the age of 9, his father set about betrothing him, hoping thus to ensure a useful alliance between family and clan.

The Mongols were exogamous — that is, they looked for a spouse among a tribe of a different clan, without any ancestor common to themselves — and polygamous. William de Rubrouck explained it in this way:

As far as their nuptials are concerned, I can tell you that no one here takes a wife without buying her; therefore, sometimes young girls reach quite an advanced age before they are married, because their parents have kept them until they can be sold. They observe the first and second degree of affinity. In fact, they can marry two sisters simultaneously or consecutively. Among their people, no widow remarries, because they believe that all who serve them in this life will serve them in the hereafter. Thus, regarding a widow, they believe that after her death she will always return to her first husband. This explains the shameful custom whereby a son sometimes marries all his father's wives, with the exception of his mother.

In his *History of the Mongols*, Giovanni da Pian del Carpini confirms these matrimonial customs:

> Every man keeps as many wives as he can keep; one may have a hundred, another fifty, or less or more. A Tatar may marry any member of his family, except his mother, his daughter or his sister born to the same mother, but a sister by the same father and the wives of the latter are not excluded. The youngest in the family has the right to marry the widow of his brother; [if he does not do so] another member of the family is obliged to marry her. . . . After the death of her husband, the widow would have difficulty in contracting another marriage if her brother-in-law refused to marry her.[1]

The practice of polygamy might lead one to believe that in Mongol tribal society some men would, voluntarily or not, have remained celibate, for there seems to have been no significant surplus of women. In fact, polygamy was closely linked with wealth, only the richest men being able to afford to keep several wives. It was also linked with social rank, with the economic interests of the family, and indeed with political loyalties.

Yesügei, having previously gathered some information from his own people — perhaps even from his own wife — decided therefore to make a series of calls on neighbouring yurts. The chronicle tells us that on the way he came across a camp of the Onggirad, the tribe to which Hö'elün belonged. Yesügei set out the purpose of his journey before the chief of the nomads, a man by the name of Dei Sechen—Dei the Wise: he wanted to find a fiancée for his eldest son. In fact, it is probable that Yesügei already had some information about his host and had not simply encountered him by chance. Dei the Wise greeted Yesügei kindly and, seeing Temüjin, said to him: 'This son of yours is a son with fire in his eyes and the spark of brilliance in his face.' Then he related his latest dream: a white gerfalcon, 'holding both the sun and the moon', came to sit on his wrist. For him, this dream was a premonitory sign of this happy meeting and the gerfalcon could be no other than Temüjin. Singing the praises of the famous beauty of Onggirad women, he insisted on presenting his own daughter to his guest, for he too wished to betroth his child. This girl, aged 10 years, was called Börte, which meant 'blue of the sky', the same colour as the mythical wolf from which Temüjin was descended. The chronicler specifies that the little girl was pretty and that 'she had the spark of brilliance in her face and fire in her eyes'.

The next day, Yesügei, on behalf of his eldest son, asked for Börte's hand in marriage. Being a prudent man, Dei the Wise proposed a deal: he accepted, but expressed the wish that Temüjin remain for some time in their camp. Doubtless he wanted to assess the qualities of his future son-in-law. Yesügei agreed, adding just one piece of advice: 'My son is afraid of dogs; do not let the dogs frighten him.' Having thus arranged Temüjin's betrothal, Yesügei rode away towards his own camp. He was to meet a tragic fate *en route*.

# 3
# The Lone Wolf

*They have their herds which they must guard and milk and,*
*most important, move to new pastures. In the space of a few*
*weeks, sometimes within a few days, the grass that surrounds*
*the camp is cropped short; it is time to leave, to break camp . . .*
*to make butter, curd,* koumiss; *to look after the horses, the*
*camels . . . Pillage is one of the tribe's normal occupations; and*
*requires certain careful preparation, such as the training of the*
*horses.*

**Captain Mayne-Reid,** *Odd People*

## Temüjin Fatherless

As he was returning to the family yurt, Yesügei crossed an area called
Shirake'er (the Yellow Steppe), which has been identified: it is a
mountain situated between the lakes Buyr Nuur and Hulun Nur. This is
where the Mongol and Onggirad tribes lived their nomadic lives. The
Tatars, who lived further south, must have come here on forays, for it
was, according to the chronicle, at a Tatar encampment that Yesügei met
his fate.

Yesügei jumped from his horse. The Tatars crowded around him.
There were some among them who still recalled the face of the *kiyad* clan
chief. But Yesügei did not recognize his old adversaries. He was offered a
drink. To this drink someone had taken the precaution of adding a
slow-acting but fatal poison. Personal revenge or political assassination?
Nobody knows. Whatever the case, Yesügei began on the way home to
feel the lethal effects of the liquid he had been treacherously offered. For
three days he managed to remain mounted on his horse before he took to
his bed in the tent in the Onggirad camp. Then, suddenly, he saw the veil
of death descending before his eyes. A young boy, Münglig, bent over the

man as he lay in agony, just in time to hear him say: 'I am ill within myself
... See to it that you take care of your younger brothers whom I leave
behind me and who are still small, and of your widowed sister-in-law.
Send my son Temüjin to me, O Münglig, my child.' And, laconically, the
writer of *The Secret History* adds: 'Thus saying, he passed away.'

Yesügei's last words concerned the orphans he was leaving behind, his
young widow, and Temüjin, who had remained with his future in-laws.
We do not know the relationship between Yesügei and those who were
present during his last moments, especially with this Münglig, whom he
charged with bringing Temüjin back to the family. The boy, who was
hardly older than Temüjin, apparently carried out the dying man's last
wishes and rode to the encampment of Dei Sechen to collect little
Temüjin.

When he came to Dei Sechen, Münglig concealed the death of Yesügei,
saying no more than that the father was missing his son intensely. This
was a wise move, for, if it was known that the boy no longer had a father,
Dei Sechen could have compelled him to stay with his own family in the
role of an adoptive son. However, Temüjin was given permission to leave
immediately. True to his promise, charmed by the boy, and thinking that
he might make a good husband for his daughter, Dei Sechen kept the girl
and groomed her for this marriage for a further four years. What were
Temüjin's feelings when, on the journey home, he learned of the tragic
passing of his father? Floods of tears of childish grief, dumb misery or a
sorrow soon to be stifled by the desire for revenge? *The Secret History*
remains silent on that point.

Fatherless at the age of 9, and the oldest of several young children,
Temüjin was to experience difficult times. He became 'head of the
family', while Hö'elün, his mother, had somehow to keep the household
afloat. With six children the task was onerous, even if she could count on
the help of several servants. At once she now collided head-on with the
law of patriarchy that pertained among the nomadic tribes. In Mongol
society one was born a member of a clan and of a tribe, even before one
was an individual, so fundamental was it to belong to a social grouping. In
losing her husband, Hö'elün also lost all authority. Yesügei had succeeded
in making his mark on his own circle of family and friends, and his
prestige as a warrior had spread to other clans and neighbouring
encampments, but his sudden death only triggered their desertion of his
bereaved family.

Rivalries and animosities were soon to arise, threatening to isolate the family of the late Yesügei. Bravely Hö'elün faced up to adversity. But she had become a poor relation whom people avoided. One incident hastened the process of setting the young woman in conflict with the two widows of the Tayichi'ud khan, Ambaγai, who would not accept the authority of the deceased man's family: the affair came to a head at the time of a religious ceremony, at which the ancestral souls were to receive nourishment. The two widows neglected to invite Yesügei's wife to the sharing of the offerings: besides being a personal insult, this excluded her from a traditional clan ritual and therefore branded her an outsider to the community. Hö'elün took the bold step of going to the ceremony, thereby publicly reproaching the two women for the insult they had paid her. The quarrel intensified; the women exchanged insults until the entire Tayichi'ud clan were ranged in opposition to Hö'elün. 'If we wish it, we shall move to new ground and abandon the mothers and sons in the camp and go without taking you with us,' they hurled at Hö'elün and her family.

The break was clean, brutal and immediate: the Tayichi'ud gathered up their belongings scattered around the yurt, tied up their bales and saddled their animals. The women and children swung themselves up into the saddles, driving their flocks before them, and abandoned their former chief's nearest and dearest to stark solitude. Only one old man, Charaqa, father of young Münglig, protested, running behind the riders and trying to make them stay. He succeeded only in drawing ungrateful abuse: 'The deep water has dried up, the precious stone has crumbled.' Their treachery was compounded by a spear thrust in the old man's back. Mortally wounded, old Charaqa crawled to Hö'elün's tent, then, calling one last time on the memory of Yesügei the Valiant, he inveighed bitterly against his assailants. To fall from social grace was, he said, inevitably to suffer the ultimate penalty. Temüjin, sobbing, rushed from the tent and ran away: this tendency to withdraw and be alone as soon as he was confronted with a difficulty is the first of his personality traits to be revealed by *The Secret History*.

Hö'elün was to prove herself a woman of character. A widow, without resources, with a brood of brats, deserted by her own people — one might have thought that she would have been crushed. Nothing of the sort: in epic style the chronicle tells us that, determined to fight adversity, she proudly flourished a banner to rouse the servants who remained faithful to her and gave orders for the move to higher pastures to proceed.

## The Years of Wandering

Pulling her *boqtaq* [woman's cap] down over her head and tightening
the belt on her jacket, and running upriver and downriver along the
course of the Onon [Onon Gol], by day and night, gathering apples and
wild cherries, she fed her young. Born brave, the *eke-üjin* [dowager]
found food for her venerable sons; she fed them by picking juniper
berries and hazel nuts, by digging up pimpernel roots and club-rush
tubers. The sons of the *eke-üjin*, nourished on wild garlic and wild
onions, rose from these poor beginnings to become sovereigns.

Thus does *The Secret History* describe the years when Hö'elün and her
children fought for survival.

Shortly before the dawn of the era of Genghis Khan, the Turco-
Mongol tribes were divided essentially into two groups. On the one hand
were the hunter-gatherers and forest people (*oi-yin irgen*) who occupied
the wooded zones around the shores of Lake Baikal, and around the
sources of the great Siberian rivers Yenisey, Irtysh, and Balkhash. Side by
side with these tribes there lived pastoral nomads, the *kegere-yin irgen*, who
practised transhumance between the western spurs of the Altay massif
and lakes Hulun Nur and Buyr Nuur, a vast steppe region extending
almost unbroken for 1,500 kilometres. Other groups still lived a nomadic
life beyond the Gobi desert and even in the vicinity of the Great Wall of
China.

The forest people rarely left their territory, which offered them a
variety of resources. They lived primarily by hunting, using the skins of
animals they had killed or trapped to make clothes, and working animal
bones, sinews and horns for different domestic uses. Congregating in
scores of widely dispersed little clusters, they lived in huts of wood or
bark, often partly buried, and moved about on skis during the cold season.
The forest people knew which animals offered flesh and milk high in
nutritional value, including various types of cattle (yaks, cows) and deer
(reindeer); when they found themselves near a water course, they fished
with harpoon or net. But they were as much gatherers as they were
hunters, and the taiga provided them with supplementary food or
medicinal resources (nuts, rhubarb, potentilla).

At some distant and uncertain epoch — several centuries, indeed more
than a thousand years, before the Christian era for the Scythians or the
Huns; a little before our era for the forest people of what used to be called

Tannu Tuva (now Tuvinskaya ASSR) in the Siberian Altay — certain tribes of hunter-gatherers began to drift gradually further and further away from the gloomy taiga and to take up stock farming. We do not know the motives for, nor the precise circumstances of, this fundamental stage in human activity. Climatic or ecological disturbances, demographic growth encroaching on the resources of the forest, the discovery of new animal products? A significant increase in population seems the most likely explanation for this change; unless there are substantial breaks where stands of trees have been cut down, or clearings offering scope for even a primitive sort of agriculture, the forest cannot provide subsistence for a population of any size. The breeders gradually domesticated the animals whose flesh they were already in the habit of consuming: the horse and the reindeer. Then, probably between the tenth and the seventh millennium BC, without abandoning hunting and gathering, most of the Mongol tribes began to domesticate small and large livestock.

Far from being an economy limited to survival or given to aimless wandering, nomadic pastoralism is a structured way of life which obeys the imperatives of climate, the laws of economics and precise social rules. It is based on stock farming without stalls or stables and, being extensive in nature, requires periodic removals within the pastoral territory of one or more clans; these territories are allotted according to tradition or, quite often, following violent conflicts. The allotted pasture area is called *nutu γ* by the Mongols, but is better known by the Turkish name, *yurt*.

The Mongols are primarily nomads in the original sense of the word. The word 'nomad' comes from the Greek *nomos*, one who leads livestock to graze, a shepherd. This definition is, however, inadequate nowadays, for it encompasses people who engage in no activity connected with stock farming. This is true of those who practise slash-and-burn cultivation; of the hunter-gatherers of Asia, Africa or Australia; of the 'sea gypsies' of the Malay–Indonesian archipelagos; or indeed of the ten million or so gypsies scattered throughout the world, some of whom are adopting a sedentary existence. Consequently, there is a tendency now to refer to a person as 'nomadic' who obtains a livelihood from various different types of economic activity in regions where the soil has a low yield or is, indeed, unsuitable for any agrarian use; 'nomadic' is also applied to groups of people without a fixed habitat, loosely connected and so having no cohesive 'statehood'.

Nomadism varies considerably according to the fertility or poverty of the soil, the density of population, the know-how and technical expertise of the stock farmers, the frequency of epidemics among animals, and so on. The minimum strength of the herds, that is, the minimum from which a pastoral population can feed itself, obviously depends on all these factors. The Russian Mongolist Palladius calculated that in the eighteenth century a Kalmyk family of five persons needed to maintain between fifty and a hundred animals to ensure their subsistence. At the beginning of the twentieth century, according to Zhetetski, a family unit of five stock farmers in central Asia needed to own a stock of about fifteen horses, eight sheep or goats and three camels. More recently, the Soviet journal *Narody Srednei Azii* (*Peoples of Central Asia*) informs us that in the 1960s a family of pastoral nomads needed a minimum of fifteen horses, two camels, about fifty sheep and six other large stock animals to ensure adequate provision of 'grey foods' (meat, nearly always eaten boiled, hence the grey colour) and 'white foods' (fresh or fermented dairy produce), but also that the stock had to be expanded from time to time through breeding. Obviously it is difficult to estimate the number and quality of the animals raised by the Mongols in the twelfth century, but we do know that when they went into battle each horseman could be accompanied by two, three or even four remounts, indicating that the herd was plentiful in number, and also explaining the numerous horse-stealing episodes recounted in *The Secret History*.

William of Rubrouck, who discovered how this pastoral life functioned, a century after the birth of Genghis Khan, described it with some accuracy:

> They [the nomads] have no fixed residence and never know where they will be the next day. Between them they have shared out Scythia, which extends from the Danube to the Levant [Asia]; each captain, according to the number of men he has under his command, knows the limits of his pasture lands, he knows where he must graze the stock in winter and in summer, in spring and in autumn. In winter, they go down towards the warmer areas in the south; in summer, they head back north towards cooler regions. In winter, when it snows, they use pasture lands where there is now water, since the snow serves the purpose instead.

The seasonal calendar which the stock farmers observed embodies all the local variations connected with altitude, amount of rainfall and richness of the pasture itself. Before they undertook any major move to other pastures, the farmers sent out some of their men on a reconnaissance to establish the fertility of the fodder in the pasture lands or to assert their traditional claims to the use of the valleys or the alpine meadows where their yurts were situated. Without grasses, there would be no fodder for the animals, no increase in the stock and no resources for the people: grass is the true richness of the steppes. A Mongol proverb underlines the point: 'The grass is there for the animals and the animals are there for the men.' It was said, with exaggeration, of Attila, 'the scourge of God', that 'the grass no longer grew where his horse had passed by.'

As they contemplated their moves from one pasture to another, the nomads — whose herd was their principal asset — had to be fully alert to the weather. In the cold season, sudden falls in temperature accompanied by snow posed a constant threat to the stock. Snow in blizzards can be so deep that it restricts the animals to one place and cuts them off from their food supplies. Since the pastoral nomads do not keep reserves of fodder, small livestock can perish in the course of a night. Only yaks and horses manage to survive, the former because they are protected by their very thick hair and can uncover food with their hooves; the latter because their hooves lift them clear of the ground and they therefore run no risk of being buried in the snow, and also because they instinctively head down towards drier ground. There are other hazards: a sudden thaw can swell the water courses and cause some animals to drown; equally, a sudden cold snap can seal vegetation inside a casing of ice, and the animals cannot therefore get to their food.

On his way to Tibet, the Swede Sven Hedin noted how the rigours of nature can decimate the flocks:

> The camels arrive up at the col absolutely exhausted and half suffocated . . . The animals cast a melancholy eye over the panorama of sterile rock that they find there; they seem to have lost all hope of ever finding rich pasture . . . With each passing day the animals waste away. Strenuous marches and a starvation diet; these are the very animals that are accustomed to thin pasture and can find sustenance among rocks and debris, where other animals cannot find enough to eat.

Aridity is the main obstacle to the development of livestock. In summer, in some places, burning winds can plane the ground, scraping the thin shoots off the steppe surface. The grass dries out, losing all colour, and crumbles like dust when the animals begin to browse.

The harshness of the physical conditions demands clever adaptation to nature on the part of men. Unlike agriculturalists, the Mongols were not able to space out their sowings, to turn to crop substitutes or to live off their grain reserves. Wherever they went in their seasonal migrations, the tribes had first and foremost to find pasture suitable for the animals: horses being taken from alpine meadows to foothills had an exceptional need for rich grass, while sheep and goats made do with the driest soils, on which grew artemisia and bulb plants. The yaks got their nourishment by scaling the alpine slopes, while the camels preferred the vegetation of the dry places. These migrations, this ceaseless search for sources of drinking water, this complex of care involved in keeping domesticated animals were the survival conditions under which the Mongols lived.

Temüjin and his brothers busied themselves with pursuits that demanded skill as much as strength, such as gathering and fishing with hooks or nets. However nimble these young hunters were, their daily fare can hardly have been very plentiful. No doubt Yesügei's young widow owned a modest flock: a few dozen sheep or goats, a herd of horses and some beef cattle which were yoked to carts for transport. Although there were relatively few mouths to feed — some relatives, some friends and a number of servants partly recruited from among those who had once been captured and pressed into service — their existence remained precarious. Felt tents, clothes, cooking utensils, tools and curried leather, vehicles: the nomad not only has to make and repair all these things with his own hands but he also has to carry all his belongings with him. Rubrouck's list of daily tasks that the nomadic Mongols had to perform bears witness to the fact:

The women's work consists of driving the waggons, loading their houses on and off these waggons, milking the cows, making butter and *khuruud* [curdled milk], preparing and assembling animal skins; for this they use a needle made of sinews. They divide the sinews into thin threads, then they twist them together into a long thread. They also sew shoes, pattens and other kinds of garment . . . They also make the felt and cover their houses with it. The men make bows and arrows, bits, bridles, saddles: they hew their wooden houses and trucks, they look after the horses and milk the mares; they beat the *koumiss*, that is, the mares' milk; they make the leather bottles in which this is kept, they keep the camels and load them up for travelling. Together they watch the sheep and the goats, which are sometimes milked by the men, sometimes by the women. They prepare the skins with the sour milk of ewes, curdled and salted.

From an early age, Temüjin, together with brothers and servants, participated in these daily tasks. He learned very young to sit astride one of the horses of that unusual breed that the nomads had been domesticating for about 3,000 years. For it was customary to learn to ride very early in childhood and to spend such a large part of one's life mounted that it was said that one stayed in the saddle 'until the stirrups fell to pieces'. A domesticated brother of the famous *taki*, or Przewalski's[1] horse, which vanished from the West but was discovered in central Asia by the Russian explorer (Przhevalsky) whose name it bears, it is a short animal with stubby hooves, usually cream-coloured or light bay. But is this *taki* of the steppe really a horse at all? It weighs only 350 kilos (the females often no more than 300 kilos) and stands about 1.3 metres (approx. 13 hands) high at the withers, a size which classes it as a pony or even a miniature pony.

The animal is generally castrated when it reaches the age of 3 years, and it is this gelding which is used for riding, the stallions being reserved for the augmentation of the herd. The *taki* is broken in on a tether or mounted before being saddled. This little horse, indispensable to every pastoral migration, is very strong. These animals that amble (*joroo*), lifting two hooves on the same side at the same time (like a nag), have always been especially prized by the Mongols, who claim that the horse seems to glide as though on ice, so smoothly that one can trot along on one holding a full cup and not spill any of the contents. The Mongols often ride their horses standing up in the stirrups. A little over 50 years ago, Namnandorj achieved some feats of endurance with fresh high-quality horses: they covered a distance of 320 kilometres in a week and 1,800 kilometres in 28 days.

The nomad and his horse are inseparable; for him the horse is synonymous with mobility, speed and freedom. This veritable passion for horses is encountered again and again in Mongol legends and songs. The bard Pajai today still sings:

> He has two ears [similar to those] of the wolf,
> His eyes are [like] the morning star.
> He has withers of miraculous precious stones,
> His nostrils are pearly white. . .

*[He gallops] at twice the speed of the cold wind.*
*He can crush all living things underfoot.*
*He is full of strength,*
*A horse [such as] he is the leader of all geldings,*
*yes!*

## Inside and Outside

Accustomed as they are to wide open spaces and to a land that is constantly windswept, the Mongol nomads invented an original type of habitation that is adapted to their mode of existence: the tent. Apparently rudimentary and fragile, even primitive in the eyes of settled peoples, the nomads' tent nevertheless constitutes the only type of habitation that permits the extensive exploitation of cattle which are in constant need of new pastures. The traditional tent of the Mongols — and also of the Kalmyks, the Buryats, the Kazakhs, and other Turco-Mongols — is still in use today, even among more or less settled populations, as is the case in Mongolia. This tent, called the *ger*, has changed hardly at all since the Flemish traveller William de Rubrouck described it:

> The house they sleep in is built on a circular base of woven sticks; the carpentry-work in the house is also of sticks that meet at the top in a circular opening from which emerges a pipe similar to a chimney; they cover the house with white felt which they coat frequently with chalk or white earth and powdered bone to heighten its pure whiteness. Sometimes too they use black felt. The felt around the upper opening is decorated with a fine variety of designs. In front of the door also they hang a piece of worked felt, artistically embellished. They sew felt on to felt, multicoloured motifs representing vines, trees, birds, and animals. These houses are sometimes built so large that they measure thirty feet across.

The nomads make their tents with materials they have to hand: felt and wood. The sheep, of which 'nothing is wasted' (meat, milk, skin, bone) is the principal source of felt, thanks to seasonal shearing. The felting, which is neither woven nor spun, is obtained by placing layers of wool on a stand previously dampened and coated with greasy substances. The animal fibres are then compressed and, depending on the methods used, the felt has elasticity and strength in varying degrees.

The tent is in two parts: the covering felt and the framework. The essence of the framework is a trellis (*khana*) of light wood, often juniper or willow. Stripped branches are split lengthwise to make thin, slightly curved laths. These are then crisscrossed in a regular pattern and bound together to make latticework, similar to the mesh of a net, which can be folded. These pieces of latticework constitute the outer 'wall' of the tent and rise to shoulder height. Between two such trellises a space is left in which is inserted a door frame; in summer the door is replaced by a felt curtain or even a piece of cloth. Around the circumference of the 'wall', the nomads place long poles at regular intervals; these converge at the top of the structure, like the ribs of an umbrella: they then fit into a ring of heavy wood, whose weight provides stability and therefore steadies the whole structure. Around this framework the Mongols place large rectangular or trapezoidal sheets of felt (*kashma*). Depending on the climate, they put on four, five or even eight layers of felt, held in place by cords. Finally, as William of Rubrouck notes, the felt is whitened and rendered impermeable with fat.

Thanks to its massive, cylindrical shape, the Mongol tent is remarkably resistant to the inclemencies of the weather. The felt part generally lasts five years and the framework perhaps fifteen years. Two people can erect it without any difficulty inside an hour. The whole thing weighs about 200 kilos, the felt alone weighing 150 kilos. This habitation has the advantage of being transportable on a waggon which needs only two animals (oxen, yaks, camels) to pull it. If they need to leave precipitately, the Mongols lift the tent completely erected on to a waggon: travellers in the Middle Ages noticed formal tents being transported on waggons drawn by ten or twenty draught animals. Occasionally, the tent is moved in its erect state to avoid an accumulation of ashes or waste material. Care is always taken to orientate the tent according to the prevailing winds, but also according to the advice of the shamans relating to propitious or ill-omened cardinal points. More often than not it is placed in such a way that the door faces south 'to welcome the sun and friends'. It is forbidden to touch the door frame or the ropes in the doorway, which are considered taboo: Rubrouck reports the anger shown by the Mongols to a monk, Friar Barthélémy, who by mistake broke this code.

The tent interior is arranged in accordance with precise rules and is divided into four parts: at the back, opposite the entrance, are the quarters of the master of the house, his wife and his children; to his right, still facing the door, is the place of honour; visitors, depending on their sex, share the two remaining front sections: women on the eastern side, men on the west. An imaginary line separating the men from the women represents a barrier that may virtually never be crossed. Domestic servants and poor relations have quarters near the entrance, not far from the small livestock which often shelter here in winter. At the back of the tent is a sort of communal bed. The hearth is obviously in the centre of the tent. Here the women do the cooking. Above the fire, the smoke stack that sits on top of the tent's central high point also serves to let fresh air into the dwelling.

Domestic objects are arranged in a traditional way: around the circumference are sacks and leather bottles containing food reserves, boxes of clothes, and utensils. Dairy products are always kept on the coolest side of the tent. It is the usual practice to separate 'masculine' objects (saddles, weapons) from 'feminine' objects. If the head of the household is wealthy, the interior is decorated with carpets, cushions and felt embroideries usually with animal designs: he may also own several 'service tents' in addition to the main one, where he can store his belongings and lodge his servants. Lastly, there is a corner of the tent, behind the place of honour, where idols are placed: 'Above the head of the household,' notes Rubrouck,

> there is always an image, a kind of puppet or statuette made of felt which they call 'the master's brother', and another similar object above the head of the mistress, which they call 'the mistress's brother'; they are fixed to the wall; and, higher up, between these two, there is another figure, small and thin, who serves as the guardian of the house.

Giovanni da Pian del Carpini adds more detail on this sacred part of the Mongol tent:

> The Mongols believe in a God who created the visible and invisible world and who, on this earth, dispenses favours and inflicts punishments; but they neither pray to nor praise Him and perform no rites in His honour. Nevertheless they make felt idols in man's image and place them on both sides of the entrance to the tent, on top of another object of the same material, which is in the shape of breasts. These gods are considered guardians of the flocks; they provide the milk and make the animals' young grow.[2]

This form of idolatry appeared fairly late among the Turco-Mongols.

The nomads symbolically fed these little felt figures by wiping their mouths with fat and invoked their powers when someone was ill. The breasts of these guardian deities are evidence that they were regarded as having gifts of fecundity. Doubtless they also had another purpose. Rubrouck observes that the Mongols termed them relatives of the householders ('master's brother' and 'mistress's brother'), and Pian del Carpini notes that it was forbidden on pain of death to steal the deities placed on a waggon at the side of the tent. Certain anthropomorphic figures belonged in certain specific households, a fact which suggests that they were symbolic representations of ancestors, who were accorded some kind of cult status.

We might add that the air vent through which the wreaths of smoke from the hearth passed out of the tent also had a religious significance: this is where the light of the heavens passes through into the tent and it is through this orifice that the deities were thought to penetrate into the tent interior. This hole in the roof is the eye of heaven through which light enters. Thus, it will be remembered, was Genghis Khan conceived.

## Growing and Cooking
'There is food only in the evenings,' notes Rubrouck.

> In the morning we were given something to drink or we were allowed to take some millet. But in the evening we were given meat, a shoulder of lamb together with the ribs, and some meat bouillon to drink in measured quantities. When we had drunk our fill of the meat bouillon, we felt perfectly revived, and this seemed to me the healthiest and most nourishing of drinks . . . Sometimes we had to eat meat that was half cooked or almost raw, because they lacked the stocks to keep the fire going.

Domestic animals provided everything: building materials, food, work materials. The Mongol economy was based on this close bond between man and animal. For even though hunting and fishing provided appreciable additions to their diet, and though shepherds sometimes swapped agricultural products with settled farmers, they lived almost exclusively off their flocks, which served both as a means of production and a consumable item. Dairy products and meat were the staples of their diet. The Mongols preferred sheep and goats because they reproduced most quickly and required care for only a short period. They ate their meat roasted, more often boiled, sometimes flavoured with wild herbs. However, at that time, there was no great abundance of food because the livestock had to be conserved, especially when the animals were not very fat. Nowadays the official figure for meat consumption by the Mongols is half a kilo a day!

Temüjin and his contemporaries can certainly not have consumed this amount. Travellers who have described the Mongol menu paint a picture of a rather defective diet: 'On the subject of their food and nourishment, it is a fact that they are equally prepared to eat the meat of animals they have found dead or have killed . . . From the meat of a single sheep they can feed fifty to a hundred men: indeed, they cut it into small dice into a bowl and add salt and water; they add no other sauce to it,' observed William of Rubrouck. The Franciscan Giovanni da Pian del Carpini, envoy of Pope Innocent IV, admits frankly a disgust for Mongol fare: 'Everything edible is included in the Mongol diet: dogs, wolves, foxes, horses, if necessary even human flesh . . . The people eat even the excrement of mares and colts. We have seen them crunching up insects to eat . . . We have even seen them eating mice.'[3]

The French mansions from which these two clergymen came unquestionably offered rather finer fare. Even if Pian del Carpini was exaggerating, there are other accounts which confirm that the Mongol table could hardly be described as very refined gastronomically. Certain writers have described with revulsion the astonishing practices connected with food, particularly among the Huns: the habit of warming and tenderizing raw meat by squeezing it between their thighs and the rump of their horse, or of placing it under the saddle. Ammien Marcelin, who conducted a campaign against Parthian nomads, and also Jean de Joinville, a companion of the French king St Louis (Louis IX), mention these practices in connection with the Mongols. Even admitting the barbarism of Mongol customs, it is still hard to believe that these reports contained any truth: for one thing, raw meat is hardly likely to gain in taste or flavour when it has been coated in dirty hair or soaked in sweat; for another, this method seems a highly ineffective and improbable way of tenderizing meat!

Rubrouck gives us details of a method of preparing meat that was peculiar to the Mongols: 'If a cow or horse happens to die, they dry the meat: they cut it into thin slices which they hang exposed to the sunlight and the wind so that they will dry as quickly as possible without being salted and without emitting any smell whatever.' This may explain the origin of 'steak tartare'. Meat treated in this way is rather similar to the buffalo pemmican prepared by the American Indian hunters, the smoked wild cattle meat of the Caribbean people or the pork *chà bông* of the Vietnamese. This dried flesh is pressed, fermented, and sometimes salted. Dehydrated meat keeps well and is very high in nutritive value; it is eaten by being chewed until it is reduced to stringy morsels or powder and these are then thrown into a bouillon. A few pieces of smoked meat hung on one's saddle and a bottle of curdled milk, as dry as plaster, provide a complete diet and are very suitable battle rations for horsemen on expeditions to distant places. At a time when armies lacked any kind of supply administration, and when men found it difficult to fill their stomachs in the countries they had conquered, this self-sufficiency in food and drink must certainly have facilitated the progress of Genghis Khan's troops.

Another essential food for the nomads was milk and all its derivatives ('white foods'). Every year nanny goats, ewes, cows, she-camels and mares yielded milk, which the Mongols collected in leather bottles or buckets made of skin. The yield must have been rather poor: in a steppe environment, a cow today gives only 350 litres of milk a year, that is, about a litre a day. A mare can give more than two litres of milk in five or six daily milkings, always carried out by the men. To keep it longer, it is made into curdled milk, buttermilk, yogurt (a Turkish term meaning 'to thicken'), cheese or *koumiss* (fermented milk, usually from mares). Known since Neolithic times, when curdled milk was kept in wooden receptacles, cheese is one of the most ancient processed foods. Because of its nutritional value, this food, which is almost complete in itself, has always found favour among shepherds. The Mongols boiled butter to get rid of the water content and kept it in this form until the winter. They let the milk residue turn sour, brought it to the boil, and then made from the curds they obtained rounds of cheese which would harden like stone. This soured curdled milk (*khuruud*, hence the word 'curd') was then moistened with water and churned until it was smooth, and this is the way it was drunk.

Temüjin saw the servants, and perhaps his mother too, preparing *koumiss*, this drink which is served at almost every meal. The milk is kept in leather bottles and exposed to the sun or kept under the tent skin. To activate the process of fermentation, it is stirred with special ladles; stopping for a moment to stir the contents of one of these capacious bottles is a polite gesture on the part of a visitor entering the tent. Once soured, slightly fermented and warmed to above 5°C, it constitutes a complete food, the core and basis of the diet, thanks to its protein and vitamin content. This refreshing drink, also known as *airag*, leaves 'the taste of almond milk' in the mouth, according to Rubrouck, and the Mongols consume enormous quantities of it.

The Flemish Franciscan also mentions *caracosmos*, a drink apparently reserved only for noblemen. This was a black *koumiss* (*qara qumis*), so called because the milk was taken from mares with black coats. One might also mention *bal*, a type of mead, and the rice beer which was obtained from China. Lastly, there was also *arkhi*, which originated in India and entered Mongolia via Turkestan by the same route as did Buddhism, and at the same time. This alcoholic drink, the manufacture of which we find mentioned in the second half of the thirteenth century, was obtained by slowly boiling sour milk in a cauldron equipped with a device to collect the condensed alcohol vapour, the soured milk here serving as a bacterial agent. Palladius notes that the Kalmyks made it by keeping the milk in the belly of a slaughtered sheep. These drinks could be transported, and the *History of the Yuan Dynasty* describes the *yundu*, or 'hairy carts', virtually bottles on wheels that were drawn by mares.

## In the Steppes of Central Asia

Gathering, hunting on the edge of the taiga, keeping constant watch on animals that were always under the covetous eyes of thieves, branding the animals, jobs large and small — these were the stuff of which Temüjin's days were made.

Faced with an environment so unfavourable to agriculture, the nomad grazes his domestic animals on poor soils. Hence the constant coming and going of men and animals on soils where grass grows or withers along with the rhythm of the seasons and according to the type of pasture. Alps and valleys, hillsides and waterholes, all belong to no one. For the nomad, the whole earth is a vast communal field. Having to make do with the bare necessities, the Mongol shepherd owns nothing that he cannot transport with him: his flock and a few waggons containing his tent, his belongings and his utensils: to accumulate any more would be to impede his mobility. It is a part of his nature to feel light and free. Every site to him is only a temporary resting-place. But these migrations, far from being mere vagrancy, conform to rules. There is a long tradition relating to pastoral territory and the nomad operates within his domain: customs, rights and privileges allot him several yurts, according to a system of 'branding' that is based on the seasons or on custom.

Although the peasant in the Middle Ages lived in a social space with definite limits, the nomad had at his disposal pastoral land that contracted or expanded along with dry and rainy periods. The cultivator is anchored (to his village) and restricted (to his tillage). For the peasant, the land, divided into enclosures, in accordance with property rights, is an element of stability. The life of a settler depends on geometry; that of a nomad on geography. The former leaves his land and his village only in rare circumstances: war, epidemics, expropriation. The latter is attached to a particular place only as long as his herd is grazing there.

At the end of the twelfth century, in Asia as in the West, peasant societies ceased to be wholly self-sufficient in their means of obtaining a livelihood. Agriculturalists ensured the subsistence of other social classes: artisans, clergymen, a nobility, merchants. Whether owned or rented, worked by free men or serfs, the earth now yielded considerable wealth. For the medieval peasant, the nomads, having neither hearth nor home, were nothing but intruders and as such posed a real threat. Had not centuries of Hun, Germanic and Slav invasions put nomads beyond the pale as far as settled societies were concerned?

True, the settler had also, in the course of the centuries, altered the hand nature had dealt him by nibbling at virgin soil to transform it into sown farmland. His walled villages, his fortified towns limited the nomads' freedom of movement and the cultivated ground reduced the steppes to the smoothness of leather. We have here two types of civilization that are fundamentally opposed to each other. In the eyes of the Mongols — or of other nomadic peoples — who cannot imagine such an intimate involvement between man and the earth, the umbilical tie between the peasant and his land seems shocking. While the cultivator waits on his land for a season propitious for harvesting, the nomad makes tracks for a place further away where he knows he will find plenty. The peasant has time on his side, the nomad has space. To the nomadic shepherds, the agriculturalists are nothing but slaves of their land. They take pleasure in making fun of them, saying that the peasant 'cannot stray any further than a pregnant woman can go to urinate'.

This mutual hostility between nomadic and settled peoples goes back thousands of years and still persists in various parts of the world: one has only to think of the defensive reflexes exhibited by most settled populations in Europe towards the gypsies. This antagonism was to raise its head again, as we shall see, when the Mongols mounted their attacks on the vast Asiatic empires. While continually clashing with settled peoples over centuries, they had, at the same time, their own social codes. Their way of life implies a particular state of mind and original modes of expression. In addition, because of their mobility, the Mongols had two activities that go hand in hand with this: trade and war. The former allowed them to procure goods which they did not themselves possess: grain and manufactured goods, especially cloth. The latter was a contingent means of obtaining complementary resources: herds, slaves, and weapons.

**Fratricide**

For Hö'elün's family, subsistence was not always easy: a squirrel, a fish or some fruit from a wild strawberry tree constituted a treasure for the whole yurt where they erected their felt tents. As soon as such a find was made, a row would break out among the children. The chronicle tells us that Temüjin, then no doubt aged 12 or 13, and his brother Jochi Qasar were once fighting with Bekter and Belgütei over a fish caught in a stream, the former accusing the latter of having stolen their catch. They went to find Hö'elün to ask her to arbitrate. She, being a wise mother, would not take sides with either pair, and told them that unity is strength, especially when one is faced with misfortune: 'How can you, older brothers or younger brothers, act like this towards one another? We have no other friends than our own shadows.'

But Temüjin and his brother Jochi Qasar would not accept these words of wisdom. Their violent temperaments and their spite were soon to provoke a crisis. One day, when the boys were arguing about a lark that they had just killed, Temüjin and Jochi Qasar took up their bows and arrows and shot and killed Bekter. According to *The Secret History*, the murder was entirely premeditated: Temüjin, hiding an arrow behind his back, went up behind his half-brother while Jochi Qasar approached him from in front. Bekter pleaded with them, reminding them of the words of their mother. In vain. The two brothers shot him as though they were merely doing 'target practice'. Seeing Temüjin and his brother returning, hanging their heads, Hö'elün was quick to realize what horrible deed they had done. Defending against her own sons a child whom she herself had not brought into the world, she showered them with insults, called them tigers and giant snakes; comparing her elder son with the 'gerfalcon which swoops down to attack its own shadow', she accused him of having behaved like 'a dog that bites its own placenta', a 'mandarin duck which devours its own ducklings'.

This cold determination, taste for revenge and scorn for the lives of others seem to be, even from the time of his adolescence, the dominant character traits of Temüjin. Many more instances of proof were to come. For this boy who did not hesitate to kill someone who offered him resistance, even if it was his half-brother, this was only the beginning.

# 4
# The Coat of Sable

*Sciendum est quod qum vident hostes tunc vadunt ad eos et unusquisque iacet tres sagittas vel quatuor contra adversarios suos. et si vident quod eos superare non possunt retro regrediuntur ad suos et hoc faciunt in fraudem ut adversarii eos sequuntur ad loca ubi insidias paraverunt et si eorum inimici insequuntur ipsos ad predictas insidias circumdant eos et sic vulnerant et occidunt.*

(It is a fact that when they [the Mongols] see the enemy, they approach him and each of them shoots three or four arrows in his direction. And if they see that they cannot gain victory over him, they retrace their steps, a ruse to draw the enemy to follow them to the place where they have prepared an ambush, and if the enemy does pursue them to the trap they have set they surround him, wound him and kill him.)

**Giovanni da Pian del Carpini,**
***Historia Mongalorum; il viaggio di frate Giovanni***
***da Pian del Carpini ai Tartari***
[***History of the Mongols***]

When Hö'elün admonished her quarrelsome sons, telling them that their only friends were their own shadows, she was not mistaken. Toughened by the many trials they had lived through, often as ravenous as young wolves — the chronicle reports that they fed on 'fish that were weak or injured' — Yesügei's children were gradually becoming men. Misfortune did not succeed in crushing their spirit. But this resilience in the face of life's rigours, this capacity to brave fate, was soon to come to the attention of Tarγutai Kiriltuγ, the khan of the Tayichi'ud, the very man who had given the order to abandon Hö'elün and her circle, leaving them open to the ostracism of the clan. Kiriltuγ perceived a threat from this quarter, for he knew perfectly well that he had been responsible for the decline of the family of his former chief, Yesügei. 'The brats have grown up,' he said to himself, and he decided, while there was still time, to crush the clutch of eaglets.

## Temüjin Abducted

One day, therefore, a group of Tayichi'ud horsemen galloped over the horizon. The occupants of Hö'elün's few tents were quick to sense the danger. But what were they to do against several armed men bent on tearing them apart — except to flee? Temüjin, now about 15 years old, felt the threat most keenly. He ran away to hide in the nearby woods as quickly as he could. His brothers followed. With all possible haste, they made a pile of branches behind which they could shelter and from which let fly their arrows against the enemy. But the Tayichi'ud, apparently not caring to lose any of their men in a skirmish, preferred to negotiate their retreat in exchange for the surrender of Temüjin. He, aware that he was the stake in the bargain, was off into the woods that crowned the neighbouring hills. Seeing the tangle of vegetation in which the youth had hidden, the Tayichi'ud dismounted and began to climb up the pine- and larch-covered mounds. Kiriltuγ posted his colleagues at intervals in the open spaces. Lookouts watched the approaches. They were counting on hunger, thirst and fatigue to flush the fugitive out, to force the wolf to leave his lair. Temüjin, who still had his horse with him, made a few hurried attempts to get out, but each time he was spotted. *The Secret History* tells us that he spent nine days and nights in the forest before creeping under a shelter where, by a stroke of bad luck, his pursuers were lying in wait for him. Temüjin was immediately bound with leather bands and taken before the Tayichi'ud chief.

Kiriltuγ, who could have had him put to death on the spot, chose to show clemency. Did he recognize the boy's courage, did he feel pity for him, or did he perhaps merely decide to postpone his revenge until later? We do not know. What we do know is that he ordered his men to place a pillory around the neck of the captured youth. This form of punishment, which had been in use in China for centuries, was particularly hateful because it weighed down the prisoner, forcing him into a grotesque and humiliating position. Temüjin was made to remain for some days with his head and hands imprisoned in this heavy block of wood, and the Mongol chronicler recounts how he was paraded from tent to tent, where everyone came out to ridicule or insult him.

Temüjin, boiling with humiliation and rage, braced himself for the revenge he so keenly sought, while at the same time looking for a way to make good his escape. On the 'sixteenth of the first summer moon, on the day of the red disc', the Tayichi'ud were holding a festival on the banks of the Onon Gol. A young boy had been appointed to guard the prisoner, but

Temüjin was quick to see that with a little patience and daring he now had a good chance to get rid of his frail little jailer: there was a lot of drinking and loud singing; nobody was taking any notice of the prisoner. Temüjin seized his chance: he went up to the jailer, leapt at him and threw him to the ground; then he disappeared. The river was close by. Without hesitating, he jumped in, his head and arms still locked into the pillory, and let himself float along with the current.

Once the alert had been raised, the Tayichi'ud lost no time in pulling themselves together and giving chase. They scoured every reed-bed and beat every thicket. The moon was full. The pursuers, torches in hand, signalled to each other, excited by this impromptu manhunt. *The Secret History* gives few details of the incident, but one can imagine Temüjin squatting by the river's edge, trying to hide among the aquatic plants while the men shouted to each other and their oaths smothered the splashing noise of the black water where the fugitive was hiding.

It was at this point that fate looked kindly on Temüjin: one of the pursuers suddenly saw him, still imprisoned in the heavy block of wood that almost disabled him. Now, for some unknown reason, this man, one Sorqan Shira, a Tayichi'ud vassal, kept silent about his discovery. Was it out of pity, perhaps, or a debt towards Yesügei, or conflict with the Tayichi'ud? The chronicle says that Sorqan Shira busied himself sending the pursuers off in the wrong direction while hiding Temüjin from them. Wearying of their fruitless search, the Tayichi'ud abandoned the chase and went back to their tents, meaning to resume the hunt the following day. A man impeded by a wooden collar, with no horse and unarmed, how far could he get after all?

Sorqan Shira had advised Temüjin to rejoin the family encampment using out-of-the-way paths, but the boy was in no mood to listen. Impetuously, he climbed out of the water and then managed to creep along to his rescuer's dwelling. This was a wise move for, if his host had refused to hide him now, Temüjin could always have threatened to betray the truth if the man were accused of failing to hand him over. Sorqan Shira refused to offer the escapee refuge, for fear of retaliation. But his sons beseeched him to accede to Temüjin's demand. Soon they had taken off his collar, given him food and drink, and agreed, after all, to hide him.

The next day the Tayichi'ud intensified their hunt, searching every thicket and combing through the flocks in case Temüjin was sheltering among them; then they decided to search the tents. Sorqan Shira made his visitor leave and hide in a waggon full of fleeces that was standing near

71

the yurt. Just as a man was preparing to search the vehicle by plunging a pike into the pile of wool, Sorqan Shira again came to Temüjin's rescue, saying, as to nobody in particular, that no one in his right mind would hide under a heap of wool in this blistering heat and run the risk of melting. The observation seemed to make sense to the man, and he and his fellows moved off elsewhere. Soon afterwards, Temüjin made his escape from these dangerous parts, taking some provisions with him — a roasted lamb and two bottles of milk. Sorqan Shira had proved himself generous and given him also a bow and two arrows and a saddled horse. Temüjin then galloped off towards the family encampment, following the tracks the Tayichi'ud had made on the day they had taken him captive; nomads were known to be able to recognize tracks left by animals and to distinguish male tracks from female and the tracks of injured animals; they could even garner information from these on the men who had been accompanying them.

Back amongst his family, the boy probably received a hero's welcome and resumed his place among his own people. The family decided to break camp and move elsewhere so as to be as far as possible from the Tayichi'ud. It was not long before they were installed in a mountainous region near the Blue Lake in the Hentiy massif. There they resumed a daily life like that they had had before; caring for the livestock, milking, churning milk and cutting firewood occupied the greater part of their time.

**The Hunt**
They had few enough diversions, except for horseriding, racing without bridles, and games such as are still popular among nomads today: trying to catch a cap or piece of cloth between one's teeth while remaining in the saddle, or striking a stake driven into the ground with a pole while on a fast-trotting horse. Another pursuit that offered excitement and fun was hunting, which added an extra spice to life. Besides small animals caught in traps, there were wild horses to be hunted, the *taki*, and steppe donkeys, called *qulan*; these were caught, after being run down, using lassos fixed to long poles. Later, when he had tens of thousands of men under his command, Temüjin was to retain a pronounced liking for hunting and would organize *battues* on a giant scale.

Temüjin would certainly also have taken part, from his earliest years, in hawking parties with falcons, such as those organized by Kublai Khan, Temüjin's grandson, which were described in extravagant terms by the Venetian Marco Polo:

After he [the emperor] has stopped at his capital city those three months that I mentioned, to wit, December, January, February, he starts off on the first day of March and travels southward towards the Ocean Sea, a journey of two days. He takes with him full ten thousand falconers and some five hundred gerfalcons, besides peregrines, sakers and other hawks in great numbers; and goshawks also to fly at the water-fowl.

Falconry occupied a place of privilege among the Mongols. Hunting with birds of prey requires a mastery of very ancient training skills as well as intimate knowledge of the habits of predatory birds. The first step is to take certain varieties from the nest, usually goshawks or falcons, but sometimes also eagles, which are capable of pursuing larger game, particularly deer and similar animals. While it is still young and unable to fend for itself with regard to food, the falcon depends on its master. Every day, the master trains the bird of prey to seize decoys made of balls of feathers or of fur rubbed with animal fat, which he shakes and throws into the air in front of him. The bird, having a natural predatory instinct, swoops down on this artificial bait and very soon learns to swoop on real prey which is pointed out to it. Most of the time, moreover, the prey chosen is the bird's natural food, and the raptors are chosen for training on the basis of their instinct to hunt certain species: game of fur or feather, rabbit or quail. On the day of the hunt proper, after weeks of trials and failures, the hunters take out their birds perched on a leather-gloved wrist. Being heavier, eagles perch more often on the horse's saddle, since their weight would be too much for the hunter's wrist.

The hunt may last for hours. Horsemen and birds scan the landscape, the former avoiding the slightest noise. Sometimes it is the man who espies the prey first, sometimes it is the bird, which has had its blindfold, a leather hood, removed. As soon as the hunter catches sight of the animal, he 'throws' the raptor: the falcon takes flight and on the wing stirs up the partridge or the furry balls scurrying to hide among the pebbles. For a moment the bird hovers above his victims, noting the speed and direction of their movement, instinctively picking out the animal that is slowest and most vulnerable. Then he swoops down on it, seizes it in his talons and strikes it on the head with his beak to kill it. Whether the prey is a hare surprised near its burrow or a quail snatched in full flight, the bird of prey grounds it and immediately takes up a characteristic stance indicating possession, intimidation and threat, and spreads his wings to cover the dead quarry. His master must jump from the saddle as quickly as he can to snatch up the remains, which the raptor will already have begun to tear with his beak. The Mongol rider pulls a piece of meat from under his coat, the head of a fieldmouse, perhaps, which he substitutes for the quarry. This scrap of carrion is the falcon's only reward. Quite often the bird misses his target. Those goshawks and eagles are rare which kill several animals in a row; either they tire quite quickly or, having feasted, they refuse instinctively to return to the hunt. It is only men, after all, who take pleasure in hunting.

Time without number Temüjin must have taken part in these chases, these ritualized games in which everyone strove to compete with the swiftest riders. Yet times were still hard for his family, who, according to the chronicle, owned a sum total of nine cream-coloured geldings. Then one day some Tayichi'ud horsemen stole eight of these. This type of theft, which was very common, used to cause feuds that sometimes endured for generations. Although the livestock were branded and there were dogs guarding the flocks, raids were launched to replace sheep lost through epidemics or eaten by wild animals or, just as frequently, out of the sheer thrill of rustling.

The theft of the eight horses had a devastating effect on Temüjin's family. What were they to do without mounts? They could not keep watch over their flocks on foot. Temüjin was left with just one horse: he jumped astride and set off to track down the thieves. For eight days he followed their traces. By chance he met a shepherd who told him he had seen a troop of riders driving eight horses in front of them, and was able to remember the horses' colour. This piece of information was enough for Temüjin, who galloped off to retrieve his property, accompanied by the young shepherd. The youths eventually caught the rustlers and recovered the stolen geldings without the incident's degenerating into a real confrontation.

Now that he had found his herd again, Temüjin offered to share it with the young shepherd, whose name was Bo'urchu. But the boy refused, saying that he had wanted nothing more than to be of service. His generosity touched Temüjin deeply, and thus began a friendship between the two which was never to be broken. Bo'urchu then took Temüjin to meet his father. Afterwards, having feasted with them on roast baby lamb, he went back to the family camp.

These are modest enough exploits, one may think, and probably embroidered by the author of *The Secret History* to cast a favourable light on his adventurer hero. But let us not forget that Temüjin was then still a youth and that these were but his first campaigns.

## A Promise Kept

As the years went by, Temüjin and his family seem to have begun to live appreciably better. It was hardly opulence, but they had a herd that was growing stout, some fine stallions grazing the grass, and a promising flock. They moved to higher pastures as usual, into the upper reaches of the Onon Gol and the nearby Onggirad territory, where the Selenge Mörön flows into the lake Hulun Nur.

It was hereabouts that Temüjin, now grown to manhood, again took up the thread with Dei the Wise, the Onggirad whom he had not seen since the death of Yesügei, some seven years earlier. Temüjin had not forgotten that he had been betrothed to Dei's daughter. One fine day, therefore, he went to meet the Onggirad, accompanied by his half-brother Belgütei, to seek out his betrothed, young Börte, now aged 16 years. Although many years of trouble had elapsed and despite the tragic death of Yesügei, Dei the Wise confirmed the understanding he had reached with the latter and, true to his word, agreed to give his daughter in marriage to Temüjin. When he put young Börte's fate in Temüjin's hands, he gave her the customary dowry of servants and goods.

*The Secret History* gives hardly any details about the wedding ritual. Pian del Carpini, like Rubrouck, reports that the Mongols bought their wives and that the young bridegroom carried his fiancée off in secret back to his family: 'abducted her by force and took her to his house, as though having to use violence'. The Turco-Mongol game of *kökböri* (blue wolf), better known by its Persian name of *bozkashi*, in which horsemen fight over the skin of a goat or a sheep, is probably a vestige of the wedding ritual.

We do not know how much Temüjin paid for his bride, but she brought a present, the so-called *sitkül*, in her dowry for her future mother-in-law. This was a truly royal gift: a coat of sable, which was to play no small part in the rise of Temüjin. The union between Börte and Temüjin speaks of a marriage of convenience as much as of an affair of the heart. *The Secret History* clearly says that the Onggirad girls were renowned for their beauty.

So Temüjin became a married man. Though he was not wealthy, he could from now on count on the support of family and clan. After the hard years of wandering, the flight from powerful enemies, and the captivity and humiliation, the time had come for him to forge useful alliances so that he could exert some influence beyond the bounds of his own yurt. It was from the very moment of his marriage to Börte, indeed, that the man began to assert himself. His wife was unquestionably a not irrelevant adjunct to this process. Besides offering the support of her people, she brought to him the strength of her character. Intelligent, firm and wise, Börte proved to offer excellent counsel to Temüjin; there were some occasions, indeed, on which her influence on him was to be decisive. Temüjin was to take several other wives and concubines, but he always remained attached to his first wife.

## Tents and Tribes

Now, as the twelfth century was coming to an end, central Asia was passing through a period of political upheaval and excitement: from the Pacific coast to the Caspian Sea there coexisted great states of settled peoples, formed out of ancient civilizations, as well as unruly, often short-lived principalities, comprised of nomadic peoples.

Immediately after the fall of the Liao dynasty (1125), the situation in China was complex: the entire south, right up to the western marches, belonged to the Song empire, whose nerve centre was the metropolis of Hangzhou, which was situated on its marine frontage. Founded in 960 by edict, the Song dynasty restored civil power and brought glowing international esteem to the empire: during this time, China experienced a golden age. The north of the country, that is, the provinces traversed by the Huang He (Yellow River) and a large part of Manchuria, were in the hands of the Jin dynasty, founded in 1115 by the Ruzhen (or Jurchen) on the ruins of the Liao (Khitan) dynasty. The Ruzhen, Tungus in origin, and nomads of long standing, formed an alliance with the Song to invade the far north of China, and eventually, having become thoroughly Sinicized, adopted also the civil and military administrative systems of the Chinese.

Farther west, in the region of the great loop of the Huang He and in northern Kansu, the Xixia held sway. These people, who were closely related to the Tibetans, established a court at Ningxia, the capital of the Minyak empire.

In western high Asia, to the south of the Aral Sea (now called Aral'skoye More) and as far as the Persian Gulf, an area that included present-day Iran, part of western Afghanistan, and the Soviet republics of Turkmenistan (now Turkmeniya) and Uzbekistan, extended the vast Moslem empire of Khwārezm, peopled by Turco-Iranians.

Flanking the latter to the northeast and corresponding roughly with the Soviet republics of Kirgiziya and Kazakhstan, but going beyond into the desert zone of the Chinese Taklimakan Shamo, was another empire: that of the Qara-Khitai, headed by an aristocracy of Mongol stock but heavily influenced by China. Towards 1140, this empire succeeded in subjugating the Turkish Qarqanid principalities occupying Transoxiana and part of the Taklimakan Shamo, as well as Khwārezm, before that state expanded at the beginning of the thirteenth century, at the expense of neighbouring kingdoms and principalities. The Qara-Khitai, for their part, dominated the Uighur, a partly Christianized Turkish people.

On the margins of these great states, vast steppes formed the ever-moving and turbulent domain of the nomads. Stretching for nearly 3,000 kilometres from the eastern limit of Manchuria to Lake Balkhash in the west, it put its stamp on all the region that included the sources of the great Siberian rivers Irtysh, Ob, Yenisey, Vitim, and Ergun He (Argun). Largely because of their lack of the written word and the absence of cities, the history of the nomadic peoples remains obscure to this day. Proto-Tungus from Manchuria and western Mongolia, Proto-Turks from Mongolia and the vast zones extending towards the Altay and Lake Balkhash, and, later on, Proto-Mongols together constituted a complex ethnic mosaic. For some 3,000 years, these peoples maintained an intense rivalry with the settled peoples who, by repulsing them, forbade them to practise transhumance on their lands. Nearly fifteen centuries before Christ, Chinese settlers must already have been pushing these nomads back: the chronicler Sima Qian reports how the populations of the principalities of the far north were forced into repeated exodus, and how the nomads mounted raids on virgin lands cultivated by Chinese peasants.

This deep hostility between the two types of peoples with their conflicting ways of life has remained engraved in their consciousness and has even appeared in Chinese writing: for example, right up until the reforming decade of the 1950s, the Chinese referred to 'barbarians' with words whose roots often derived from the notion of bestiality. These ideograms implicitly designated nomads as 'dog-men', 'bird-men' or 'insect-men'. To settled peoples, could these people, with their unknown and consequently disturbing customs, who were constantly on the move, who had no cities and apparently no laws, could they really be human? In their eyes, a person who has no roof over his head is faithless and lawless. Only 100 years ago, Captain Mayne-Reid described the practices and customs of the Turkmen nomads in these terms:

These vagabond tribes, who belong to a great variety of races, and of whom the best known are the Mongols, the Tatars, the Turkmen, the Uzbeks, the Kirghiz and the Kalmyks, display different characteristics, both moral and physical . . . Many of them have a bloodthirsty temperament and evince qualities no less fierce than the most odious savages in other parts of the world.

These are nevertheless the very 'savages' who founded principalities and kingdoms, though sometimes short-lived ones, assembling and disbanding as political circumstance demanded.

The nomads of central Asia belong, therefore, to three main groups: Tungus, Mongols, and Turks. But this classification is subject to a high degree of vagueness and overlap, partly because of the diversity of subgroups and partly because of their extreme mobility in time and space. The Xiongnu are thus sometimes considered to be Proto-Turks (according to Hambis, Pelliot and Shiratori in his first hypothesis); sometimes to be Proto-Mongols (Shiratori's second version). The Tatars, for their part, are certainly Turks, but they have sometimes been designated Proto-Mongols who have undergone Turkish influence and intermarriage. The difficulties of categorization magnify when one takes into account the fact that several of these peoples were at times ruled by a foreign aristocracy.

Of the first Proto-Turk empires we have some acquaintance, if not a great deal, with the Xiongnu who, between the third and the second century BC, formed confederations of clans: they often found themselves in conflict with Chinese power, which on many occasions countered their attempts to extend their territory. Beaten back by military might — and, equally, defeated by Chinese diplomatic trickery which took skilful advantage of divisions among tribes and played them off against one another — the Xiongnu eventually dispersed. One subgroup established themselves in the vicinity of the Great Wall, while others were gradually absorbed into China. Still other groups emigrated to the area of the upper Irtysh, where they pushed the Vogul and Ostyak peoples back towards the forests of the far north. These last contributed to stamping a Turkish imprint on the steppe zones of Kirgiziya. It was the Xiongnu who were to creep over towards the Ukraine in the second century and who, two centuries after that, were to rise up in the West and even invade Gaul, under the name Huns.

As for the Proto-Mongols, they made a hazy appearance around

150 BC, with the emergence of the Xianbi (Hsien-pi), who occupied a vast territory extending from Manchuria to Turkestan. These nomads crushed the Xiongnu, who were torn apart by internal rivalries, in AD 93 and very quickly became embroiled in conflict with China.

From the fourth to the sixth century, the empire of the Ruanruan (Avars) was founded between Korea and the Irtysh on land that had once been part of the Xiongnu empire. Then, from the eighth to the ninth century, a Uighur khanate of Turkish stock entrenched itself in a huge area of the two Mongolias that then existed. The Uighurs, who had ousted another Turkish people, the Tujue, set up their capital at Qara Balγasun, on the Orhon Gol. Influenced by the China of the Tang dynasty and by Sogdiana, they attained a high level of civilization, but they were unable to resist the Kirghiz (in 840), who were themselves conquered around 960 by the Khitan, a people of Mongol stock. The Khitan occupied northern China, along with parts of Mongolia and Manchuria, but were not really able to subdue the tribes of upper Mongolia, with the exception of the Tatars and the Merkid.

On the threshold of the thirteenth century, before the armies of Genghis Khan burst upon the scene, Mongolia was like a huge frozen sea on which the tribes drifted aimlessly like ice floes: sometimes they would join together in a confederation, only to disperse again when it weakened or lost its authority. Neither the Khitan, who were under threat from the Chinese empire, the kingdom of Korea and the Uighur simultaneously, nor the Uighur themselves, who were also in conflict with unruly principalities, were in a position to assume political and military control over the immense Mongol steppes. Others, the Kereyid and the Naiman, for example, were to disappear before the onslaught of Genghis Khan. Mongolia, that huge theatre over which no one succeeded in gaining overall mastery for any length of time, remained a place where tribal groups periodically met and fought without any real hope or intention of holding the reins of power.

## A Moving Ethnic Patchwork

It was in the Tang era (618–907) that the Mongols first made their appearance under the original name of *Meng-wu*. According to Chinese annals, this tribal population belonged to a more important grouping that lived along the upper reaches of the Amur river, the She-wei. These were no doubt a fairly diverse collection of people, comprising Proto-Mongols and Tungus. The Chinese of the tenth century, who were at that time

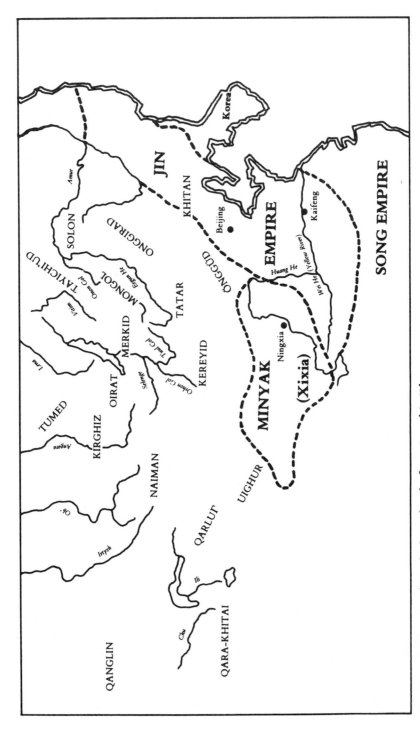

Map 3.   Mongol and Turkish Tribes before Genghis Khan

going through an undoubted upsurge in their cultural life, depicted them as savages of the most despicable kind and even went so far as to accuse them of being cannibals who ate raw flesh. The volumes of the *History of the Liao* have given us the names of various Mongol subgroups (*Hei Ta-ta*, or Black Tatars; *Bai Ta-ta*, or White Tatars, etc).

What, then, were the ethnic groups scattered over those spaces that lay unclaimed or had been forsaken by settled peoples, at the end of the twelfth century? Southwest of Lake Baikal, near the sources of the huge Irtysh and Ob' rivers which slice through Siberia, lived the Naiman, wandering as far as the upper reaches of the Selenge Mörön and Orhon Gol. They were Turks who had some Mongol blood and at that time spoke Mongol dialects. However, influenced as they were by their Uighur neighbours, they used their own language in official documents. Though shamanist originally, they had adopted Nestorian Christianity. Their prince bore the title *da wang* or *tai wang* (in Chinese: great king), a fact which leads one to believe that they owed just as much to the influence of the Sinicized Ruzhen.

To the south of the Selenge, and along the course of the Tuul Gol, we find the Kereyid. In the beginning they were most likely a loose confederation of Turkish clans. Their sovereign, To'oril, had a Turkish name, however, and some historians believe that at the beginning of the epic that was the era of Genghis Khan the Kereyid spoke a Turkish dialect. Nestorian Christianity spread among these people from the twelfth century onwards, as is demonstrated by the Christian names given to some of the Kereyid aristocracy.

Along the banks of the Selenge, to the south of Lake Baikal, lived the Merkid, cheek by jowl with the forest tribes with whom they were constantly in conflict. This unruly tribe held out for a long time against the Mongols and the Chinese. Lastly, near the lakes Buyr and Hulun, on the right bank of the Ergun He, there lived the Tatars, already speaking a Mongol dialect, even though it was of Turkish origin. Well known even in the West for their aggressiveness, the Tatars were later to clash with the Ruzhen who ruled northern China and Manchuria.

The Mongol tribes proper — altogether they probably numbered fewer than a million souls — lived around Lake Baikal and the sources of the great north-flowing Siberian rivers. They were splintered into many clans, some important, some not, and were forever in the throes of political turmoil, despite the fact that traditional divisions of territory clearly allocated summer and winter pastures to this or that clan. Failure to observe verbal agreements regarding the distribution of pasture lands, repeated theft of animals, robbery of all kinds and rivalries among clan chiefs all gave rise to an endless string of grudges, feuds, and vendettas whose participants could, at times, not remember what had caused them. Tribes united for the duration of a season or the duration of some conflict, or even for several years, and then, for some obscure reason, they parted company, each clan or subclan staking its own claim to independence and its own rights and becoming the rival of the other.

From the tenth century onwards, upper Mongolia was riven by profound anarchy, each tribe being full of mistrust for its neighbour. Ever in flux, these Mongol tribes — Onggirad, Merkid, Tatar, Oirat, Önggüd or Barula — were close in origin, in language, above all in their way of life, but they evidently did not constitute a nation. Having no real institutions and no law of succession, there was no prospect whatever that they might be capable of forming a confederation. To unite them it would have been necessary first to impose some kind of rigid framework on them, and that could be done only by the authority or the charisma of a prince. Many times throughout history, we see how the death of a khan caused the break-up of any tribal unity or organization. Therein lay the weakness of the Mongol feudal system, which was nearly always unable to take advantage of any system of hereditary succession such as existed in the khanates. Among the Mongol tribes, power rested wherever the khan's tent had been placed, whereas in the same era, among settled societies, royal power was associated with a capital city which, if not fixed, was at least honoured by tradition.

For over 2,000 years, the Chinese had been in contact with the Mongol or Turkish nomads, sometimes doing battle with them, sometimes reducing them to servitude: depending on whether they remained thoroughgoing enemies or had been pacified, the Chinese often termed them 'raw barbarians' or 'cooked barbarians'. But at the same time they maintained commerce with them and, in particular, were regular buyers of their horses for their own troops.

The Khitan and the Ruzhen, ancient peoples who had traded nomadism for a settled way of life and become the founders of powerful empires, were also in contact with these 'barbarians'. The Sinicized Ruzhen (Jin dynasty), once installed in Beijing (1153), established diplomatic relations with them, thus entering into a highly ambivalent position vis-à-vis their dealings with the nomads. More often than not, they would strive to heighten internal rivalries so as to be able to take advantage of them. It was clearly in Beijing's interest, if not to be allied with the nomads, at least to profit from the benevolent neutrality of these tribes which formed a protective buffer along the imperial frontiers. To make these people favourably disposed towards the empire, the Jin rulers often had only to send their chiefs manufactured goods made by Chinese artisans which could not be found on the steppes. On other occasions, they would send courtesans who were past their prime and could no longer hope to find favour at court. Again, honorific titles would sometimes be dispensed to minor nobles among the barbarians. This delicate diplomacy inevitably entailed compromises, not to say compromising acts. It also stirred up undying hatred among different groups of the nomads, who stood disunited and defenceless against Chinese intrigues. Around the year 1150, the Tatars handed over to the Beijing authorities a Kereyid ruler, Markuz Buyiruγ Qan, and then a Mongol prince, Ökin Baraqaγ, son of the first 'unifier' of the Mongols, Qabul Qan, reputed to be the ancestor of Genghis Khan. They also gave up to their powerful neighbour the chief of the Tayichi'ud, Ambaγai, the man whose two widows quarrelled with Hö'elün, Temüjin's mother. These acts of treachery were to stick in the great khan's mind.

These encounters, interspersed with political trickery of the lowest kind, gave repeated impetus to the formation of bands of guerrillas among the Mongol tribal groups — a situation which was, to say the least, hardly conducive to unification.

## Languages of the Altay: The Word and the Seal
The constant mixing of the nomads of central Asia, their temporary alliances followed by slow or sudden separations, all contributed to miscegenation and to the assimilation of some groups into others to whom they may or may not have been related. Lacking the art of writing, these nomadic peoples could not always record all their migrations, invasions, and dispersals; but the study of their languages enables us to shed light on their origins. Although the vast majority of the populations of high Asia speak related dialects — belonging to the Altaic family — this huge region has no true linguistic unity. Because of the often very significant distances between the tribal groups, in view of their constant migration, and, lastly, because of their political fragmentation, the nomad populations use numerous languages or dialects.

The linguistic family that prevails over the bulk of Siberia and central Asia is known as Altaic, and includes languages spoken today by nearly

80 million people, the vast majority of them closely related to Turkish. This family comprises three distinct groups: Tungusic, Mongol and Turkic. They are distinguished by their simple system of sounds, rich in vowels and poor in consonants, and they conform to the law of vocalic harmony. Their construction is agglutinative — simple words are combined to express compound ideas — and they have a complex system of declensions.

The Tungusic languages (Solon, Orochon, Olcha, Evenki, Manchu, etc) are spoken principally in the extreme eastern part of high Asia, in an area that goes beyond the modern provinces of northeast China (Liaoning, Jilin and Heilongjiang, as well as the left bank of the Amur river), and in part of the far north of Korea. But the Tungus dialect spoken by the Ruzhen, who then ruled northern China, did not fully develop until the ascendancy of Manchu power in the sixteenth century.

The Turkic languages were spread over a much larger geographical area, covering the whole of central Asia, from western Mongolia to the European border. The Xiongnu were Turkic-speaking, as were the Hephthalite Huns who, around AD 500, held sway over part of central Asia, between the Aral Sea and the upper Indus. Also Turkic-speaking were most of the peoples who, in the following centuries, founded the great central Asian kingdoms (Qarqanid, Uighur, Qara-Khitai, and Khwārezm). With the outward thrust of the Mongols, the Turkic language was gradually pushed westward. There remain, however, various doubts about the ethno-linguistic origins of several of these peoples: thus, one hesitates to designate the Merkid and the Naiman as Mongolized Turks or, conversely, as Mongols who had come under Turkish influence.

In short, the Mongol languages were spoken over an area that was broadly coterminous with that over which the Altaic group of languages extended. This explains the many Turkic or Tungusic borrowings into Mongol and, equally, the Mongolization of other Altaic linguistic groups. At the time of Genghis Khan, the various Mongol dialects were already dominated by the western dialect, because it was this that was used in the peripatetic imperial court. Later, when the Mongols acquired the art of writing, at the beginning of the fourteenth century, it was this dialectal form that was set down and developed throughout Mongolia.

At the end of the thirteenth century, the Mongols often had recourse to scribes, either among settled peoples with whom they traded, or among caravaneers, or even among foreign prisoners. They would also have recruited interpreters, who had long since created an important role for themselves in establishing contacts between tribes. As Genghis Khan's power spread over a huge part of Asia and stabilized, and especially as the · Mongols came into contact with the Chinese and with Sinicized peoples, so the idea of creating a body of public records — and therefore writing — began to emerge.

Rubrouck and Marco Polo both commented on the use the Mongols made of the *paizi*, tablets of wood, jade or gold stamped with an imperial seal. These 'tablets of authority' (*paizi* or *pai-mian* in Chinese, *paiza* in Mongolian) probably originated in China. They consisted of two symmetrical pieces of wood or metal bearing first some notches (*fu*), and then some engraved inscriptions or decorations. One of these pieces would be kept by the authority who received the documents; the other would be handed back to the messenger or to the envoy who served as go-between. The messages were considered valid if one half of the *paizi* corresponded with the other, thus guaranteeing authenticity on the part of both sender and recipient. *Paizi* were given only to the most trustworthy people, and to be asked to transmit one was considered an honour. The use of 'tablets of authority', which was like that of the chancery seal, was known to the Mongols from the time when they came into contact with the Khitan and the Sinicized Ruzhen, that is, from the beginning of the ascent of the Genghis Khan dynasty. According to the Japanese historian Haneda Toru, it was Temüjin himself who, on meeting a Khitan captured in Beijing in 1215, Yelü Chucai, introduced the use of the *paizi* within his empire. These were the first fruits of writing.

The Uighur also played a fundamental part in the cultural development of the Mongols. The Uighur had come to prominence between 754 and 850, founding a khanate that compared in importance with the two contemporary Mongolian khanates. They had formed an alliance with the Chinese of the Tang dynasty, and this, combined with the influence of Mazdean missionaries from the Persian borders, had given them access to a refined culture which was further enriched by incoming caravans. These caravans not only brought valuable merchandise but also spread new techniques and ideas drawn both from Turco-Iranian civilizations and from the rich Buddhist culture which flourished in central Asia. Along with the Chinese, the Uighur became the educators of the still rough-and-ready nomadic Mongols. They had also created an alphabet which replaced that of their Tujue predecessors: adapted from Sogdian and an earlier form of Syriac, this permitted the notation of the Turkic sounds that occurred in their language. Syriac script, incidentally, introduced into high Asia by Nestorian missions, was derived from ancient Aramaic, the Semitic language of the Middle East.

Perhaps because of the influence of Chinese, the new Uighur script was written vertically. The chanceries of Turkic and Mongol monarchs in central Asia were soon to employ the services of Uighur secretaries; history records the name of one of the first such assistants who served the imperial bureaucracy of Genghis Khan, that of Tata Tong-a. This form of writing developed by the Uighurs was in common use under Temüjin and his successors until his grandson Kublai undertook a reform of the written language. Kublai called on the services of a lama who, taking inspiration both from Tibetan and Chinese, invented a new graphic system. After the fall of the Yuan dynasty (1368), when the Mongol conquerors began to spread back towards the steppes from which they had come, Uighur script, slightly modified, was reinstated. In the seventeenth century, a Mongol lama created another form of writing which came to be used in the Tien Shan and around the area of Qinghai Hu (Koko Nor); the Kalmyks of the Volga went on using this until the twentieth century. This Uighur script is still used today by the Mongols living in China (Inner Mongolia), but in the Mongolian People's Republic it has been replaced by the Cyrillic alphabet, to which have been added certain letters that are used to record the phonic peculiarities of the language.

**First Moves towards Hegemony**
Despite the endless clashes between tribes and constant centrifugal impulses, certain Mongol tribes had taken the first steps towards what may be called tribal confederation, following the triumphs of the Mongol armies. Between 1139 and 1147, the Jin dynasty in China crumbled before the onslaught of the nomads and several Mongol chiefs, skilled in strategy, were evidently able to gain the upper hand. Various epic poems glorifying their exploits bear witness to this success. Without stating as much explicitly, Chinese and Persian texts indicate, between the lines, that the Mongol tribes at the end of the twelfth century, inspired by some of their chiefs, were beginning to 'stir'.

From the episodes recounted, with a certain grandiloquence, in *The Secret History*, there emerge from the shadows certain chiefs crowned with military glory. One such was Qaidu, who founded the Borjigin clan and was therefore an ancestor of Temüjin. Another was Qabul Qan, considered to have been the founder of the first unified Mongol kingdom.

*The Secret History* says that 'Qabul Qan had the government of all the Mongols', and the Persian chronicler Rashīd al-Dīn mentions him in an episode tinged with farce: a guest at the court of Beijing, Qabul Qan did sufficient justice to the banquet organized for him, but, having drunk considerably more than was wise, he began to indulge in some rather crude familiarities towards the emperor of China and even went so far as to tug his beard. The latter declined to take offence at this little drunken joke because, says the Persian chronicler, he had been rather amused to watch his guest's gluttony. It is more likely that the Beijing court preferred to avoid any misplaced response to this boor for fear of provoking a diplomatic incident. None the less, the Mongol sovereign was conducted respectfully back to the imperial frontiers.

Afterwards, Beijing invited Qabul Qan again, this time with the intention of seizing him. Apparently he was wise to the intrigues of the Chinese and mistrustful of their intentions, so he contrived a diplomatic absence on the pretext of some unforeseen occurrence. Nevertheless, he was followed and caught by Chinese envoys, who had instantly been transformed into secret agents. Qabul Qan managed, however, to get away and, rousing his followers, enticed his enemies into a tent, where he had them promptly executed. The farce turned into tragedy, and Beijing could no longer tolerate the insult and injury done both to the sovereign and to those in his service.

The conflict which erupted between the two sides was conspicuous for its indecisive battles, but it concluded with a victory for the Mongols. In 1147, the Chinese Jin empire was forced to sign a peace treaty, under the terms of which it abandoned about thirty fortified positions and undertook to hand over to the nomads not only manufactured goods, as had been the practice, but also, henceforth, grain and livestock. In addition, the Mongol chief had an honorific title bestowed on himself. Qabul Qan, this tragicomic petty king, seemingly succeeded in bringing the Chinese empire to its knees by force of arms, after having made a fool of the sovereign with his clownish behaviour. In fact, the episode is still a matter of controversy, and it is not even certain whether the Sino-Mongol treaty was really signed in the reign of Qabul Qan.

*The Secret History* traces Temüjin's genealogy back to Qaidu, but he does not seem to have been descended from Qabul Qan, the first 'unifier' of the Mongol people. It must therefore be conceded that, even if a latent desire for hegemony existed in the time of Qabul Qan, it did not fully surface on the Mongol scene until the time of Temüjin.

## Alliance with To'oril

Gradually Temüjin began to forge anew alliances that had lapsed with the death of his father. During the years when his powers were at their height, Yesügei certainly helped To'oril, who had proclaimed himself sovereign of the Kereyid, to regain his throne. Temüjin cleverly chose an opportune moment to remind To'oril of his existence. While this was a shrewd move, it was also a risky one, since Temüjin had had no contact with the Kereyid for years. He had therefore to act with caution.

Accompanied by Jochi Qasar and Belgütei, his brother and half-brother, Temüjin rode to the banks of the Tuul Gol, which flows into Lake Baikal, the world's deepest lake. This was the nomadic home of the Kereyid, whose origins are shrouded in controversy and of whom nothing is known before the twelfth century. Rashīd al-Dīn, the Persian, records the genealogy of some of their rulers. The man who united the Kereyid was Markuz Buyiruγ Qan, who was probably of Turkic stock and is often claimed to have been a Christian, since his name was derived from that of Mark. The Kereyid, united under the same sceptre of imperial authority, were in part converted to Nestorianism. In the fifth century, the Nestorian Christians, followers of Nestorius, the bishop of Constantinople, had adopted the heresy that Christ was divided into two persons, intimately connected but still distinct. The Syrian bishop Apollinaris, the School of Antioch, and the Council of Ephesus were all engaged in debate about this doctrine, which was a Christology of a decidedly esoteric nature. We do not know exactly how Nestorianism spread across central Asia, but we do know that Christian missions were set up in Persia, Kurdestan and India.

It was these Nestorians that Temüjin, somewhat hesitatingly, approached. He took with him, as a present for their king, To'oril, the coat of sable. To'oril received the son of his old ally Yesügei, apparently pleased to observe the young man's servile manner of introducing himself: 'Once you were the *anda* [sworn brother] of my father; you are therefore just like a father to me. I have taken a wife and I bring you the gift she brought when she first came to me.' Flattered, To'oril accepted the present and, to show his magnanimity, offered Temüjin his services. He assured the young man of his support and, better still, offered to restore the common heritage which the people had possessed under his old comrade in arms, Yesügei. The prospect of personally pulling together many Mongol clans could hardly have been more appealing to Temüjin. 'I will bring back to you your straying kinsmen,' declared

To'oril to his guest. 'I will reunite your scattered people. I will bind them to you with an unbreakable bond. This thought will always be uppermost in my mind and nearest to my heart.'

This lavish promise came as a surprise. For, after all, what significance did Temüjin have in the eyes of the king of the Kereyid, who had power over a far-flung collection of tribes and was assured of a glorious place in history? True, Temüjin was the son of a clan chief who had achieved his own moments of glory, and therefore he was of noble origin. But for now he was nothing more than a small stockbreeder, owning fewer than ten horses! What high reputation could he possibly enjoy, apart from his birth? He had to his credit some exciting exploits on horseback, but these were, when all was said and done, minor retaliatory ventures against cattle rustlers. The conclusion we must draw is that the Kereyid king thought so highly of his former ally Yesügei that he was moved to offer to the son what he had not given to the father. Be that as it may, one cannot help admiring the audacity and resourcefulness of Temüjin, coming as he did, with sable coat under his arm, to renew an old alliance with a respected ruler who gave orders to several thousand men. Temüjin found himself a protector at the same time that he found an ally. The eaglet had cleverly sought protection under the wing of the eagle.

The news travelled quite fast around the Mongolian vastnesses. When he returned to his family's yurt, Temüjin and his companions were approached by an old man of the Urianqadai tribe, one Jarchi'udai Ebügen, in the company of his son, Jelme. The old man, apparently out of long-standing loyalty to Yesügei — or because he had heard of the friendship struck up between Temüjin and To'oril — came to offer the services of his son; Jelme was to prove himself one of Genghis's most courageous military leaders.

Thus, although he had just become the Kereyid king's vassal, Temüjin was assuming the command of a band of faithful followers, the first of many in his later entourage. Was it his leadership qualities that made fortune so smile on him? Or should we conclude that those around him foresaw that this daring young man would one day have the bright star of good luck dawning over his head?

# 5
# Entering the Fray

*'I have put on my leather-fastened armour,*
*And seized my hilted sword;*
*I have cut my nocked arrow.*
*I am ready, let us fight to the death*
*Against the Uduyid-Merkid!'*
*Give them this message! After my brother To'oril-qan has set*
*out and, coming from the southern side of Burqan Qaldun, has*
*passed my sworn brother Temüjin and* joined forces with
him, *let us meet at Botoqan-bo'orji at the source of the Onon*
*river.*

**The Secret History of the Mongols**

## The Merkid Abduct Börte

In about the year 1184, Temüjin, then not yet 30 years old, was beginning
to think about ways of restoring the gilt on his coat of arms, so badly
tarnished by the Tayichi'ud, when he was confronted by a sudden twist of
fate: the abduction of his young wife.

The felt tents of his encampment had been erected in the area around
the upper reaches of the Kerulen, and all its members were attending to
their daily chores with the livestock or in the dwelling. Suddenly, an old
woman who served Hö'elün said she thought she detected some kind of
threat. When she pressed her ear to the ground, her fears were
immediately confirmed. Anxiously she announced that a strong party of
riders was approaching the yurt. In an instant, the Mongol camp prepared
to meet an attack by pillagers. Nobody registered much surprise: the
camp had long expected the Tayichi'ud to attack them.

What they saw now, however, was a group of about 300 Merkid
horsemen. These believed they had an account to settle with Temüjin's

late father who, it will be remembered, had snatched Hö'elün from them. It was past history, going back 20 years or more. The chronicle does not say so, but this abduction had probably given rise to one of those common feuds that poisoned relationships among clans and tribes. This time, the Merkid had come to strike back with a vengeance by seizing some women in their turn. Temüjin and his people were not slow to realize that, with their mere nine saddled horses, they were incapable of resisting such a large party. They all leapt onto their mounts: Temüjin and his brothers, as well as Bo'urchu and Jelme, Hö'elün with her daughter Temülün riding behind. There was no horse left for Temüjin's wife Börte, nor for Yesügei's second wife, who lived with Hö'elün.

It may seem surprising that the men appear so thoughtlessly to have abandoned members of their family to their fate, one of whom was a young married woman who would doubtless arouse some desire in many of the Merkid riders. How to explain their precipitate flight? Perhaps they were simply terrified by the prospect of the enemy riders bursting on the scene; or perhaps they harboured little regard for women. Or could it be that Temüjin — supremely cunning, as ever — chose to leave his own wife behind as a kind of bait in order to let the rest of his entourage escape? Calling reassuringly to those already galloping away, an old servant said she would hide Börte. This she did by concealing her under some bales of wool heaped on a waggon.

The Merkid riders reached the deserted camp soon afterwards and, according to *The Secret History*, seized Yesügei's wife without striking a blow. Then, catching sight of the servant, they pressed her to explain why she was in the yurt. The woman maintained she had come to take a waggon of wool back to her own encampment. Unconvinced, the Merkid started rummaging in the vehicle, where they very soon uncovered Börte. It is not difficult to imagine their shouts of triumph and their laughter of greed and lust when they came upon their lovely quarry. The riders dismounted, entered the tents and swept up everything they could carry. Failing to discover a single man, they recognized some male tracks but these ran out where the men had plunged into thickets or swamps by the forest; the riders therefore had, with bad grace, to give up their idea of inflicting a lesson on Temüjin and his comrades. They had their booty: Börte and Yesügei's widow. Their honour was satisfied.

Temüjin and his brothers did not re-emerge from the woods until they were quite sure that the Merkid had gone. Indeed, Temüjin remained in hiding for several days, sheltering under a hut of branches, fearful lest the enemy return. Eventually, when the danger seemed to have passed, he summoned up courage and returned to the camp. The chronicle relates that, to thank the gods for having saved his life, Temüjin faced the sacred mountain of Burqan Qaldun and spoke the following words: 'Thanks to old Qo'aγchin and her ear of a weasel and her eye of a fox, I have escaped with my life, I have reached Mount Burqan, and I have made myself a hut of willow branches; I had to run away to Mount Burqan Qaldun like a poor louse. Every morning I shall offer a sacrifice to Burqan Qaldun, and every day I shall invoke it; let the sons of my sons know of this and understand!' Then, in accordance with the custom of his religion, he undid his belt and hung it around his neck and, beating his chest with his fist, prostrated himself nine times in the direction of the sun.

Not much is known about the religious beliefs of the Mongols at that time. Jean-Paul Roux has shown in *La Religion des Turcs et des Mongols* that nomads and forest dwellers practised cult worship of certain natural elevations, such as hills and rocks:

> Every elevated feature, be it a simple rock in regions of flat plains, is invested with meaning. It represents some embryonic thrust of earth towards heaven, and ascending it is an upward step towards God. Prayers are more likely to be heard from a high point, and the wandering souls of the dead less distant from the eternal life they seek.

For the Turks and Mongols, mountains, which were supposed to be the progenitors of a clan's animal ancestors, and which were believed to ensure the protection of one of their heroic founding fathers, were sacred. Mount Burqan Qaldun, to which Temüjin addressed himself, was no doubt one of these holy places. It is, in fact, located in just the same place as the sources of the sacred water courses where the ancestors of the Mongols first drew breath. At the very beginning of *The Secret History*, there is an episode which suggests that a Cyclops haunting Burqan Qaldun had united with a Mongol woman:

> Duua Soqor had only one eye in the middle of his forehead; [with this eye] he could see three stages into the distance. One day, Duua Soqor left Burqan Qaldun with his younger brother Dobun Mergen. From the top of Burqan Qaldun, Duua Soqor, looking into the distance, saw far off a group of people moving their herds to new pastures and coming [into the area]. He said: 'In the midst of those people . . . there is a

beautiful girl at the front of a "black" cart. If she is not yet spoken for, we will ask to have her for you, my younger brother Dobun Mergen.'

Thus Mount Burqan Qaldun brings us to another myth concerning the origin of the Mongol people: the mountain was somehow the 'magic mountain' which sired the Mongols. The remoteness of mountains, their difficulty of access, and their majestic summits capped with perpetual snow, are no doubt at the heart of the fascination they exert over men, and, as a logical consequence of this, of their being invested with sacred qualities.

As for the cult of sun worship also mentioned in *The Secret History*, this fitted in with astral veneration, probably associated with the broader cult of worship of the 'Everlasting Blue Sky' (*Köke Möngke Tenggeri*). Burqan Qaldun, the supposed site of the union between a legendary hero and a Mongol woman, and a symbol of verticality directed heavenwards, played a very important role in Mongol mythology, and Temüjin is known at various times in his life to have turned to it.

No sooner had Temüjin thanked heaven for having saved his life than he set about recapturing his lovely bride and avenging the affront he had suffered at the hands of the Merkid. It was natural for him to appeal to To'oril, his lord paramount of recent date, and remind him of the promise he had made to reunite Temüjin's people. The Merkid were quite powerful, and this was no mere case of recovering a few stolen horses. To attack them was to enter into serious conflict, with the attendant risk of bloodshed. Nevertheless, when Temüjin went to ask for his help, To'oril proved true to his word: 'We shall get your wife Börte back for you, even if we have to face all the Merkid tribes at once.'

The war began. Initially, its impetus derived from one cause: the beautiful eyes of a young bride.

## An Anti-Caesar Emerges

The Merkid comprised three main ethnic groups: Uduyid, Uuas, and Qa'ad. These groups and the neighbouring tribes lived as nomads, usually in the northern basin of the river Selenge Mörön, between Lake Baikal and the Altay range, a region of steppes dotted with forests becoming gradually denser the farther north one goes. To judge from the pasture lands they occupied, there were some tens of thousands of Merkid, but no more than that.

Before summoning his followers, To'oril took steps to protect his rear. He called on a Jajirad tribal chief called Jamuγa, a man of Mongol stock. An orphan raised in a noble family, Jamuγa had been a childhood friend of Temüjin and the two had, after the ritual exchange of blood, proclaimed themselves *anda*, sworn brothers. Now Jamuγa had apparently become a powerful chief in command of several thousand men. To'oril showed considerable wisdom: letting Temüjin take the initiative in and the responsibility for hostilities against the Merkid, he asked him to propose an armed alliance with Jamuγa:

> Go and speak with your young brother Jamuγa. Young brother Jamuγa is said to be at Qorqonaγ Jubur. I will have two *tümen* (20,000 men) on horseback and I shall be the right arm of the column; brother Jamuγa also should have two mounted *tümen* and be the left arm. Jamuγa should appoint the place where we should meet.

*The Secret History* indicates how many were involved on both sides. To'oril and Jamuγa each mobilized two mounted *tümen*. Altogether this made 40,000 warriors, a huge army, suggesting a very advanced level of organization and captains with highly polished manoeuvring skills, but no doubt the bard considerably exaggerated the size of the effective forces. In any case, Jamuγa was in a position to put into action as many *tümen* as the Kereyid ruler, and the latter even left the choice of meeting-place to him, which means that Jamuγa, as head of the Jajirad, was a sufficiently powerful figure to be treated as an equal by To'oril.

One wonders what strategic role Temüjin played in all this, remembering that in all he possessed a total of nine horses! Nevertheless, accompanied by his brother Jochi Qasar and his half-brother Belgütei, he went before Jamuγa to plead his cause. The Jajirad chief was certainly aware of the deal and the alliance against the Merkid which had been plotted. Whether he wanted to stay loyal to Temüjin, or whether he perceived some advantage in defeating the Merkid — the two arguments are not mutually exclusive — Jamuγa responded positively to his *anda*:

> When I learned that my *anda* had been left with an empty bed, I was sick at heart; when I learned that his breast was half rent in two by sorrow, I was sick to my liver. To vindicate his revenge, I shall destroy the Uduyid and Uuas Merkid and shall rescue his *üjin* Börte

(Lady Börte); to cleanse his wound, I shall break the Qa'ad Merkid and shall save him by bringing his Lady Börte back to him.

Uttering these words like a noble knight, Jamuγa unveiled his plan of attack. He appears to have had knowledge of the enemy's effective forces and positions. Acting as commanding officer, he set forth his cavalry arrangement, then, having given his orders, he decided to concentrate his forces. But To'oril and Temüjin, in violation of the agreements previously arrived at, did not rejoin Jamuγa until three days later and he laid stern blame on his allies:

> Did we not agree amongst ourselves that even in the event of storm we should not be late in arriving at the assembly point, nor yet in the event of a torrent of rain delay meeting at the appointed place? When Mongols say 'yes', is it not tantamount to having sworn an oath? Did we not unanimously say that we should expel from our ranks anyone who delayed in honouring his 'yes'?

To'oril, at a loss, apologized and admitted his error, and asked Jamuγa to mete out suitable punishment. But the latter, whether from magnanimity or a wish to maintain the alliance intact, declined to punish his allies. The reunited forces then pushed forward towards the Merkid. Study of a map of the operation shows that the military campaign was no mere raid undertaken lightly. The horsemen covered several dozen kilometres, over undulating ground punctuated with forests and rivers which could only be crossed by raft. Having gone over the passes of the Malkhan mountains (now Malkhanskiy Khrebet), the assembled forces at last came to the Kilγo valley, in the heart of Merkid country. From here they launched an attack on the encampment of Toγto'a Beki, chief of the Uduyid. But, having been forewarned by sable hunters and fishermen in the area, Toγto'a Beki had already fled; he left all his goods and belongings and a large number of his people to the mercy of the enemy.

**The Bride is Rescued**
From the moment battle commenced, the Merkid realized that the game was up: their camp had been overwhelmed by a surprise attack; their chief, with Mongol riders in hot pursuit, had disappeared during the night along the Selenge Mörön. A great number of the Merkid succumbed to the fury of the enemy. Men rushing from their tents were mercilessly

stabbed; others tried to creep away under cover of shadows. The air was full of cries of distress, the death rattles of the mortally wounded, the moans of the injured and the howling of women. Throughout the yurt, the bodies of the dead littered the ground.

The chronicle says nothing about Temüjin's role in this battle except that he kept apart from the fray and tumult to run and find his wife. He found her among a group of fleeing Merkid and, calling her name at the top of his voice, managed to make her hear him. Temüjin, concerned only with his wife's safe return, then asked To'oril to call a halt to the battle so that they might make camp on the battlefield. The young warrior abandoned his sword for the call of love and its joys, and *The Secret History* evokes the romantic image of the couple clasped together in the clear moonlight.

The chronicle does not tell us whether the pair were able to reach some understanding of the circumstances of the young woman's abduction by the Merkid some weeks before. On the subject of Temüjin's flight, Börte remained silent. But her husband had chivalrously made up for his previous lack of daring by at once going to war to rescue her. In any case, one thing was certain: Börte was pregnant, no doubt the work of her abductors; when the child was born a few months later, he was given the name Jochi, meaning 'guest'.

It will be remembered that, at the same time as abducting Börte, the Merkid also took Suchigil, the mother of Temüjin's half-brother. In his attempts to find her, her son, Belgütei, ran hither and thither in the devastated enemy yurt. On questioning a man taken prisoner, he succeeded in tracing her. She, however, being dressed in rags, refused to appear before her son. Before fleeing into a nearby wood, she just said that she had been living 'as man and wife with a bad man' and that she could never again 'look her son in the eye'. Belgütei looked for her for a long time, and it seemed certain she was going to meet her death, an end brought about by shame and exhaustion. Wild with rage, Belgütei drowned his sorrow in murder: with his own hands he massacred all the prisoners who had taken part in the abduction of his mother. For good measure, he also killed their children and grandchildren. The Merkid taken prisoner became part of the Mongols' war booty. These atrocities were to fan into flames the first flickers of an inextinguishable hatred between the Mongols and the Merkid.

Still, in the midst of the carnage, one could detect, here and there, a note of humaneness. The Mongols were capable of showing kindness towards children. So it was that Temüjin picked up off the battlefield a little boy of 5, dressed in furs. He had 'eyes of fire' and he was taken away, with the idea of raising him and making of him a serving boy for Hö'elün.

## A Strange Friendship

For Temüjin it was now a matter of urgency to return to his familiar pasture lands. Before doing so, he went to see his two generous allies to renew his pledges of friendship and to show them his gratitude. Then he poured libations to the divine rulers of the world beyond: to Tenggeri, the All-Powerful Sky, and to 'Mother Earth', to thank them for their help in this triumphant campaign.

Although Temüjin and his companions returned to their own lands, To'oril and Jamuγa decided to press their advantage and undertook a new offensive against another Merkid tribe, the Uuas, who were moving their herds from the Selenge Mörön to Orhon Gol. Having crushed the Uuas, To'oril returned to his camps situated around the upper Tuul Gol, not far from present-day Ulan Bator, while the paths of Jamuγa and Temüjin, strange to say, crossed again. For nearly two years, these two were yoked together in pursuit of a common destiny. They herded their flocks together near the river Onon Gol, and at the same time became inseparable comrades in arms.

At this point in the narrative of Temüjin's life, *The Secret History* allows an intimate note to creep into the text, and with it a marked sentimentality. We are told first that Temüjin and Jamuγa were for a long time childhood playmates, and that at the age of 11 they gave each other presents — a roebuck knucklebone and a 'copper-coated knucklebone' (probably as an amulet or item of jewellery) — and at the same time swore mutual friendship. Later, when they were in a hunting party, the two friends exchanged arrows, one of the whistling type, the other decorated with a juniper berry. After their victory over the Merkid, the two *anda* again began to offer each other tokens of friendship. Temüjin gave Jamuγa a golden belt he had snatched from Toγto'a, and also offered Jamuγa the chance to ride his own bay mare. Jamuγa for his part let his friend ride his courser and made him a present of a valuable belt. For months, the pair shared a carefree existence, savouring the pleasure of riding and celebrations. *The Secret History* notes that the friends decided to merge their two existences into one life; again and again, their close friendship is thus underlined.

[Temüjin and Jamuγa] had heard sages and old men say that *anda* men have [between them] but one life and that they never desert each other; thus they say: 'This will be the safeguard of our life.' Such is the love they bear for each other. Now the two renewed their *anda* union and said, 'We love each other.'

A later passage returns to their exchanges of gifts and then to their relationship:

In front of the Quldaγar Qun of Qorqonaγ Jubur, by a bushy tree, they declared themselves *anda* and swore love for each other, they rejoiced with feasts and banquets, and at night they slept together under the same blanket. Temüjin and Jamuγa loved each other; they loved each other for a whole year and half of a second year.

Rarely has the chronicler of *The Secret History* spoken so effusively or at such length about love.

But one day, when the two *anda*, followed by their families and their flocks, were drawing near some welcoming pasture land, Jamuγa cried: '*Anda, anda* Temüjin, let us dismount near the mountain; our grooms will find suitable ground there to pitch their tents. Let us dismount near the river; the men who tend our sheep and lambs will find food there for their bellies.' At first glance, it appears that Jamuγa wanted to call a halt so that the sheep might graze and the men who cared for the horses could find a good place to erect their tents. Yet, at this apparently banal suggestion, Temüjin now uttered a few words full of menace and foreboding; then he fell into a grim silence and rode off quickly to rejoin his mother in the thick of the travellers. But, before Hö'elün could even open her mouth, Börte said:

*Anda* Jamuγa, they say, is a man who becomes weary; the moment has come when he is weary of us. Those suggestions that *anda* Jamuγa has just made conceal some hidden motive against us. Let us not dismount. We would do best to take advantage of our movement and make a clean break; we should travel even by night.

This unexpected, even precipitate utterance by Temüjin's wife seems to have been so convincing to him and the others that they all decided on the spot to separate from Jamuγa. It had taken only a few words to say what needed to be said, and from that moment the two men became enemies. A strange episode, this seemingly innocent suggestion from Jamuγa interpreted in such a suspicious way by his companion! A surprising sequel, these enigmatic words of mistrust spoken by Börte! And, more astonishing still, this brusque separation of the two *anda* without a hint of explanation being offered by either side!

Apart from thinking that this passage in *The Secret History* may have been corrupted, how is one to make sense of this rupture? The Russian Mongolists Vladimirtsov and Barthold have put forward the following explanation: that there were two classes in Mongol society that were opposed to each other, one raising horses — and this class, to which Temüjin belonged, formed an aristocracy; the other, which included Jamuγa, was dedicated to rearing small livestock.

This Soviet school of thought, basing its case on a later passage in the chronicle, considers Temüjin to have been a conservative and an aristocrat and his rival to have been an innovator, perhaps even a man swayed by democratic feeling, for he was able to 'love what was new and despise what was old'. Having no claim to royal descent, Jamuγa could have been seen as an opponent of the 'establishment'. Attractive though this interpretation is, it rests on some imponderables. The preponderance of horse breeders, the aristocrats of the steppes, over shepherds is a point that has not been proven. An inequality between rearers of large and small livestock is a matter of supposition and, in any case, of less consequence than, say, the climatic conditions and the value and quality of the livestock itself.

But, in that case, how is one to interpret the puzzling break-up of the relationship between the two sworn brothers? A biographer of Genghis Khan, Prawdin, raises, almost by accident, another hypothesis. While taking account of the Soviet historians' view of the possible conflicts between shepherds and horse breeders practising different methods of transhumance, he hints that Jamuγa was suspected by Temüjin's wife and mother of having ignored 'proper manners and customs'. Is this to be understood as an allusion to the private habits of Jamuγa, a man who the chronicle contentiously asserts was of capricious and ambiguous character and who could weary of his most intimate friend? Did the 'sworn brotherhood' conceal some other intimacy? Like the Sinologue Arthur Waley, the Mongolist Paul Pelliot claims not to know the significance of the line, 'they slept together under the same blanket'. However, the clause 'they loved each other', repeated four times in just a few lines, lends weight to the theory that this was a special kind of friendship taken to its conclusion. One cannot speak with any certainty on this point: failing another version of *The Secret History* from a different chronicler or any other relevant texts, however, there is only one inference to be drawn.

A little later, after Temüjin had separated from Jamuγa, the chronicle relates an odd omen, something between a dream and a moral tale, which adds to the ambiguity surrounding the anti-hero, Jamuγa. The shaman Qorchi said that Jamuγa was born from the same womb as himself, but from a different seed. Then he related to Temüjin how a cow had one day collided with Jamuγa, breaking a horn as it did so. Conscious of having been weakened, the beast raised itself up before him, lowing: 'Bring me my horn.' A bull, lacking horns, came lowing to be yoked to Jamuγa's cart. It was then that Temüjin rose up, like a *deus ex machina*, to be greeted as their leader by all his people, who instantly recognized his power. The shaman's prophecy does little to dispel the equivocal character of Jamuγa.

When Temüjin made the sudden decision to break with his old friend, he was followed by many who were loyal to him and by Mongol clans and subclans listed at some length in the chronicle. Great names from the aristocracy fell in under his banner, giving him the tools with which to forge new power. Temüjin's new adherents had quite a surprise in store for their leader: near Mount Gürelgü, in the upper Kerulen valley, they proposed to their young chief that they make him khan!

Since the fall of the tribal chief Qutula, one of the presumed descendants of Qabul Qan, there had been no incumbent khan. The idea of restoring the khanate with a single ruler over so many different tribes was an earnest of multitribal unity to come, a forerunner of confederation. The shaman and soothsayer Qorchi, who had forecast Temüjin's imminent rise soon after the break with Jamuγa, sought an assurance of his own welfare when he asked the future khan: 'If you become master of the people, what happiness will you give me for having foretold it?'

# 6
# Birth of an Empire

## Temüjin is Elected Khan

'We will make you khan,' they said. 'When Temüjin is khan, we will fling ourselves like the lightning upon your foes, we shall go with you and keep you and we shall give you for your *ordo* the fairest girls and ladies of the enemy . . . When we hunt wild animals, we shall drive the animals out of the steppe and capture them and give them to you . . . If we disobey you on the day of battle, take our flocks from us, our wives and children, throw our worthless heads out on the desert earth. If we have disregarded your advice in peacetime, take our men and our servants away from us, take our wives and our sons, and abandon us leaderless on the bare earth . . .' When they had finished exchanging these words and spoken these oaths, they proclaimed Temüjin *qan*, calling him *Chinghis Kaan*.

Thus, according to *The Secret History*, was Temüjin designated Genghis Khan (or *Chinghis Kaan*), the name under which he has passed into posterity. There is general agreement that the term should be taken to mean 'ocean khan' or 'oceanic khan', that is, 'ruler vast as the ocean', 'universal ruler'. The word 'genghis' could be Turkish and, according to Pelliot, a variant form of the Tibeto-Mongolian *dalai lama* ('oceanic lama'). There is little doubt that the notion of ocean contained in this title has a cosmogonic significance of some sort: for the Mongols, as for their Tibetan neighbours, the ocean was foreign to their geographical environment and therefore, very likely, endowed with a mythical quality. Alternatively, some people may accept the meaning which the Persian Rashīd al-Dīn gave to the word 'genghis' (or *djinkiz*): powerful.

As for the term 'khan' (also *qaghan*, or *qahan*), it made its appearance, borne by chiefs of the Ruanruan (Avar) tribes — Mongols — towards AD 500. The title was perpetuated by the conquerors and successors of the Ruanruan, the Tujue Turks, towards the end of the sixth century. Between the tenth and the twelfth century, a khan was a 'strong man' chosen by his peers to lead a military expedition or a great hunt. Most often, this was a clan (*oboγ*) chief or a tribal (*irgen*) chief who, by virtue of his personal authority or his skill as a warrior, was chosen by the tribal council (*quriltai*) made up of hereditary nobles, the wealthiest men in the tribes and their vassals. The title *khan* was therefore ephemeral and did not rest on any legal foundation. Moreover, it was subject to negotiation: the chronicler of *The Secret History* reports in this vein that, before he would elect Jamuγa, one of his followers demanded to have the command of 10,000 men and to be given 'thirty beautiful wives'. Certain tribes elected several khans simultaneously: it is a fact that the *wang khan* To'oril, while the most powerful, was not the only khan of the Kereyid. Although it was temporary in nature and not likely to be passed on, the title *khan* allowed an ambitious holder to increase his authority over a broader range of tribal peoples. Temüjin was very quick to seize this opportunity and turn to his advantage the unstable nature of the tribal confederations.

Who were the men who gave their mandate to Temüjin? In traditional Mongol society, in which everyone who was descended from the same 'bones' (*yasun*), that is to say, from a single common ancestor, was a member of a given clan, every family, be it nuclear or extended, therefore represented a clan subgroup. As in every society, the hazards of existence threw up some outstanding personalities. Between the tenth and the twelfth century, the chiefs were in the first instance skilled hunters — bringing prosperity to the clan — or skilled warriors — allowing the clan to snatch more livestock. These men, the *noyans*, sought to inspire the loyal submission of clans and tribes and to dominate the pastoral economy. They adopted surnames, foreign or honorific titles, which they usually coupled with their own names: *ochigin* (young keeper of the hearth), *bökö* (athlete), *mergen* (champion archer), *baγatur* (valiant). They formed a kind of 'aristocracy of the steppes'. Their wives also took titles: *eke* (mother), *üjin* (lady).

Members of neighbouring tribes or clans would unite around these *noyans*. These adherents might be opportunists who had taken up residence in the victor's camp, or the poor and weak who sought his protection. These 'born vassals' (*unagan boγolchud*) formed a kind of body of servants; they might become part of the dowry of a noble girl, but they were allowed to keep their domestic goods and their own livestock. They carried out a variety of jobs for their masters: watching the flocks, work in the pastures, and maintenance and repair of carts and tents. During the hunting seasons, it was they who acted as beaters; and if an armed conflict broke out, it was they who were drafted into the service of the *noyan*. Below their rank were the *ötele-boγolchud* and the *jala'ut*, semi-slaves who could be freed. These were jacks-of-all-trades who performed the most menial tasks and who, according to Rubrouck, often lived off leftovers and scraps.

Although no titles were bestowed in any formal written form, certain clans, by way of their power or wealth, or because of the fame of their chiefs and the real or rumoured exploits of their members, enjoyed enhanced prestige. Even though it is difficult to speak of a true feudal nobility — possessing fiefdoms — in the usual sense of the term, it must be acknowledged that the clan or tribal chiefs who headed a patriarchal society (*ulus*) — of which there were several hundred numbering some thousands of individuals — were considered an aristocracy. The chief of an *ulus* did not have the ownership of the land, but he did have the right of usufruct in respect of it. For, since he was the owner in his own right of an assemblage of people, he was also able to reserve his rights over a domain (the *nutuγ*, better known by its Turkish name of *yurt*), which was sufficiently large to support men and animals. Each noble could thus lay claim to a portion of the clan's pasture lands.

The rights of the *noyans* and the way in which these affected their relationships with their vassals differed from the customs that pertained amongst cultivators. In this nomadic society, it was control over transhumance and the distribution of pasturage that lent the noble his feudal function. 'Nobody may stay in an area which has not been assigned to him by the emperor,' noted Pian del Carpini. 'He himself decides where the chiefs are to reside, the chiefs assign emplacements to the commanders of the chiliarchiae [1,000 men], these commanders to the centurions, and the centurions to platoon leaders.'[1]

It was probably in 1197 that the *quriltai* met to elect Temüjin, then aged about 40 years. In some ways the choice was a surprising one, for, if one accepts that he was descended from Qabul Qan, he came from a younger branch of the family. Furthermore, if his biography is to be believed, apart from the war he waged, with the assistance of his allies, against the Merkid, Temüjin's only claims to fame were some fairly inconsequential skirmishes. And even then, says *The Secret History*, he was literally propelled forward over the heads of others better placed than himself, beginning with Jamuγa. Perhaps the latter seemed too much of an innovator or too inconstant? *The Secret History* remains tight-lipped on that point. About the time between Börte's abduction and the break with Jamuγa, the chronicle says nothing, as if history had suddenly picked up speed. The lapse of time between the two events is about 20 years. Certain passages of the biography have indubitably disappeared; it is equally certain that other episodes were deliberately omitted.

Since 1150, the time when Qabul Qan had tried to unite the Mongol tribes, the ancient khanate had fallen into disuse. The heirs apparent of the khan had not been able, or wished, to rally the nation of tribes (*ulus irgen*) under their banners. Now here we have the clan chiefs asking Temüjin to revive the title. Among them were men from his father's clan — the Kiyad — but also from the Ba'arin, the Jalayir, and even the direct heirs of Qabul Qan: the princes Altan, Quchar and Sacha Beki. Are the first signs of Temüjin's charisma to be seen in his election to khan? Probably. For to see him as a puppet in the hands of the nobility is a hypothesis with little credibility. The man had shown himself sufficiently energetic, zealous and daring not to be content to play a secondary role, and certainly not to allow himself to be manipulated. To read *The Secret History* one would think that Temüjin was made khan in order to lead clans and tribes on traditional skirmishes whose main aim was to organize hunts and raids. No power offered a serious threat to the Mongols and the Tatars did not, it seems, represent a real danger to their neighbours. Temüjin was undoubtedly elected by his peers quite simply because he seemed to them to be the most suitable leader of the entire pack.

Religious considerations may also have entered into the calculations of these men, whose minds were open to signs from heaven and to the various prophecies to which they gained insight through the shamans.

Had not one of these, Qorchi, forecast the near miraculous attainment of the supreme power that was to come to Temüjin? And similarly, Muqali, one of Temüjin's loyal generals, had revealed a strange coincidence to his leader: Temüjin had sat down one day to rest under a tree in a place called Qorqonaɣ Jubur. Now this, Muqali informed him, was the exact spot where Qutula Qan, the last tribal chief to have previously held the title of khan, had made a halt to celebrate his accession. These fateful signs only heightened the aura surrounding Temüjin's elevation to power.

Once installed as khan, Temüjin seems to have taken his new responsibilities seriously. In the first place, he already enjoyed the confidence of his followers. But, thinking that this was not enough, he surrounded himself with a team of faithful supporters. Among them were Jelme and Bo'urchu, who had helped him in the difficult years and were still his friends. Having sung their praises, Temüjin offered them promotion to positions of high office in which they were, according to *The Secret History*, 'in charge of everything'. Sübetei and the other men who had chosen to abandon Jamuɣa to follow the new khan were rewarded with official functions, which again amounted to promotions. The young captains thus gained positions of command within the new corps of 'quiver-bearers' (*qorchin*): chosen for their competence and loyalty, they were soon to become the crack division of the force that the new khan was to raise among the pastoralists of the steppes. Temüjin, an ambitious manipulator of men, knew how to use them to good effect.

**Consolidation of Power**
One of the first steps Temüjin took to secure his power was to establish himself as the new spokesman within this riotous assembly that was the Mongol people. He therefore sent envoys to King To'oril, his old protector, to tell him that their master had acceded to the khanate. The king's response was, however, laconic, and he did not have any gift sent to Temüjin. Did he already see the eagle developing from the eaglet he had helped to take flight? Or, more simply, did he judge that, since the new chief had assembled under his colours only a few of the Mongol peoples, the event was not really an event at all?

When Temüjin's envoys went to try to knit bonds of neighbourliness with Jamuɣa and his allies, diplomatic relations became fraught with ambiguity. Temüjin had left his friend with precipitate suddenness, and it may be supposed that Jamuɣa harboured a sombre resentment against him, the more so since several thousand men had taken his rival's part and gone with him. Now, on hearing of the election of the khan, Jamuya did not flinch. He did, however, reproach the princes Altan and Quchar for their treacherous conduct which, in his view, led to the separation of the two *anda*.

Altan and Quchar, you two coming between *anda* Temüjin and myself, why, by stinging *anda* Temüjin in the side and pricking him in the ribs, did you make us separate? And now what is the thought that was in your mind when you made him *qan*? Altan, Quchar, you two, remember the words you spoke and how you put the *anda*'s mind at rest. Now that you have thrown in your lot with my *anda*, at least serve him well.

Jamuya's main sentiment seemed to be regret for a lost friendship; he did not condemn his old friend for having departed. Temüjin, as he saw it, had been the victim of a conspiracy.

'You cannot have two bears in the same cave,' runs a Mongol proverb. And indeed, the ordinary theft of some horses set the grass alight. A relative of Jamuya's who had stolen some of Temüjin's mounts was put to death by the owner's men.

If we are to believe the chronicle, Jamuya mobilized 30,000 horsemen to avenge this murder! The first conflict between Temüjin and Jamuya took place in front of Mount Gürelgü, on the site of Dalan-Baljut (the Seventy Marshes). Temüjin came off worst, but retreated in good order and entrenched himself in a defile with the same number of men. Furious at having let him escape, Jamuya subjected sixty-six of the enemy captives to a horrific punishment, which no doubt had originated in China: bound hand and foot, the victims were thrown into enormous cauldrons and boiled until their screams were muffled by the clouds of vapour. Another chief was decapitated and his body, tied to the tail of Jamuya's horse, brutally dragged behind and mutilated. Jamuya's victory did not, however, encroach upon the prestige of his opponent. Entire clans, the Urut, the Mangyud, the Qongqotadai, and many others, deserted and joined the new khan.

In the course of this terrible battle that was played out on the edge of the Siberian taiga, many of the Mongol clans began to sense which way the wind was blowing. Nevertheless, if the khan was to succeed in rallying the tribes behind him, there was a need to achieve a much higher degree of unity, or simply of discipline, among these nomads who professed allegiance to Temüjin. The independence of the clans, their fondness for plunder as a substitute for the unreliable natural increases in their herds, the ravages of animal disease, the feuds and personal quarrels were all permanent obstacles to any attempt to construct a confederation of any kind.

Customs were primitive and the nomads clung above all else to violence and superstition. Cruelty alternated with maudlin sentimentality, fits of anger with bouts of remorse. They acted without self-restraint; brawls and murderous attacks broke out seemingly for the most futile of motives. The chronicle relates how, during one of those banquets where feasting degenerated into gorging, the ladies of the nobility hurled some insults and then set upon one of the cupbearers who had inadvertently served them after serving a concubine. Also in the course of the feast, the half-brother of the khan surprised a thief, who favoured him with a vicious sabre slash. Quarrels between shrewish women, scuffles between stablemen and bloody disputes between drunken shepherds, these were the stuff of life in this rough and boorish society, in which people were better acquainted with the art of cudgelling than with that of dainty eating.

Was it a dispute of this kind which served as a pretext for the larger conflict that drove To'oril from his throne? In 1197 or 1198, To'oril had several of his brothers murdered. Two of the survivors, Jaqa Gambu and Erge Qara, succeeded in escaping and found refuge with another Mongol tribe, the Naiman, who were then living in the foothills of the Great Altay range. The Naiman chief, perceiving some self-interest in taking the fugitives' part, mounted an attack on To'oril, who, in his turn, had to flee. He took refuge in the Qara Khitai capital; their ruler, who was doubtless a Mongol by origin though Turkish in his way of life, bore the title Gür Qan. The sovereign soon made it clear to the exile that he could not stay any longer on his land. Now *persona non grata*, To'oril wandered around the steppe lands of the Uighur and the Tangut before re-entering Mongol territory. It is related that the only things he could call his own were five goats whose milk he drank, a camel which, when its side was slashed, would yield a little blood for him to drink, and — a stroke of extreme bad luck for a nomadic prince — a blind horse. It was in this destitute and weakened state that he was met by some envoys of Temüjin who came to tell him that their master was prepared to receive him. To'oril accepted this generous offer and soon was restored — though a ruin of a man for a time — to a position of respect at the side of his former protégé.

At the same time, Temüjin took part in a military expedition against a people who had long had a fearsome reputation: the Tatars or Tartars. In the West, especially in Russia, their name has been given to many nomadic, Asiatic invaders. Because they were known as the 'sons of hell' and because their name is akin to the words 'barbaric' and 'barbarian', they inspired the pun attributed to St Louis: 'We shall hurl the Tartars into Tartarus.'

This western-Turkish tribe, who spoke a Mongol dialect, probably owed their reputation for bellicosity to their situation. They lived as nomads between the Khingan mountains (now Da Hinggan Ling) in the east and the Kerulen (Herlen Gol) to the northwest and, together with the Önggüd and some lesser tribes, were the Turco-Mongol tribe that came most frequently into contact with the Chinese. It is well known that China, then under the domination of the Jin dynasty, lived under the constant threat of incursions from barbarians, Tungus or Turco-Mongols. For centuries, China had maintained the same political stance towards the nomads of the far north: divide and rule; use barbarians against barbarians. The Jin rulers were very clever exploiters of the divisions and rivalries among the nomads for the purpose of protecting their empire. There were times when they had to dispatch contingents beyond the Great Wall, but for most of the time the indigenous nomads served as a kind of territorial army that effectively screened China from incursions from the steppes.

The Tatars, for their part, were playing a game of deceit. They were an undisciplined and thoroughly unreasonable lot and Beijing decided to get rid of them by pushing them northwards to where the Mongols lived and where Temüjin had just imposed his rule. Now the Tatars, compromised in their alliances with the Chinese, which were as shaky as they were short-lived, gradually became the enemies of the Mongols. As early as 1150, they had handed over to the Chinese some members of the family of Qabul Qan, and then, in 1161, while still in league with Beijing, had contributed to the downfall of the first Mongol confederation. Around 1167, it was, again, one of their clans that committed the treacherous act of poisoning Yesügei, Temüjin's father.

The Tatars were therefore, as far as the majority of the Mongol tribes were concerned, traitors. Accordingly, when a Chinese army attacked the Tatars from the southeast and Beijing, overturning its existing alliances, turned to To'oril for help in destroying them, Temüjin was able to take advantage of the situation and reinforce his own position by securing an easy victory over them on his own ground. Quickly he roused his followers to hurl them against the hard-pressed enemy: 'Since time immemorial the Tatar people have killed [our] forefathers and [our] fathers; these are people against whom we have grievances; [let us take advantage] of the occasion to catch them in a pair of pincers.' Not much is known about the battles which took place that year — around 1198 — near the river Uuldza Gol. Temüjin was supported by the troops of To'oril, who wanted to avenge his grandfather, who had been assassinated by the Tatars. Temüjin and To'oril launched a violent attack on the Tatars, who dug themselves in behind a barricade of branches. But the Mongols, forcing the defences, killed the Tatar chief, Megüjin Se'ültü, and seized his gold- and pearl-ornamented bed.

The Chinese general, having cleverly pushed his adversaries into the hands of the Mongols, now distributed honours to his new-found allies. He conferred on the Kereyid sovereign the Chinese title of king (*wang*, probably pronounced *ong* by the Mongols). To'oril tagged this title on to the one he already had, calling himself henceforward *ong khan*, the 'king khan'. Perhaps confusing the name and the title of the Kereyid king, Chinese scribes in their annals refer to him by name as 'Ong Khan'.

This pleonasm was to reverberate down the years and was the origin of the famous legend of King (or Prester) John: taking up the Nestorian scribes' error in translation that had rendered *wang khan* as 'King John', the bishop of Byblos, in 1144, sent a missive to the pope telling him of the existence of a Christian monarch by that name who was powerful and an implacable destroyer of Moslems. These rumours led Marco Polo to reintroduce into Europe the idea of the existence of this Asiatic monarch, with whom the West strove in vain to forge an alliance: 'But there was no sovereign in the land. They did, however, pay tax and tribute to a great prince who was called in their tongue UNC CAN, the same that we call Prester John, him in fact about whose great dominion all the world talks.' It was this same hypothetical character who in European lore became eventually transposed to Abyssinia in the form of the Christian Negus.

As a reward for his victory over the Tatars, Temüjin received from the Chinese only the more modest title of 'deputy commissioner for peace', a sign that Beijing did not think a great deal of this minor unknown. By all accounts, these titles meant little to the court of Beijing and the prodigality with which they distributed them rather resembled later practices of strewing glass beads among the natives; the titles were honorary rather than honorific and were good only for flattering the barbarians' vanity. The booty which To'oril and Temüjin snatched from the Tatars no doubt represented a more tangible reward for them. While looting the Tatar camp, Temüjin for the second time found and took from the battlefield a little boy who had been abandoned, Shigi-Qutuqu: he wore a sable coat and a gold nose ring. Hö'elün took him in as her adopted son.

Rich with Tatar booty, the khan returned to his lands near the sources of the Kerulen, in the area around Lake Qariltu. There he was met with an uprising of the Jürkin clan, who had refused to take part in the campaign against the Tatars. In an act of revenge for the insult they had suffered during a riotous banquet at which too much had been drunk, the Jürkin had killed in cold blood a few dozen men belonging to the khan's entourage. The latter saw no other possible response but to mete out the most rigorous of punishments. The Jürkin rebels were cornered, overcome and then captured. Among the prisoners were two princes who were presumed to be direct descendants of Qabul Qan: Sacha Beki and Taichu. They were decapitated. Already Temüjin had the temerity to dispose of anyone, even of noble birth, who laid claim to power. It was a precedent.

A little while afterwards, Büri Bökö (Büri the Athlete), another rival of the khan and also a prince by inheritance, became another subject for this policy of elimination. The occasion arose during a wrestling contest, a sport of which the Turco-Mongols had always been passionately fond. Belgütei, the khan's half-brother, challenged Büri and soon the two men, with naked torsos and legs encased in breeches, were in a clinch, trying to unbalance each other with arm holds. Forming a circle around the wrestlers, the spectators stamped their feet, spurred on their favourite, and loudly cheered the best trick holds. *The Secret History* reports that Büri, who was a veritable giant of a man, deliberately fell before Belgütei in order not to offend Temüjin. The khan, who was watching the match, probably with keen interest, 'bit his lower lip', a sign Belgütei had been waiting for. Belgütei threw himself on his opponent's back, 'crossed his hands on both sides of Büri Bökö's neck and pulled, at the same time kneeing him in the back'. This 'double head hold' broke Büri's spine, thus cutting short any ambition he may have harboured to stake any kind of legitimate claim to the khanate.

This barely camouflaged execution took Temüjin a step further up the ladder towards supreme power. The khan was, however, still far from having imposed his rule over all the nomadic tribes. In 1201, a league was formed against him: it probably numbered several thousand men: Merkid,

Tayichi'ud, Naiman, Tatar and other tribes besides. This 'army' had been set in motion under the orders of Jamuγa, who had retained such political power that the aristocracy of these confederated clans had proclaimed him Gür Qan. Jamuγa thus became sole leader of the great tribal league against Temüjin's rule.

Rallying behind the Gür Qan Jamuγa were some of Temüjin's old rivals: the Merkid Toγto'a Beki; an Oirat chief, Qutuqa Beki; the chief of the Tayichi'ud, Tarγutai; and lastly a Naiman. This coalition represented an important point in Mongol history: at the beginning of the thirteenth century, numerous tribes, sinking their traditional differences, had gathered together under the leadership of a single prince. The election of Jamuγa to an alternative and parallel khanate suggests that the nomadic tribes were beginning to have some aspirations towards unification of some kind. Opposite Temüjin were ranged in the league some groups that were quite distant from each other; no longer were they simply a collection of neighbouring clans having some degree of kinship. From the slopes of the great Khingan range (Da Hinggan Ling) in the east came the Tatars to join the league; from the sombre northern taiga regions came the Oirat; and from the Altay mountains in the southwest there advanced the most dangerous of all, the Naiman.

**War against the Naiman**
Partly Christianized Turks in the process of Mongolization, the Naiman, neighbours of the Kereyid, lived between the upper Irtysh and the region of Karakorum, in the Great Altay range. At that time they were going through a crisis of succession. Their chief had just died and his two sons had quarrelled over a concubine. In the end, each of the enemy brothers had raised a party of followers. The first, Buyiruγ, had stirred up the plains tribes while his rival had found allies among the mountain clans. Out of this feud was to spring a terrible and bloody war.

On learning of this dissension, Temüjin and his ally To'oril decided to strike quickly. They assembled several thousand horsemen and animals to mount an invasion of the Naiman territory. Having crossed the Hangayn Nuruu mountain chain, they dug themselves in in the Kobdo, a lake region. Buyiruγ, preferring to avoid a conflict, fled before the advancing Mongol threat. Temüjin learned from his scouts that the way was free through the passes of the Altay range, and he used this passage to penetrate enemy territory. The passes reach an altitude of nearly 3,000 metres; they cannot be crossed except in summer. But, like Hannibal who had crossed the Alps 1,000 years before, the khan had no hesitation in taking his cavalry across the mountains of central Asia, along with carts carrying the men's baggage and even sheep to feed the army. Coming down from the mountains on the far side, the Mongols reached the valley of the Ulungur He, not far from the lake of the same name. There, in a swampy area notorious for miasmas, they entered into battle with the Naiman and killed their chief.

The day after this easy victory, the Mongols turned around and went back across the Hangayn Nuruu. They made very slow progress across inhospitable valleys and wild gorges, and there they were attacked by the Naiman tribes who were waiting in ambush in a narrow gully. Night fell on this landscape in which every rock could conceal an opponent, every escarpment could endanger the horses' progress. The scouts had marked the location of the most hazardous spots, but the Mongols hesitated to go on. The men in the front lines conferred together and agreed to await daybreak before engaging the enemy in any further action.

Now the next day Temüjin and his lieutenants, having unwisely advanced onto the territory of the mountain Naiman, discovered that they had been betrayed by To'oril, Temüjin's faithful ally who had helped him to secure the crown, and who, as Yesügei's former companion-in-arms, had fought the Merkid clans to help his son retrieve his captured wife. To put Temüjin on the wrong scent, To'oril had lit watch-fires at their positions and then had quietly slipped away with his troops, abandoning Temüjin in hostile terrain. To'oril's sudden defection is not readily explained. The chronicle claims that Jamuya instigated this act and deceived the Kereyid chief by making him think that Temüjin was secretly in league with the Naiman. What is clear from the chronicle, in any event, is that the troops of To'oril and of Temüjin acted independently of each other.

At dawn Temüjin was enraged to discover his flank exposed and the Naiman, positioned on all the strategic high points, in mastery of the situation. The khan did not hesitate for a moment. Realizing that he was 'like a fish swimming in a pot', he pulled his forces back. The Naiman, who held the passes, showered arrows down on the Mongols. These, lacking the protection of the Kereyid, had great difficulty extricating themselves from the dead end in which they were cornered. Nevertheless, a retreat was effected, and they arrived at a site called 'Donkey Back Steppe' on open ground. It was then that Temüjin learned that To'oril was in difficulties. To'oril, who had made his troops perform an about-face, was being harassed by the Naiman and was on the point of abandoning several members of his family to the enemy. The khan, whether out of magnanimity or political cunning, decided to send some contingents to To'oril's aid. His 'Four Coursers' — Bo'urchu, Muqali, Boroγul, and Chila'un, brave men all — at last succeeded in rescuing the Kereyid and re-establishing the situation.

Once he was out of danger, To'oril expressed his gratitude to his ally. He asked heaven's blessing on this man who had helped him to pull back from the brink of disaster. To Bo'urchu, one of the Mongol khan's best officers, he gave ten gold pieces and a garment of the finest materials. Shortly afterwards he was to utter these words, which perhaps explained his conduct: 'I am old now; when, in my old age, I rise over the heights . . . who will govern all the people then?' Old and weak, To'oril sensed that his end was near. He had become the plaything of the strongest and no longer had the energy and verve of a warrior chief. Was this the reason why the Mongol khan behaved towards him with gentle compassion?

**Blood on the Steppes**

Having eliminated the Naiman, Temüjin might have thought that his new-found power would afford him some protection from the neighbouring tribes. If he did, he reckoned without Jamuγa, that eternal plotter. There is something highly fascinating about the obstinacy with which this man sought to harm one who had for so long been his most intimate friend. Was he really Temüjin's archrival or has *The Secret History* painted Jamuγa as a foil to the great khan — a situation often found in the great novels about the days of chivalry?

In the very first few months of the thirteenth century, Jamuγa again gathered together an assemblage of clans opposed to the khan's overriding power: Merkid from the lower Selenge Mörön, Tatars from the upper Kerulen, Oirat foresters, Tayichi'ud from the Onon Gol, and even some clans from among Temüjin's own circle of followers, including the Onggirad. Also attached to this rather loose coalition were the Naiman clans who had not been driven out. Jamuγa, who had been proclaimed Gür Qan, wanted to give some official credence to his bid to shift the balance of power in his direction. To this end, he brought in some shamans who performed some of the customary rituals, notably the sacrifice of horses. But Temüjin's side were watching and waiting. In the steppes, news travels fast. Whenever shepherds meet they ask questions about tribal movements, and no hunter approaches a camp without being sure that he will receive a friendly welcome. In these first months of 1200, Temüjin's power was such that he could maintain a regular intelligence corps, a body of circumspect scouts. Shepherds did not move without spying out the situation among the tribes in the region; they posted watchmen on the hilltops overlooking waterways, and examined the tracks left by the breeders who had just moved on from their summer pastures. By these means Temüjin learned that Jamuγa had mobilized dozens of clans and subclans and that he was going to have to confront his old 'sworn brother' once again.

One more time, Temüjin appealed to To'oril, his ageing and unsteady ally. The first conflict occurred on the banks of the Ergun He (Argun). The chroniclers report that Jamuγa had with him several shamans who uttered some incantations before the decisive battle, throwing stones into the water and beseeching the deities to grant their prince success. According to the Mongol sources, two of them, Buyiruγ and Qutuqa Beki, succeeded in stirring up a storm by their rites. But, it is said, 'the magic storm turned course and it was precisely on them that the magic storm was released'. Was this a bad omen? Although it is tempting to read some curious coincidence into the practices of the shamans and the cataclysm that was to be unleashed on the battlefields, the episode does not really seem authentic. Let us just say that certain of the shamans, who were keen observers of natural phenomena and very familiar with climatic variations, could no doubt have persuaded the shepherds that they had some ability to make rain or fine weather.

By all accounts, the battle which unfolded on the banks of the Ergun He was extremely violent. The opposing troops occupied the whole of a day in indecisive charges: 'They fought by returning again and again, many times, to the fray and, when night fell, they organized their defences and lay down to sleep on the field of battle.' Nightfall called a halt to the fighting, but even more compelling factors were the exhaustion of the fighters and of the animals, especially the horses.

During the battle of the Ergun He, the khan was seriously wounded. His 'neck artery' had been cut and he began to haemorrhage, but his faithful attendant, Jelme, immediately dismounted and sucked the blood from the wound. Temüjin was unconscious for half the night; then he feverishly demanded something to drink. Jelme managed to crawl over to the enemy lines to take a bottle of curdled mare's milk from one of the carts. Diluted with a little water, this milk revived the invalid's strength. Here the chronicle becomes punctilious about the facts and tells us that

Temüjin reproached his faithful attendant for having spat out the blood too close to him and having let it dry there in a little brownish puddle that looked very unpleasant. When he was back on his feet again, however, the khan gave effusive thanks to his friend who had that night undoubtedly saved his life. At last messengers arrived: they announced that the Naiman had withdrawn from the battlefield. For Temüjin, this was another victory.

On the ground where no soldier stood lay the bodies of the fallen, already swarming with flies. The wounded, exhausted from crying in vain for help, were in their death throes; many of them did die, for gangrene and septicaemia were bound to set in wherever flesh had been pierced by metal. Here and there bodies were being stripped of their weapons, a piece of jewellery or a cap. On the top of a hill a little distance away, Temüjin spotted a woman in tears. As he drew nearer, he recognized her as the daughter of Sorqan Shira, the man who had saved his life when he had been subjected to the pillory torture by the Tayichi'ud: the woman was howling because the khan's men had taken away her husband, with the intention of getting him alone and stabbing him. Shortly afterwards Sorqan Shira himself arrived on the scene: he had gone over to Jamuγa's side, but he told Temüjin that pressure had been put on his family, and he had not since been able to get away to rejoin his real allies. We read in the chronicle that the khan was very ready to pardon his old friend.

At the close of the battle, an enemy warrior called Jirγo'adai presented himself before the khan. He claimed that it was he who, with a single arrow, had struck down a courser that Temüjin had given to his lieutenant Bo'urchu. When he had finished describing this brilliant shot, he waited with great calmness for the punishment he expected to follow. But the brave archer was spared. He was given the surname Jebe, 'Arrowhead'; he was to enter the khan's service and cover himself in glory in Persia and beyond, even as far afield as the portals of Europe.

The Tayichi'ud chief, Tarγutai, Temüjin's old enemy, managed to run away. He was tracked but hid in a wood. Three of his servants grabbed him, tied him up and threw him into his cart to deliver him to the conqueror in the hope of a handsome reward. But on the way there, after a battle during which their captive was very nearly set free, they began to have their doubts about the wisdom of handing him over. They were fearful of the reaction of the khan, who, it was said, considered disloyalty to be an unforgivable act of treachery. They therefore released their prisoner, and then went to the khan's tent to inform him of their deed. Luck was on their side: they too were pardoned.

Temüjin's magnanimity was hardly limitless, however. On his orders, heads rolled, particularly those of the Tayichi'ud, for whom he had since childhood sworn the fiercest hatred. All 'who had Tayichi'ud bones' were mercilessly massacred, even small children. Capable sometimes of gentleness, even of kindness, Temüjin was also disposed towards uncontrollable and incomprehensible acts of violence. True, the era and the nomadic way of life were scarcely conducive to refined behaviour. As the thirteenth century dawned, did the khan already foresee the immense panoramic vista that he was later to survey? Knowing when to seize the opportunity is the cardinal virtue of the ambitious. This man, who was not one to be troubled about obstacles that might stand in his way and who had already twisted the arm of fate, must have been familiar with the Mongol proverb: 'When the arrow is ready at the bowstring, let it fly.'

## Fur-coated Militias

*The Secret History* gives the impression that the events that took place around the year 1200 shook high Asia to the core. In fact, the conflicts in which Temüjin and his rivals were involved were limited in scope and did not embroil the greatest of the Asiatic powers. Seen from Beijing, which was protected by army units camped along the Great Wall, these sporadic outbreaks of fighting among the Mongol tribes were nothing but distant 'trouble among the barbarians'. The kingdom of Korea was hardly aware of any Mongol activity because the Tungus acted as a screen drawn across central Asia. Like the Uighur kingdom, that of the Xixia (Minyak) was protected by the great void of the Gobi desert. Not to mention the great western powers of high Asia (the Islamized empire of Khwārezm, the Qara Khitai empire, and the sultanate of Muhammad of Ghur in the Punjab and northern India), which were a long way off and had no inkling of the existence of Temüjin and his nomadic hordes.

In the course of the skirmishes and raids related in *The Secret History*, Temüjin's army was gradually taking shape. Around 1200, the Mongols as yet had no real military infrastructure. The nomadic tribes were first and foremost livestock herders. Their main tasks were looking after the herds and exploiting the resources they provided. When they were not occupied with the work of rearing, the Mongols had to maintain their carts, renew the guys or framework of their tents, file their arrows to sharp points, and card the felt from which they made not only their tents but also coverings for their carts and waggons and some of their clothing.

Added to all these daily chores was leatherwork, which demanded some complicated expertise. The nomads had been quick to notice that the action of smoke, for example from grease, had the effect of softening and preserving skins used for clothing. It is probable that the people of the forests had observed a tanning process taking place in certain barks of trees of the taiga which, after lying for long periods in swamps, had undergone slow maceration. Archaeological digs in Kerch', in the Crimea, as also in Uzbekistan and various parts of southern Siberia, have revealed that in ancient times nomadic populations, such as the Sarmatians or the Sacae (Asian Scythians), were dressed in very much the same way as the Mongols: leather tunics that fitted fairly closely and trousers, also of leather, attached to the ankles by thongs; on their feet they wore knee-high boots. At the Pazyrik site in the Altay, and on the borders of Mongolia, Soviet archaeologists have uncovered a great variety of leather objects — often parts of a harness — that were buried in funeral mounds (tumuli). These finely crafted artefacts, 2,500 years old, show that some nomadic peoples practised leather currying of high quality: the pieces found carry bas-reliefs superimposed on layers of leather.

Skins and wool used by the Mongols came principally from sheep and goats: sometimes tanned in salt, they were made into ankle-length or knee-length pelisses which were fastened around the chest and crossed to the left, in Turkish style; then later on, to the right, Chinese-fashion. The wool was sometimes worn on the inside, sometimes on the outside. Underneath these pelisses, the Mongols wore garments of lined woven material or of soft flannelling, stolen or otherwise acquired from settled people, since the nomads themselves did not weave. This undergarment, which was open in front, allowed the wearer to mount a horse with ease, and was never taken off. All observers noted that this garment was constantly soiled and greasy. In fact, if they were thoroughly saturated with grease, the skins kept their suppleness and strength for longer!

The men's legs were covered in a type of loose-cut trousers that slipped inside soft boots with curved toes, such as one sees on the Chinese paintings of that period. When the weather was very cold, they sometimes wore a second pair of felt boots, lighter in weight than the others, which served rather the same function as long culottes. Various types of cap completed the outfit: felt skullcaps of the type still worn by some people in central Asia, hats with earflaps like the Russian *uchenka*, or turbans. Rubrouck describes in great detail the garb of the Mongols he encountered on his journey:

> As to their garments and style of dress, you will know that they receive from Cathay [China] and other countries of the East and also from Persia and other southern lands stuffs of silk and gold and cotton cloths in which they dress in summer . . . In winter they wear at least two pelisses, one with the fur worn on the inside, in contact with the body, the other with the fur on the outside against wind and snow: usually these are skins of wolf, fox or dog-faced baboon [lynx?]. When they are at home, they wear a lighter version of the same. Poor people make pelisses for outdoor wear from the skins of dogs or goats. They make trousers from these skins too. The rich line their clothes with silk tow. . . . The poor line theirs with cotton cloth.

Girard de Rialle, at the turn of the twentieth century, offers us an almost identical description:

> Their clothes consist, for both sexes, of trousers, cotton or sheepskin robes belted at the waist, felt coats or fur pelisses for the winter; on their heads they wear little skullcaps of silk or vividly coloured cloth, trimmed with fur in cold weather; on their feet they wear big thick-soled boots.

The women wore similar clothes that were perhaps just a little longer. Their tunics of coloured linen were acquired by barter with caravaneers. After their marriage or during ceremonies, the ladies of the nobility exhibited a showy elegance, particularly in their hairstyles, which amazed travellers: they wore twisted fringes that spilled down from a tall framework of individually decorated wood or bark. The whole thing looked like a kind of hat sitting on a plateau or some sort of complicated scaffolding rather like cow horns holding the hair in place; and it was decorated with ribbons, gold or silver jewels or semiprecious stones. Odoric of Pordenone compared this female hairdo with a 'man's foot', adorned with pearls and feathers. Up to the beginning of the twentieth century, explorers reported that the fashionable women of the steppes attended to their occupations without seeming to be hampered by this cumbersome headgear, which bore certain distinguishing tribal features.

'As for the women's apparel, this is remarkable for an exceptional type of hairstyle,' wrote Captain Mayne-Reid at the end of the nineteenth century. 'The front of the monstrous hat they wear is decorated with gold and silver pear-drops, with little hand-bells, with rows of sequins and buttons, with sheep-bells, with chains, with hearts set with precious stones, in short, with a mass of ornaments which seem more suited to a horse's harness than to the dress of a woman.'

Very common among both sexes were plaits, which might be tied up or left to hang about the shoulders. Another custom — this one a male fashion — was noticed by medieval travellers: they shaved a large area of their skulls and plaited the rest of the hair, which fell around their ears or down the nape of the neck. It was like a kind of upside-down 'pudding basin', where the whole area that was 'underneath the basin' was carefully shaved.

Hygiene certainly cannot have ranked very high as a consideration among the Mongols, for water was scarce and subject to various taboos. Rubrouck underlines the point in talking about Mongol women: 'They never wash their clothes because they say it annoys God, and there would be a thunderstorm if they hung them up to dry . . . They never wash their cooking bowls either; moreover, when the meat is cooked, they wash the meat-serving dish with bouillon from the pot and then tip the bouillon back into the pot.' Likewise, the coarseness of the Mongols' table manners amazed the Flemish Franciscan: 'They pass the drink around in one cup, from one to the next, men and women: sometimes they try to see who can drink the most, very sloppily and greedily. When they want to press someone to drink, they clutch him by the ears and pull hard so that his throat will open wide, and they clap their hands and dance in front of him.' Pian del Carpini provides further evidence of the same gross behaviour: 'When the fat from the meat makes the hands abominably sticky, they wipe them either on their leggings or on a tuft of grass or on whatever else comes to hand; the more refined among them use the corners of rags.'[2]

It was these boorish shepherds and grooms, these lowly specimens dressed in dirty, smelly clothing, who went to make up the cavalry battalions of Genghis Khan. In the beginning, these stockmen were not prepared for real war, even though, to defend their animals and their pasture grounds, they did manufacture various types of weapon: bows, sabres, maces and lassos, but also defensive weapons — caparisons for their horses, metal helmets, and suits of armour. The last-named was made of plates of leather from cows or other animals, stuck down on top of one another with a bitumen mixture and held in shape with the help of thongs. The metal for the helmets and armour was apparently not wrought.

Hunting was, for the steppe nomads, an initiation for war. It gave the chance to add to their monotonous daily diet, but also allowed the men to leave the clan's yurt, sometimes for several days at a time. At the edges of the woods they trapped wild animals with snares, but in the open they hunted with bows and arrows. Birds — larks and ptarmigans — and small rodents — squirrels and jerboas — were killed with arrows tipped with horn or hard wood which killed the animals without ripping the feathers or the fur, while big game — deer and wolves — were taken in large-scale, methodically organized *battues*.

For these great massed hunts, hundreds, sometimes thousands of men were mobilized. The hunters, accompanied by hounds, and sometimes by gerfalcons or other birds of prey, tame wolves and trained cheetahs, attempted to drive a large number of game towards natural traps or areas closed off by rows of archers; dziggetai, deer, wild boar, bear, sable and hare were all, according to the season, shot with arrows, or pierced with boar-spears, killed *en masse* in bouts of wholesale slaughter. 'After Genghis Khan, his troops amused themselves taking shots at animals that were so weary from the long chase that they could eventually be caught by hand. When everyone tired of this amusement, they set free the dziggetai that remained, but before releasing them those who had captured them stamped their personal brand on the animals' skin.'

These *battues* were organized like military operations, each *noyan*, each knight leading his party of beaters and bent on achieving great precision and maximum efficiency; and the game that was killed was distributed according to strict rules: the khan, in the first instance; then the princes and nobles had priority in receiving the best trophies of the hunt. Marco Polo, who was present at some great *battues* organized for lords and noblemen during the reign of Kublai Khan, found it 'truly . . . a glorious sight':

And when the Prince goes a-hunting, one of those Barons, with his 10,000 men and something like 5,000 dogs. goes towards the right, whilst the other goes towards the left with his party in like manner. They move along, all abreast of one another, so that the whole line extends over a full day's journey, and no animal can escape them.

The hunts, raids, and feuds which mobilized thousands of horsemen had the effect of welding the tribes together, of mollifying rivalries and of honing their sense of strategy. The vast hunting grounds became fields of manoeuvre for the Mongol tribes and their allies. These riders in their pelisses of sheep or wolf skin in no way resembled the men-at-arms of the great military orders of medieval Europe nor the troops commandeered by the Chinese empire, men who were often ready to sell their services to the highest bidder. The men who united under Temüjin's authority were horse breeders, sheep rearers, and nomadic shepherds, who, when it was necessary, fiercely defended their herds, their pastures and their families. To a certain extent, then, this was an armed population. Like militiamen on alert, they were usually armed because they had to face cattle rustlers, the incursions of clans or tribes out for revenge, or even troops sent against them by the great established nations. The day would come when Genghis Khan would draw all these occasional 'partisans' into his circle and turn them into true warriors who would follow him on his way to conquer the world.

# 7

# Master of Mongolia

*Then Chingis addressed the Tatars and the Moals [Mongols]
saying: 'It is because we have no leader that our neighbours
oppress us.' At the end of which the Tatars and the Moals took
him for their leader and for their captain.*

**William of Rubrouck,**
***Journey in the Mongol Empire***

## War against the Tatars and the Kereyid

By now a respected and feared leader and an intrepid warrior, Temüjin
began to realize that he would be able to extend his power only at the
expense of the clans or tribes which until then had refused to bow to his
authority. In 1202, less than five years after his election to the khanate, he
felt at last sufficiently powerful to try to bring the Tatars to their knees.
Although they had suffered grave reverses in their fortunes at the hands
of the Jin dynasty and the coalition led by Temüjin and To'oril, the Tatars
still maintained forces in sufficient strength for revenge to be considered
feasible. The khan, however, was too quick for them: in the battle that
took place at the mouth of the river Khalka, at a site named Dalan
Nemürges (the Seventy Felt Coats), he crushed a grouping of four Tatar
tribes.

The khan had exhorted his men not to plunge into a frenzy of looting
until they had completely defeated the enemy. Now Altan, Quchar and
Daritai either did not hear or chose not to hear. The khan could not
tolerate such indiscipline: when the fighting was over, he had their booty
seized, but he did not have the men executed, perhaps because they were

125

his kinsfolk. Humiliated in front of their troops, these three rarely rebelled from then on.

Among the plunder to be shared out among the victors were two beautiful Tatar girls, the daughters of a conquered chief. Temüjin found the first of them, Yesügen, to his taste and made her his concubine; then, discovering that her sister, Yesüi, was more charming still, he took her into his tent as well. Little is known about the relationships the khan had with women, but what is sure is that he enjoyed their company. The constant presence of women around the Mongol chiefs — a function of the relative freedom the women enjoyed as much as of the practice of keeping concubines — was mentioned on several occasions by observers, notably Pian del Carpini and Rubrouck, both of whom found the women extremely ugly!

When the battle was over, Temüjin called together his secret council to come to a decision about the fate of several captives of high lineage; then he delivered the verdict, which was not subject to appeal: death. One sees in the khan at this juncture his persistent wish for revenge against the Tatars, people whom he held collectively responsible for the death of his father over 30 years before. Belgütei, the khan's half-brother, inadvertently let something slip about the fate that awaited the prisoners. Having hidden knives under their clothes, they defended themselves desperately and killed a number of the khan's men who had come to attack them. As a punishment for having talked too much, Belgütei was thenceforth excluded from meetings of the secret council.

This victory over the Tatars raised Temüjin's prestige further. Soon afterwards, the Solon, another Tatar people, recognized, in their turn, the sovereignty of the khan. New allies, new pasture lands, new hunting grounds: the steady rise in Temüjin's power gradually made the Kereyid ruler uneasy. And despite his advanced age, he abandoned his benevolent neutrality towards Temüjin in favour of a malevolent neutrality. Like Marco Polo, who relates the episode, some chroniclers have explained this conflict with reference to the offence that To'oril inflicted on the khan: they were neighbours, the Mongols and the Kereyid, and they had formed good relations and sometimes alliances — even though, as will be remembered, during the battle against the Naiman, To'oril had abandoned the contest at a critical moment. Temüjin decided nonetheless to resume this alliance, and proposed to To'oril that the treaty be sealed by a marriage: for his son Jochi he requested a Kereyid princess, offering in return a Mongol princess for the son of the *wang khan*, Nilqa. To'oril, however, declined the suggestion and the khan was bitterly resentful of the rejection.

In fact, Nilqa, who bore the princely title Senggüm, given him by China, regarded a matrimonial union between the two parties with disapproval. On the one hand, there was his ageing father; on the other, Temüjin in all his glory, whom this union would elevate from the rank of vassal to that of an equal to his lord paramount. Nilqa had moreover already formed some contacts with Jamuγa, who had still not renounced the idea of becoming khan himself. Nilqa therefore tried to circumvent his father who, whether from caution or lack of energy, was not anxious to become involved. He reckoned without the obstinacy of the young and impetuous Nilqa, who was determined to oust the power he believed to be tottering. 'Honey on his lips, a dagger next to his breast', he succeeded in getting the old man to accept his demands and released his first darts against Temüjin: in spring 1203 his agents, as was a common practice, set fire to the grass where the Mongols' animals were grazing.

Shortly afterwards, on the occasion of a banquet, Nilqa decided to stir up an assault on the khan. But the plot failed, Münglig having persuaded his master not to accept the Senggüm's invitation. The latter, wasting no time, gathered his men together for a lightning operation. Again, his plans failed; a man who had taken part in the council of war was unable to hold his tongue in front of his wife and the plans, overheard by a servant — probably an enslaved Mongol — were reported to the khan, who was able to take steps to protect his camp.

The response to the alert was rapid. To prepare for the worst and delay any possible surprise attack, Jelme was charged with the task of forming a rearguard corps, while Temüjin took refuge in a semidesert region. But To'oril and his allies, Jamuγa and his men among them, managed to find him. *The Secret History* relates at great length how the best warriors from each side engaged in attacks and how the most valiant fought duels. There were bloody breaches, precipitate- retreats, chivalrous exhortations. These pages recount in epic form the brutal confrontations that took place, and describes men charging with lance or sabre, sowing confusion and death among the enemy, seeking out human flesh in order to run it through with metal.

The conduct of Jamuγa during the battle was, once again, a surprise: when To'oril suggested to him that they launch their troops in a full frontal assault, he refused. Not only did he refuse, but he also sent messengers to Temüjin to inform him about the movements of To'oril and his allies. Temüjin's incontestable tactical sense must be remarked on here. He never attempted any desperate manoeuvres, or any wild charges that would have cost him dear in terms of men. He was, on the contrary, restrained; he knew when to pull back if he was in a weak position and he would let his troops retreat to safer positions if they were under threat. All the khan's strategy was already evident at this time: impetuous attacks when the occasion favoured, retreat and withdrawal from the field when the pressure became too great. Temüjin, economical with his troops, understood that it was sometimes necessary to 'bend the bow without releasing the arrow'.

During the fighting, the khan learned that several officers were absent. Among them were Bo'urchu, Boroγul, and his own son, Ögödei. Having drawn his troops back to secure positions, Temüjin sent back some scouts to try to discover some sign of the missing officers. In the grass trampled underfoot by the horses' hooves, bodies were turned over. The search was in vain; *The Secret History* paints the picture of Temüjin mad with grief, beating his chest with his fists and calling on heaven to witness his distress. Then, suddenly, swarms of horsemen appeared on the scene. Among them, perched on a packhorse, was Bo'urchu, whose courser had been slain, and, hard on his heels, Boroγul and Ögödei. Ögödei, with a serious arrow wound in the neck, had lost a good deal of blood, but his companion had managed to bring him back. Everyone hastened to his aid and Temüjin himself, using a poker held until red-hot in a flame, cauterized the wound. And, in front of his officers, the khan shed some tears over the son who had been returned to him.

As his men were exhausted, Temüjin decided to call a retreat. On the Kereyid side, the troops were not in the best of states. They had finished with their displays of strength, their bold challenges and their vengeful exhortations. To'oril and his son were arguing about the reasons for their failure; bitterness at last gave way to a general exhaustion, even though one of the Kereyid captains, Achiγ-Shirun, flung a passionate challenge to his chief: 'Let us march on them and soon we shall be scraping them up like dung!'

Followed by several thousand still able men, Temüjin went down the river Khalka again in the direction of Buyr Nuur. Having no reserves of food in their carts, the men had to organize hunts to drive out some game; in the course of this hunt, Quyildar, a man loyal to the khan, died of exhaustion. Temüjin then divided his men into two groups and so reached the territory of the Onggirad, the tribe from whom his wife Börte had originally come. He immediately despatched messengers to these tribes to order them to receive the Mongol army in retreat. Out of fear of reprisals, opportunism or loyalty, Temüjin's hosts complied with a will and put at his disposal their reserves of food and firewood. The khan's troops had been given a good beating by the Kereyid, and he was anxious to tend their wounds. But in those distant yurts he was also to experience a short period of hard times.

## The Khan's Lament

The passages in *The Secret History* which mention the feelings of the principal personalities are regrettably rare. Yet here, leaving aside the glorification of the Mongol heroes, the chronicle gives us some clues and insights into the complexity of Temüjin, a man seemingly made of bronze. Temüjin could feel pity when the life of his own son was at stake, but then that was a shock dealt to him in the fury of the battlefield. But here, in the place of refuge he had found between Buyr Nuur and Lake Dalai, Temüjin felt the sting of despair. Beneath the apparent invulnerability of the hero lay hidden a feeling of impotence, of depression. The man of iron was revealing himself as a weak man too. The khan's long lament is addressed as much to his adversary as to adversity. The chronicler of *The Secret History* relates it in a remarkable lyrical style, suggesting that this episode was perhaps meant to be recited. The Persian Rashīd al-Dīn and the Chinese annalists have left us other versions, which do not in all instances tally.

From the depths of his hideaway, Temüjin sent two envoys to To'oril to tell him of Temüjin's deep disappointment in the person he had taken pains to establish in the role of adoptive father. And despite his vexation and resentment, Temüjin did not load his reproach with any threats. In his long list of grievances, one senses his indignation but, keener still, his disappointment in the Kereyid's fickleness. To the Mongol khan this was a sign of the influence of some evil force, which alone was capable of creating a breach of loyalty in an alliance. 'Khan my father,' said Temüjin sadly, 'have you not been pricked by someone near you, have you not been provoked by someone standing in your way? Khan my father . . . were we not agreed in this: "If a serpent with teeth rouses us [against each other], we shall not lend ourselves to this arousal; we shall believe what we shall verify with our own teeth and our own mouths"? Were we not agreed on that?'

Temüjin reminded the man whom he still considered his lord

paramount of his odious defection before the Naiman enemy. He reproached To'oril for his lack of gratitude when Yesügei, Temüjin's father, had helped him to repossess the throne; he reminded To'oril that he, Temüjin, had picked up the sceptre from the dust and put it in his hand, saying that his conquest of tribal territories had been nothing but the act of a vassal. Finally, Temüjin gave To'oril a lesson in loyalty by showing him that an alliance cannot be broken so lightly: 'If a cart with two shafts breaks its second shaft, its ox cannot pull it; am I not your second shaft? If a cart with two wheels breaks the second wheel, it cannot roll along; am I not your second wheel?' This declaration, which so clearly revealed his personal feelings, drew up a detailed balance sheet of all the services that had been rendered to To'oril. Was it intended to bring home to him that he, Temüjin, was not one to go on indefinitely personally supporting and cleaving to a lord who was so inconstant and so ungrateful?

But behind the khan's message there lay perhaps also a threat, a 'diplomatic manoeuvre of consummate skill', as René Grousset called it. Temüjin harboured grievances not only against the Kereyid king but also, by extension, against his relatives and allies as well. He made his claims and complaints plain to the other players in the drama too. He took exception to the ambition of To'oril's son, Nilqa Senggüm, to displace his old father prematurely from the throne, thereby stirring up distrust between the two men. He made it clear to the princes Quchar and Altan, who had gone over to the Kereyid side, that since they had elected him khan it was to him that they owed their allegiance, and that he would have showered them with gifts had they acknowledged this. Lastly, he complained to Jamuγa of his having sought to supplant him in To'oril's affections. His catalogue of complaints was intended to cause trouble among his opponents, to give some a bad conscience and to divide others.

There was every advantage to Temüjin — betrayed, threatened and isolated as he was — in presenting himself as the outraged lord and master. All the virtues of the nomads, which he trumpeted so loudly — the vassal's loyalty, the habit of keeping one's word and respecting that of others, the sense of honour and the attachment to the indissoluble bonds of blood and clan — all these he attributed also to himself, no doubt in good faith. In fact, he was not to demonstrate these qualities until the occasion brought them out. Does not every sharp politician seek to convince himself of his rightness on every point?

Temüjin's message, which implied a restructuring of alliances, found no response except with To'oril. As an earnest of his good intentions, the old man declared that he would rather have his body entirely drained of blood than to betray Temüjin once more. And, in a symbolic gesture, he made a gash in his little finger with the knife he used to sharpen arrows, and poured a little of his blood into a birch-bark container, which he sent to Temüjin. This pledge of loyalty did not, however, meet with the favour of To'oril's son, Nilqa Senggüm, who was furious at Temüjin's allegations, wherein he claimed to see 'two faces and three knives'. Younger and more impetuous, Nilqa, with the stronger side behind him, wilfully tossed the agreement aside. Another war was inevitable.

**The Death of To'oril**

It was a weakened Temüjin that came face to face with To'oril, the *wang khan*. But already the tribal chiefs who were allied with To'oril, accustomed to seasonal alliances and short-term pacts, were thinking of deserting the *wang khan*. Rashīd al-Dīn tells us that Daritai, Jamuγa, Altan and Quchar were scheming to do away with To'oril. Having been warned in time, To'oril repulsed the rebels, who with their followers turned tail and fled. Daritai found refuge in Temüjin's camp. The other plotters rejoined the Naiman. Suddenly To'oril saw his star beginning to fade.

Temüjin had withdrawn to the banks of a marshy pond, very probably located in the area of the Borshchovochnyy Khrebet mountains, north of the Onon Gol. There, according to the Persian chronicler, he swore to share with his faithful followers all his future trials whatever their outcome, good or bad. Since there was nothing else to drink there but slimy water, each man squeezed the liquid from the mud in the pond to fill his cup. Now, in this inhospitable retreat, fortune smiled on Temüjin. In quick succession he received a reinforcement of Γorula nomads; some provisions, thanks to the arrival of a caravan with a thousand sheep, led by a Moslem merchant; and, finally, the help of Jochi Qasar, his brother, who had escaped from the Kereyid camp in mysterious circumstances. Having just come from the enemy lines, Jochi Qasar was able to devise and set a trap to trick the old Kereyid ruler and draw him into an ambush at the far end of a defile. The Kereyid fought for three days and three nights before capitulating, but the *wang khan* and his son miraculously managed to escape.

Temüjin dug deep into the booty they had taken from the Kereyid to reward his faithful companions-in-arms. To two herdsmen who had warned him of an imminent attack during a previous confrontation, he offered the *wang khan*'s tent and all the riches contained within it. The two shepherds were also given princely privileges: the khan named them 'quiver-bearers', which gave them the right to raise their own personal guard, to keep their weapons with them during banquets and also, on such occasions, to have their own individual jugs of drink; in addition, he authorized them to keep any game they killed during the season's great hunts. These favours promised and honours given must have inspired a great deal of loyalty towards the great khan.

The victory over the Kereyid strengthened Mongol power, by giving Temüjin the upper hand over more and more nomadic tribes. From all over central and eastern Mongolia tribal chiefs came to his tent to seek to ally themselves with him and become his vassals. Old adversaries, too, swore their allegiance. As soon as he could, the khan made new supporters of his old enemies, using diplomacy in his best interest. One cannot help but be struck by the volte-face all these men performed: whether fate had dealt them victories or defeats, they changed camp and fought desperately against those who only yesterday had been their allies. Like all nomads, the Mongols had little allegiance to an idea, a nation or a territory: they served a master. This concept is to be found also in medieval Europe of the same era, where hierarchical relationships were basically regulated by principles of suzerainty and vassalry. Small societies were united not only by tradition but equally by personal bonds and goodwill.

The defeat of the Kereyid sealed their fate. Clan by clan they became dispersed among other tribes and became the servants of the conquerors. Historical sources make no mention, however, of massacres or revenge against To'oril's people: perhaps Temüjin in his heart of hearts retained some remnant of the old armed fraternity he had once had with the *wang khan*. Consequently, quite a number of the Kereyid rose to positions of confidence. This benevolence on the part of Temüjin had its origins in the particularly close links between himself and To'oril's family. He had taken to wife a Kereyid noblewoman, Ibaqa Beki, daughter of a brother of To'oril. His own son, Tolui, was married, for the second time, to Ibaqa Beki's sister, Sorgaγtani; she was to bring into the world the first of the great rulers of the Genghis Khan line who were to hold sway over the Turco-Mongol people and over Persia and China: Möngke, Hülegü, and Kublai. This Nestorian princess appears to have played an important role in protecting missionaries and in introducing certain Christian ideas into the heart of the Mongol empire. Kublai Khan, the sovereign whom Marco Polo met, protected Nestorianism and even set up an administration charged with promoting this cult; it is well known that the Mongol courts were prepared to welcome, for the most part favourably, ideas that came from the Christian West.

During the winter of 1203, Temüjin settled into quarters in eastern Mongolia in a region called 'the Steppe of the Camel' (Teme'en Kc'er). There he learned from scouts that To'oril and his heir had taken refuge among the Naiman. Believing they would find asylum there, they had wandered onto the inhospitable steppes, followed by some of their comrades in a state of deprivation equal to their own, and lived by plunder and hunting. These were the circumstances when To'oril, dispossessed yet again, was surprised by some men from a Naiman tent: their chief, convinced that he was dealing with a cattle rustler, killed him without further ado. To'oril must have made last-minute attempts to identify himself, because word soon spread that a simple camp chief had put to death the *wang khan* of the Kereyid. The news also reached the encampment of the chief of the Naiman, who ordered that the body of To'oril should be retrieved; the man who found it cut off the king's head and took it to the Naiman chief (*tayang*). Out of regret at not having been able to meet the king in his fallen state, or out of remorse at not having saved him from an ignominious end, the *tayang* then organized a macabre ceremony in honour of the dead To'oril. He had the head set in a little silver chest which was displayed on a cushion of light-coloured felt. Then princess Gürbesü had cups brought in for libations while musicians played. But legend has it that when the draught was brought close to the lifeless, deformed lips, the head of To'oril began to smile, even to leer. Superstition made the *tayang* knock the shrine down with the back of his hand and then kick it to pieces with his boot. Seized with fear at this act of sacrilege, one of the *tayang*'s lieutenants told his master that misfortunes would forthwith begin to pile up on his crown.

The heir of the wretched To'oril had found refuge in a desert region where he lived like an outlaw. Abandoned by the last of his followers, betrayed by his own equerry, he came at last to the borders of the Xixia kingdom, south of Mongolia, near the present-day Chinese province of Gansu. Friendless, penniless and hopeless, he lived by plunder until one day, in the oasis of Kucha (now Kuqa), in Uighur territory, he was killed in a fight by some villagers.

Temüjin lost no time in subduing the various tribes that had until then been allied with To'oril. By the beginning of 1204, he had brought within the ambit of his control several tens of thousands of nomads in central and eastern Mongolia. Those of the western part remained unsubdued.

## The Elimination of the Nestorian Naiman

The Naiman tribes occupied a vast part of the steppes extending on both sides of the Altay range in Mongolia and the basin of the upper Irtysh. The Naiman were Turks who had undergone profound change. 'They were halfway along the road from a Turkish-based to a Mongol-based culture,' notes Jean-Paul Roux; they had been influenced by the Nestorianism of the Uighur and at the same time by shamanism. No doubt the Naiman nobility had left behind the 'primitive' state which still prevailed among the nomadic Mongols. This statement finds support in the haughty comments of Princess Gürbesü, who viewed her neighbours as 'stinking Mongols', adding that even the most refined Mongol princesses were wholly ignorant of the habit of washing one's hands and feet. The polish of Naiman culture came from having a more developed artisan class, from closer contacts with settled peoples, and from privileged encounters with Western travellers. Rubrouck speaks of the Nestorian Naiman as 'true subjects of Prester John'.

To prepare to meet the Mongol assault, the Naiman *tayang* tried first to attack them from the south. He made contact with the Önggüd, also Nestorian Turks but Mongolian speakers, who were moving their herds to new pastures north of the Great Wall, near Suiyuan (now in Inner Mongolia). But the Önggüd refused to join forces with the *tayang* and warned Temüjin of his warlike intentions.

The khan was out on a hunting party, on 'Donkey-back Steppe', when he learned that the Naiman were making military preparations. It was the start of the loveliest season of the year: everywhere tulips, scabiouses and irises were taking over the vast expanses of the steppes; edelweiss and thyme grew where in the winter that would soon follow there would be nothing but stony wasteland. It was there that Temüjin gathered his followers around him. Apparently the khan, considering that the horses were still too thin, would have preferred to postpone action. But his brother Temüge and his half-brother Belgütei were impatient to get to grips with the enemy, and came down on the side of going to war. Nevertheless, Temüjin stemmed the ardour of his lieutenants, trying to gain enough time to prepare his offensive against the Naiman thoroughly. He had to mobilize the allied tribes and decide on a strategy.

As before every battle, the shamans performed the ritual sacrifice in front of the *tuɣ*, a banner decorated with nine black tails of bay horses, which was carried at the head of the army; before this standard, which was supposed to contain the *suldè*, the clan's protective spirit, they spread out cups of *koumiss*. Doubtless the fateful signs deciphered by the shamans were favourable, for Temüjin immediately ordered his troops out, marching towards the west, along the Kerulen. They made slow and arduous progress, crossing escarpments and rivers on the way to the battlefield in the Hangayn Nuruu. The conflict that took place there was terrible; it severely sapped the Naiman strength and limited their power.

**A Decisive Victory**
The Naiman had not succeeded in drawing the Önggüd into their ranks; they remained a threat. Other tribes had in fact joined the *tayang*: Oirat, Kereyid rebels against Temüjin's domination, but also Merkid, Tatars and Tayichi'ud, all old enemies of the Mongol khan eager to obtain their revenge. Still implacably opposed to his old *anda*, the Jajirad chief, Jamuɣa, rode at the *tayang*'s side, at the head of about 50,000 horsemen. The *tayang* was going into his last battle. The khan's forces were somewhat less numerous, but he could count on the fighting spirit and loyalty of his companions-in-arms: Jelme, Kublai, Sübetei, Jebe, his brother Temüge and his other brother Jochi Qasar. The Naiman seem to have been much surprised to see the Mongol troops in such order and showing little sign of having crossed a huge part of Mongolia. The Naiman command was divided on whether to launch an attack swiftly; once again, it was discord and treachery that brought Temüjin success.

*The Secret History* reports that the Mongols lit large numbers of camp fires to deceive the enemy. The *tayang*, falling into the trap, wavered and considered how to respond. His son, Güchülüg, was appalled at the notion of such cowardice; he called his father a woman and said that the princess Gürbesü would be a more suitable army commander than he. Indecision merely gave way to fickleness.

The first skirmishes that broke out at the foot of Mount Naqu worried the *tayang*, whose vanguard were being relentlessly harried. Hesitating to strike a bold blow, he kept his horsemen to the rear, eager though they were to enter the fray. Jamuɣa, at his side, was watching the enemy formations and at the same time trying to recognize the men in command. Two or three hundred metres separated the two armies, but from the standards, clothes or caparisons, Jamuɣa could make out Jelme, Kublai and Jebe; he pointed them out to the *tayang*, advising him on the threats they posed and on the tactical changes to adopt.

*The Secret History* gives its account of the battle in terms of the spoken word and in a tone that is reminiscent of the war between the Greeks and the Trojans in Asia Minor:

'And who are these people who rush forward to envelop us, like colts let loose in the morning of the day, gorged with mares' milk and gambolling around their mother?' asks the king of the Naiman.

'They,' replies Jamuγa, 'are the tribes of the Urut and the Mangγud. They are pursuing the armed warriors with sabre and lance, like game; they are ripping from them their blood-soaked weapons; they are turning them over and slitting their throats; they are snatching up their remains!'

'And who is that man we see behind them, like a ravenous kite, impatient to hurl itself on its prey?' the king asks further.

'That,' replies Jamuγa again, 'is my *anda* Temüjin. His entire body is steeped in bronze, forged in iron, and he has not a single joint through which the point of an awl could penetrate. Do you see him hurling himself towards you like a ravenous vulture?'

Jamuγa then describes the captains of the enemy camp who are leading a furious charge of their horsemen against the Naiman ranks. With a kind of wild excitement — and, one may think, a secret admiration! — he relates the exploits of the foe. He says that Temüjin's brother, Jochi Qasar (the Tiger), wore a triple coat of armour and was so powerful that he could lance bodies through with the force of his arrow fire. This description, as given in the Mongol chronicle, clearly reveals the strange attraction exercised on Jamuγa by this enemy whom he used to know so well. In every word one detects his tremendous fascination with Temüjin. Then suddenly Jamuγa deserted, though not without sending messengers to 'his *anda*' Temüjin to tell him so!

During the night, the Naiman had been surrounded on Mount Naqu, their forces had been dispersed and every initiative had been snatched from them. Little groups of horsemen were moving down the slopes, trying to cut a way through. In the thickets, they were attacked as they groped in the dark, and slain. That fatal night saw the death throes of the Naiman tribes and their allies. At daybreak, the Mongols launched their assault. Riders slashed the wounded with their swords and speared fugitives. The *tayang* was seriously wounded. In the confusion, a means of helping him could not be found. He was laid on the ground while his men resolved to mount a last defensive assault. But the Mongols brushed aside this brave action as easily as if they had been flicking away a strand of hair. The *tayang* died alone. It is said that Temüjin, impressed by the courage of the man in his adversity, paid his respects to the mortal remains. Only Güchülüg, the *tayang*'s son, and Jamuγa escaped the massacre. The victors raked through the camp of the vanquished, plundering weapons, jewellery and clothes, and violating their wives and daughters. Princess Gürbesü, who had insulted the Mongols, became the khan's servant. Among the prisoners was the *tayang*'s chancellor, Tata Tong-a, a Uighur, who preferred to be taken into the khan's service too. The neighbouring tribes who had been the Naiman's allies now threw in their lot with the victor, and a Merkid chief offered Temüjin his own daughter, Qulan; she was to become one of the khan's favourites.

**The Last of the Merkid**
When this campaign was over, ridding Temüjin for good of the Nestorian Naiman, his only remaining rivals were three Merkid tribal groups. Camped between Lake Baikal and the Altay mountains, in the far northern range of the Selenge Mörön, these people, mostly forest dwellers, formed a loose confederation; Temüjin's Mongols had often used them as auxiliaries. They were, however, split into a multiplicity of factions which acted centrifugally to pull them apart, and eventually they rebelled. Some of the Merkid, under the leadership of Toγto'a Beki, had even succeeded in keeping for themselves, in the interior of a region bounded by thick forest, a zone over which the Mongols had no control. Towards 1204 or 1205, Temüjin made it his business to eliminate this sanctuary, and he marched on the Ulan Daban and Tabun-uul mountains which link the Mongolian Altay with its Siberian watershed.

This rugged, broken landscape is a taiga region, with larch, fir and conifers predominating. The Mongol horsemen forced their way into the hideout of Toγto'a, who there and then met his death. The noblemen who had been with him fled, along with the chiefs of various minor clans, and managed to wage guerrilla war against the invaders. But the Mongol troops acted quickly to cut off their access to water supplies and essential communication routes. Surrounded, the Merkid were forced to spilt into ever dwindling groups, each time leaving behind more of their baggage and provisions. They were to hold out for several years, attempting occasional sudden dashes and forays, usually with some degree of success.

Around 1217, certain Merkid groups, inspired by a kind of desperate irredentism, again plunged into the wild forests. Temüjin charged Toguchar, his son-in-law, and Sübetei, one of his best lieutenants, with destroying them. It is said that on this occasion the Mongols used 'iron carts' (*temür tergen*), that is, carts with a metal armature to help them withstand the shocks dealt by rocky terrain; it seems an unlikely thing, because it would certainly have been difficult to make progress through a forested area with heavy vehicles. Be that as it may, Sübetei eventually succeeded in wiping out the last of the Merkid guerrillas. Nomads amongst nomads, ghostly bands, starved, massacred, captured, enslaved or mongrelized, the Merkid gradually vanished from the face of the earth.

Mongol and Chinese sources differ on the date of these events, which they place ten years apart, but what is certain is that Temüjin wanted to be done with the Merkid rebels. It cannot be said that this was a deliberate strategy and a prelude to other campaigns of extermination. We should remember that the Merkid and the Mongols were of the same stock; while they bartered goods, they also doubtless were involved in economic rivalries, in disputes over hunting grounds and in mutual thefts of livestock. In addition, the two groups led quite different lives, a circumstance which gave rise to misunderstandings and natural antagonisms: for the steppe nomad, to enter the forest to track down game was to penetrate a frightening universe; to confront the unknown. The forest dwellers, on the other hand, did not generally maintain livestock; they were trappers first and foremost, and did not venture out onto the plain except when a shortage of game drove them out to steal some stray goats before returning to their huts.

The enduring hatred Temüjin felt for the Merkid must also have had its origin in a personal grudge: it was a Merkid party that had snatched his wife Börte away from him and Temüjin very likely held the Merkid collectively responsible for the abduction that some of their number had carried out. His implacable thirst for revenge against them is again attested to by an anecdote: Jochi Qasar, son of Hö'elün, captured a Merkid, a skilled archer whom he wanted to keep in his service because of his expertise. But Temüjin, who was normally inclined to show generosity towards enemies who had demonstrated military or moral virtues, refused to give the captive quarter. He who had pardoned Jebe for having shot his own horse with a well-aimed arrow now insisted that the Merkid marksman be put to death!

## The Tragedy of Jamuγa

When the last of the Merkid had been destroyed, the Kirghiz of the upper Yenisey were next to submit to Mongol might. That left one last enemy. Now that the Tatars, Naiman, Merkid, Kirghiz and other neighbouring tribes had been subdued, one man of distinguished lineage, whose standing had, however, been damaged by his treachery, this one man still stood in opposition to Temüjin: Jamuγa, that outlaw whose entire army consisted of five trusty friends. Hunted over endless swampy country surrounding the Tannu-uul mountains, isolated, a turncoat without allies, Jamuγa led the life of a madman, of a lone wild boar. One day his companions in misery, weary of his authority or eager to receive a reward, seized him, bound him with leather straps, and brought him, in short stages, to Temüjin's yurt.

Once again, Jamuγa's behaviour was totally unexpected. Before his *anda*, his 'sworn brother', Jamuγa asked for the death sentence for those who had betrayed him, but also for himself. Jamuγa's five attendants, whom he had compared with black crows attacking a wild duck, were executed before his eyes. Nevertheless, Temüjin, probably moved by the misfortune of the man who had for so long been his playmate, his childhood friend, and his intimate companion-in-arms, tried to prevent his *anda* from going to his death. He recalled that it was thanks to Jamuγa that he had recovered Börte, the wife who had been taken from him by the Merkid; he recalled campaigns where he had ridden with his companion, stirrup to stirrup, sleeping at night under the same blanket: 'Once we were bound by the closest of bonds, we were as inseparable as the two shafts of a cart. And then, one day, you abandoned me. But here you are back again. Let us be united as we were before. Let us live together again, side by side. We have not forgotten the memories of our youth, let us revive them.'

Even though the chronicles accord rather too much credit to Temüjin's magnanimity, and, in order to show the latter in a more favourable light, stress Jamuγa's treachery, it is still remarkable that the khan, to all intents and purposes, offered to make peace with his old friend. More, he offered him his renewed faithful friendship. At once he pledged himself to put behind him all the treacherous acts of a man who had repeatedly deceived, pursued and betrayed him.

Jamuγa gave his reply in words that revealed incontrovertibly a greatness of soul. He praised the generosity of his *anda* and his magnanimity, which were worthy of an emperor at the height of his power. He, too, recalled those happy bygone years, and he, too, allowed a strange nostalgia to shine through: 'Once, in the days of our youth, when we became *anda*, near the stream of Qorqonaγ, we shared our meals, we said unforgettable things to each other and we slept side by side.' But Jamuγa acknowledged that he had not been able to shut his ears to malice-laden suggestions that had set him up in opposition to Temüjin; he admitted that he had been deceived and that, by virtue of that fact, it was not possible for him to look his old friend in the eye. He confessed that he was overwhelmed with shame and remorse. To Temüjin had been granted greatness and power; to him, Jamuγa, inferiority and defeat: 'You, my *anda*, you are a hero. Your mother is the soul of wisdom. Your brothers are full of ability. The seventy-three brave men who form your entourage serve you like as many faithful coursers. How I am inferior to you, O my *anda*! When I was a small child, I was abandoned by my father and by my mother; brothers have I none, and my companions have not been loyal to me. Tenggeri has favoured my *anda*, who has surpassed me in all things.'

It is difficult to resist seeing in this some kind of impulse towards failure. And it is tempting to explain Jamuγa's feelings in terms of the trials of life that he reveals: his abandonment, as a small child, by his father and mother, his destiny as a child alone, left to his own devices. For Jamuγa pursued his course to the very end and, in an ultimate gesture of self-sacrifice, demanded that Temüjin grant him death: 'Now, O my *anda*, you must be rid of me so that your soul will be at peace. But if you decide to have me put to death, I must die without blood being shed . . . And now, make a quick end of me!'

Temüjin — according to the chronicles, which may well have exaggerated his generosity — hesitated when Jamuγa's wishes were relayed to him. He explained his lack of hatred by the fact that Jamuγa had never sought to injure him personally, and declared that he retained his attachment to him who had always, in his eyes, been blessed with great qualities. And yet, on the pretext that his old companion was 'weary of life', Temüjin at last had him executed. Did he feel that Jamuγa, even when subdued and full of repentance, might still be a potential rival? It seems not. It is perhaps more plausible to suggest that some strange game was being played out between the two protagonists.

Since Jamuγa asked for death at Temüjin's hand, Temüjin was going to grant it him, recognizing, or pretending to recognize, that he was doing nothing but complying with his friend's wish. One feels that there was a tacit complicity between them to which Temüjin was responding, and that he understood in a flash that the most precious gift he could offer his *anda* was precisely that death for which he was clamouring.

Furthermore, before inflicting his expiatory punishment on Jamuγa, Temüjin wanted to find some judicial motive: several years previously, Jamuγa had frightened him while they were out stealing horses. Now Jamuγa was rejecting the pardon offered him by his old friend. Curiously enough, Temüjin's reasons for condemning Jamuγa to death were personal and without political implications.

Jamuγa was therefore put to death. Since the soul was believed to reside in the blood, custom required that a prince who had been the recipient of honours should not have his skin broken. According to one chronicle, Jamuγa was suffocated in a carpet. One legend tells us that Temüjin refused to watch his old friend die and charged one of his nephews to carry out the execution. This account goes on to say that Jamuγa demanded to be killed in a horrifying manner: the executioner was to cut off his limbs one by one — and this request was granted.

From the beginning to the very end of their intertwined destinies, the relationship between Temüjin and Jamuγa had been an extraordinary one in which friendship and hostility each played their discordant tunes. No doubt Jamuγa could have attained his greatest aspirations if, instead of opposing Temüjin, he had supported him in his designs. No doubt he could have fought him and won if he had not fallen into a kind of passion of self-destruction and permanent inconstancy. Equally ambiguous, however, is the attitude of Temüjin who began by agreeing to pardon his adversary and ended by abandoning him. The story of this strange pair and its disturbing denouement might have inspired Shakespeare.

# 8
# Genghis Khan

*Temüjin-i Cinggis-qagan ke'en nerceyitcü qan bolqaba.* (They
proclaimed Temüjin khan and named him *Genghis
Khan*.)

**The Secret History of the Mongols**

## Investiture at the Great *Quriltai*

Hard on the heels of the death of Jamuɣa, Temüjin assumed the position
of uncontested master of most of the Mongol tribes camped between the
Da Hinggan Ling (formerly Khingan) range in the east, the Sayan
mountains in the west, the spurs of the Altay range in the south and Lake
Baikal in the north. Within this vast territory, corresponding roughly to
present-day Mongolia (slightly reduced), there remained only a few
scattered pockets of dissent. At 50, Temüjin was in a position to become
leader of all 'the people who lived under felt tents'. Thus it was that, in
May 1206, he called together a new *quriltai*, the general assembly that
united the nobles from all the clans.

Because of the very loose links among the nomadic feudal vassals, and
because of the dispersal of clans over great distances, the assemblies were
held irregularly and in different places. These were in no sense any kind
of 'organized institution': matters of greater and lesser importance were
discussed there, general or particular relations between fiefdoms were
dealt with, and decisions were made about keeping peace and making
war. Sometimes, however, these assemblies were less official in nature
and were simply a good excuse for a banquet. The call for one of these

'tribal councils' would come from one or several clans, and only those people who wanted to do so would attend. At the time of Temüjin, the *quriltai* began to play a more decisive role in affairs. The great khan, holder of an almost boundless power, continued to remain faithful to this tradition of the clan council.

So, in the middle of the year 1206, some thousands of men assembled near the sources of the Onon Gol. Along with their great herds of horses, the aristocrats of the steppe would respond to the khan's bidding and come to the assembly. On the plain where the *quriltai* was to take place, their numbers soon ran into hundreds. Among them were chiefs of well-known clans, boasting eloquent surnames (*mergen*, the Skilful; *bayatur*, the Valiant; *sechen*, the Prudent). They were all there, accompanied by their wives, their concubines and their servants, in this huge encampment of felt tents, this open-air caravanserai, full of noise and colour. They had all come to perform an act of allegiance to Temüjin, whom they had adjudged most capable of seizing and guiding the destiny of the countless tribes of Mongolia, this nation that was just beginning to see the light of day.

Hundreds of horses were hobbled all around the circumference of the yurt. The nomads wandered about, here admiring a stallion, there having an appreciative look at the workmanship of a saddle or a piece of curried leather. For days these shepherd-warriors mingled, made acquaintances, formed friendships and struck up alliances. They competed with each other in horse races, wrestling contests, or archery matches; they exchanged animal skins, hunting birds, and jewels, for the huge yurt had become a sort of fair. When night fell and the noise of the animals had died down, the men gathered around *argol* (animal dung) fires to drink cups of milk and taste the alcohol of which little bottles were swapped with peasants or with caravaneers. They played games with knucklebones and with string, listened to a musician's instrument or to one of the nomads loudly declaiming an epic poem telling of a hunt, a wild bear, and a horse galloping across the steppe.

The historical sources say nothing about the reasons for this latest *quriltai*. Some twelve years earlier — in about 1197 — Temüjin had already been chosen khan by a party of clan chiefs, including the princes who, by virtue of their exalted lineage, could equally have claimed the khanate for themselves. It appears therefore that he called the assembly not only to renew his mandate but also to ratify his *de facto* power. It was inevitable that this man, who had never concealed his lust for power, should want to receive this glorious investiture. No doubt encouraged and helped by his family and friends, Temüjin had now, after slow but inexorable progress, come to the final stage of his journey towards a legally based autocracy. Proclaimed for a second time 'Genghis Khan by the might of Tenggeri', that is to say, 'oceanic khan by the power of the Eternal Sky', he could now congratulate himself on his good fortune.

The chroniclers say that Temüjin's coronation was performed with the greatest decorum. The *tuγ*, that immaculate banner on which nine tails of bay horses fluttered in the wind, was raised to the sky, and the shaman Kököchü, the 'Trusted of Heaven', personally sanctioned Temüjin's authority in the course of a grand investiture ceremony. At the close of the *quriltai*, Temüjin, to mark the advent of his lucky star, distributed honours and rewards in a riot of supreme gratitude. Faithful attendants and deserving officers received lavish presents that had been set aside from the reserves of booty.

The khan already had followers. From now on he also had courtiers. To those who had encouraged or flattered him, Genghis Khan offered promotions and gifts. Qorchi, the shaman who had laid his stake on the rise of the khan, received the present he had claimed as the fee for his prophecy: a harem of about thirty lovely women. He also obtained the command of the forest people of the northwestern marches. Muqali, who had also foretold his master's extraordinary destiny, received a princely Chinese title and 'the command of the left wing as far as the Qunchidun mountains'. Fawningly, Shigi-Qutuqu, the khan's adoptive brother, who had been brought up by Hö'elün, claimed his share of the honours: 'Have I been less devoted to you than anyone else? Since my childhood, I have grown up in your household and have never given a thought to anyone but you. You let me sleep at your feet and treated me as your younger brother. What will you give me as a sign of favour?' He was named supreme judge, a promotion which proves, if proof were needed, that the khan did not hesitate to indulge in nepotism.

Genghis Khan was also at pains to reward his trustiest followers, who were the true architects of his rise to supreme power. Jelme, Sübetei, Kublai and Jebe were generously rewarded with military citations; Münglig, l'unan and Degei were equally exalted and praised by the khan for their bravery and loyalty during earlier campaigns. Bo'urchu, the khan's childhood friend and companion-in-arms, received the following tribute from his master for his selfless devotion: 'You knew nothing about me and yet you immediately left everything to follow me . . . O Bo'urchu,

O Muqali, you helped me ascend the throne because you have always given me good counsel, encouraging me when I was right, restraining me when I was wrong.'

Not only did the khan see to it that his loyal captains shared in his glory, he also had some words of affection, even of tenderness, for the members of his family, for his four sons — Tolui, Ögödei, Jochi and Chagatai — as also for the children he had found and adopted — Shigi-Qutuqu, his adoptive brother; Boroɣul; Kököchü; and Güchü. The chronicle maintains that his most affectionate tributes of all were reserved for all those who had died in his service. Genghis Khan also offered various privileges to the children of his warriors killed in action.

## The Khan's Men
In reading the list of offices and privileges granted to his followers or their descendants, and the string of appointments and nominations bestowed on his collaborators, one sees that Genghis Khan was singularly lucky to be surrounded by men of such outstanding valour. And indeed it was 'the khan's men' who were the main architects of Temüjin's power. He relied on them constantly, and invariably sent them on in advance of himself. All of them went to the very limits of devotion to serve their master.

True, Genghis Khan encountered over the years men who betrayed him, such as the princes Altan and Quchar; the fickle Gür Qan Jamuɣa; or To'oril, the faithless king who became ineffectual as he grew old. All were of illustrious descent. On the other hand, 'the khan's men' did not belong to great families: Genghis Khan met them on battlefields in the course of daring military actions. If the rare sources on this matter are correct, many — Jelme, Badai, Kishiliɣ, Bo'urchu, Münglig, Sorqan Shira and others — were the sons of blacksmiths or herdsmen. It was on these men, who 'carried their marshal's batons in their cartridge-pouches', that Genghis Khan chose to rely to dispose of his rivals from the high aristocracy and to pursue his conquests. And it was thanks to these feudal vassals of modest family that he eliminated the Jürkin princes Sacha Beki and Taichu, who claimed to be directly descended from the glorious Qabul Qan, and other princes such as Büri Bökö, Quchar and Altan. One has the impression that in the long domestic struggles that stirred his spirit and roused him to action, the khan preferred to have feudal land-owners, chiefs of minor clans, or even simple shepherds, for his allies; once they had proved themselves, they were promoted to high office as soon as the khan had command of a proper administrative system.

The khan's men, the *nökör* (free companions), were certainly 'companions': liegemen, vassals and servants of the khan, they belonged to clan groups that were customarily allied together, and could not be considered to have been mercenaries. When military expeditions were mounted, they were among the first to be drafted into service and they quickly revealed themselves to be excellent tacticians; they received their training on cavalry charges and went on to lead their archers and lancers to the most distant battlefields in China, in Moslem lands and even at the frontiers of Europe.

Besides these formidable swordsmen, recruited in the course of intertribal conflicts, Genghis Khan found natural allies within the bosom of his family. His adoptive and blood brothers, his half-brothers and later his sons were valuable partners in his enterprises. Within this large extended family, comparative harmony appears to have reigned. Of course, the tragic episode of the murder of Bekter is an exception, but the youths who committed that act were then aged no more than about 12.

How is the loyalty of 'the khan's men' to be explained? Perhaps they merely had an acute sense of service and a particularly strong attachment to their master. Or perhaps all these auxiliaries, with their modest origins, knew that in order to rise above their lowly positions it was in their interests to serve as best they could the man who had opened the door to that opportunity? The two explanations are not mutually exclusive. In any case, the fact that the khan fairly quickly rid himself of great Mongol princes in favour of freedmen or minor aristocrats runs counter to the theory of the Soviet historian, Barthold, that Genghis Khan, coming from the conservative aristocracy, was the natural opponent of Jamuγa, who belonged to a poorer class of shepherds whose attitudes were tinged with democratic tendencies.

**The Army, the New Striking Force**
Soon after the *quriltai* of 1206, Genghis Khan took steps to bring both sceptre and sabre within his grasp: 'Once,' he said, 'I had but seventy bodyguards by day and eighty by night. Now that by the grace of Eternal Heaven the whole empire lies at my feet, the effective force of the bodyguard should be raised to ten thousand warriors, recruited from among the sons of platoon leaders, centurions and generals.' The new khan knew very well that, while his power derived from its legal basis, it

was equally dependent for its continuance on strength. It had taken him ten years to rise from the position of tribal khan to the supreme investiture. From now on, he would do all he could to maintain that position, not the least of which was to create a true conquering army.

The khan's militias had been progressively hardened in the course of skirmishes and pitched battles, and had developed into a formidable fighting force. They were not, however, in any sense a professional army. As has been said, the men who composed these militias were first and foremost shepherds and grooms who, in peacetime, concentrated on their herding occupations. But Genghis Khan could put these militias on a war footing in the minimum of time. With the help of blacksmiths, who carried their tools and materials with them into battle on their carts, the men were able to make much of their own equipment themselves. The Mongols were used to managing horses and hunting individually or in groups, and as such were strong, competent fighters: nomadic pastoralism was an excellent training for war. Thus, now, at the beginning of the thirteenth century, the tribes that were united under the khan's sceptre had, as it were, undergone a 'natural' military training.

When the *quriltai* of 1206 was over, Genghis Khan undertook the restructuring of Mongol tribal society within a new hierarchy. The clans, subtribes and tribes which traditionally formed the patriarchal population (*ulus*) of the *noyans* were integrated into a strictly numerical, militarized system. Each *ulus* was required to be in a position to put into the field a precise number of militiamen, along with their equipment. The major tribes had to be split up, while the small ones had to amalgamate with others to form larger groupings. Armed men (*cerigut*) were divided into units in multiples of 10: the *arban* (10 men); *ja'un* (100 men); *mingan* (1,000 men); *tümen* (10,000 men); *tuγ* (100,000 men). This division of the population was founded on the feudal structure.

Thus the *noyans* constituted the senior officer corps; their commander status in the military structure, which had become hereditary, was added to their status as feudal lords. Moreover, when the great khan so ordered, the *noyans* were compelled to serve on a quasi-permanent basis. Genghis Khan performed official investitures for his most capable captains and bestowed new commands on them. Several *nökör* were given oversight of logistics, including the stud reserve and military equipment (carts, armaments). These rearrangements of the occasional militias brought in their wake the removal of certain old leaders and their replacement with ambitious 'young captains'. Among the ninety-three new command positions created, the names of Genghis Khan's trustiest followers all figured: Jelme, Jebe, Sorqan Shira, Sübetei. A little later, others who were close to the great khan were also invested with responsibility for territorial divisions of the generalissimos (*örlüg*).

This rigorous organization of the old tribal militias was to form the spearhead for subsequent conquests and the thrust behind the emergence of the true mounted army that was so impressive to its contemporaries. Fifty years later, Pian del Carpini noted the rigour of this military organization, stressing the discipline that underlay the code of conduct among combatants:

> With respect to the arrangement of the army drawn up in the line of battle, Genghis Khan ordered that one man be placed in charge of every ten men. And that man we accordingly call *decanus* [platoon leader]. Moreover one man is placed in charge of ten *decani*, who is called *centenarius* [centurion or company commander]. And indeed one man is placed in charge of ten *centenarii*, who is called *millenarius* [divisional commander]. Further, one man is placed in charge of ten *millenarii*. And that man is called a shadow among them. Finally, at the head of the whole army are placed two or three generals, who however give precedence to one, and when the army is at war, if one or two or three or even many of the ten men flee then all ten are executed. And if all ten flee, then all the men in the hundred to which they belong are excuted, unless all have fled.[1]

Superimposing an army structure on the clan and tribal population, and transforming the Mongol *ulus* into a regiment, meant that traditional feudal and clan loyalty was replaced by a commitment to empire. There were only a few tribal chiefs (Muqali, Daritai) who retained their authority over their own camps. Being a methodical leader, Genghis Khan clearly found the decimal system sufficiently appealing to introduce it into his own military organization. This attracted Marco Polo's admiration:

> Their troops are admirably ordered in the manner that I shall now relate.
>
> You see, when a Tartar prince goes forth to war, he takes with him, say, 100,000 horse. Well, he appoints an officer to every ten men, one to every hundred, one to every thousand, and one to every ten

thousand, so that his own orders have to be given to ten persons only, and each of these ten persons has to pass the orders only to other ten, and so on; no one having to give orders to more than ten. And every one in turn is responsible only to the officer immediately over him; and the discipline and order that comes of this method is marvellous.

To help coordinate this army, corps of 'arrow-messengers' were created. Making use of changes of horses that were distributed over the territory controlled by the khan, they had the task of spreading the news and of communicating the orders of the *ordo* (camp). This amazing system, the *yam* (or *jam*) (from which the Russian word for coachman — *yamshchik* — derives), allowed mounted messengers to cover phenomenal distances within the space of an extremely short time: there were tales of messengers covering 3,000 kilometres per week, or about 400 kilometres a day.

Father Huc in 1846 said he had met mounted couriers in Tibet who had made over 800 kilometres in less than a week, over very rough ground. Wearing a belt to which some bells or a trumpet were attached, these 'arrow-messengers' sometimes galloped at full pelt, day and night: literally strapped to their mounts, they were muffled up in several layers of material to protect them from inclement weather. Marco Polo, not without exaggeration, tells of these mounted messengers in the service of Kublai, Genghis Khan's grandson:

At some of these stations, moreover, there shall be posted some 400 horses standing ready for the use of the messengers; at others there shall be 200, according to the requirements, and to what the Emperor has established in each case. At every 25 miles, as I said, or anyhow at every 30 miles, you find one of these stations . . . Every one of those runners wears a great wide belt, set all over with bells, so that as they run the 3 miles from post to post their bells are heard jingling a long way off. And thus on reaching the post the runner finds another man similarly equipt, and all ready to take his place, who instantly takes over whatsoever he has in charge, and with it receives a slip of paper from the clerk who is always at hand for the purpose; and so the new man sets off.

Genghis Khan instituted new ranks and new functions: élite battalions formed the corps of 'old braves' while others, composed essentially of archers, were designated 'great quiver-bearers'. To these top-ranking warriors the sovereign promised victorious conquests, lavish booty and great numbers of slaves. But in offering these favours to his feudal lords and in playing to and flattering their fighting spirit, the khan was also, as René Grousset has observed, addressing the entire collection of united tribes: 'This valiant people which has been given me to share my joys and my sorrows, this people which has pledged loyalty to me amidst all these perils, this people, the Blue Mongols,² shall I elevate above all other people on earth.'

In creating his new army of militiamen, was Genghis Khan already thinking along the lines of a Chinese saying, 'One may have to fight on but a single day a year, but an army must not cease training for a single day'? This was only the beginning: the khan had bent his bow; he had not yet released the arrow.

### The Proclamation of the *Jasaγ*

The empire had a leader. It had an ever-changing territory. It had an army. Now it needed a set of universal laws. The *quriltai* of 1206 saw the formulation of the *jasaγ* (or *yasaγ*) which set out the ancestral laws of the Mongol people. There had in fact for centuries been a considerable collection of practices, customs and legal traditions, which gave the nomadic society an institutional framework. These oral laws were fairly well attuned to the concerns of tribes and individuals; defining as they did the social hierarchy, ownership, religious rituals, and freedoms, they ratified clan prerogatives, protected the existence of the stock breeders, condemned sacrileges, and regulated human relationships.

Foreign observers have been struck by many of the prohibitions and various taboos peculiar to the Mongols, and have noted them down in the accounts of their travels. Thus the legate of Pope Innocent IV, the Franciscan Pian del Carpini, appeared much impressed by their strangeness:

Although [the Mongols] have no laws concerning the way in which justice should be done or the sins that are to be avoided, nevertheless they have certain traditions which they themselves or their ancestors have originated. One [taboo] is thrusting a knife into a fire or even in any way touching a flame with a knife, or extracting meat from a cauldron with a knife. Equally, plunging a hatchet into a fire. For they believe that the fire will in this way be robbed of its head. Likewise, using as a prop any part of a whip which is used to lash a horse. For [the Mongols] do not use spurs. Similarly, touching an arrow with a whip. Capturing or killing young birds. Likewise, striking a horse with a bridle. Breaking one bone with another. Also spilling milk or any other drink or food on the floor. Urinating within a place of abode. But anyone who voluntarily acts thus will be killed.[3]

The monk from Umbria was unable to explain these taboos, which dated from antiquity. It was in perfectly good faith that he judged and condemned — albeit wrongly — other aspects of the Mongol ethical code: 'On the other hand, killing men, invading the territory of others, unjustly appropriating to oneself another's goods, fornicating, injuring other men, or acting against the prohibitions and precepts of God are, none of them, sins among these people.'[4]

The idea of combining into a single unified code all the existing laws, rules and customs is in line with what we know of Genghis Khan's character: his sense of order, his jealous thirst for authority, were nearly always matched by an eagerness to justify his own enlightened, right-thinking position, and one often has the impression that the man had a distinct propensity for hairsplitting argument. For the khan, who now received his peers on a carpet of white felt, the *jasaγ* had to constitute a universal legal code. Mongol law would be applicable to all the other subject peoples.

The *jasaγ* (prohibitions), supplemented by the *bilig* (statutes), was officially dictated to Uighur scribes and recorded in the 'blue notebooks', unfortunately lost, which were reconstructed according to the written works of Juwaynī and of Rashīd al-Dīn. Intended to be understood by the illiterate masses, these laws rested on principles expressed in laconic but perfectly explicit terms:

> The duty of the Mongols is to come at my bidding, to obey my orders, to kill whomsoever I desire.
> He who does not obey will have his head severed from his body.

After this preliminary, which was, to say the least, Draconian, it is hardly surprising, in light of the era, to discover that the code itself was very strict indeed. The following were forbidden on pain of death: homicide, theft of livestock, receiving stolen goods or harbouring runaway slaves, the interruption by a third party of a duel and prolonged confiscation of another person's weapons. The same penalty applied to adultery, fornication, and sodomy. Certain transgressions, being considered less serious, incurred only the amputation of a limb (rape of a young girl) . . . Still others, thought to be minor, were punishable only by fines payable in kind. A good thrashing awaited those guilty of misdemeanours. Genghis Khan, who was well aware of his fellow Mongols' tendency towards drunkenness — his own son Ögödei being a case in point — recommended that no one get drunk more than three times a month!

The *jasay* also specified the role of a woman in the heart of this patriarchal society: she was expected to concern herself above all else with 'the good reputation of her husband'. Her rights and duties centred on domestic tasks as much as on loyalty to her spouse and master:

A man cannot be as the sun is, present everywhere. Thus a woman, when her husband is absent, be it at war or on a hunt, must keep her household in such good order that, if a messenger from a prince or any other traveller is obliged to stop by her tent, he sees it clean and tidy and is able to obtain a good meal there: this confers honour on the husband; one knows the worth of a man by that of his wife.

What can we say about the application of these virtuous principles? Pian del Carpini, who had little sympathy with the customs of the nomads, observed:

Their women are pure and one does not hear of any lack of chastity among them. However, certain of the men use jesting language that is licentious and even obscene. Uprisings among them are rare, if indeed they are ever seen at all. And although they get drunk very often, they never engage in argument, in word or deed, while inebriated.[5]

As for the laws that pertained during times of war, they were as explicit as they were expeditious:

The sentry who is inattentive will be killed.
The arrow-messenger who gets drunk will be killed.
Anyone who harbours a fugitive will be killed.
The warrior who unlawfully appropriates booty for himself will be killed.
The leader who is incompetent will be killed.

*Dura lex*, one may well say . . . But in all ages and in all countries martial law has counted human life cheap.

It fell to Shigi-Qutuqu, Genghis Khan's adoptive brother, to put this code into practice, for it was he who was appointed supreme judge. This code was progressively added to and improved over the years, but it was not officially proclaimed until the occasion of the *quriltai* of 1219, just after the conquest of northern China and just before the conquest of the western part of Asia.

The great khan sought to mark the affirmation of his power by an event that would establish a new era. The *jasaγ*, being a tangible manifestation of his prestige, served to confirm his legitimacy. Having brought more than twenty peoples to their knees in the name of his righteousness, the lawgiver now wished to justify his actions. We see evidence of this in an edict of 1219, engraved on a Taoist stele erected at the instigation of a Chinese monk, which justifies the acts passed by the khan and finishes with the following statement: 'I have thus received the support of Heaven and obtained supreme dignity.'

The *jasaγ*, in fact, did nothing except restate and ratify secular customs. Genghis Khan was hardly an innovator or a liberal. But in his desire to end the anarchy which he had put down, he succeeded in sanctioning the family and clan hierarchies, in regulating the system of property and inheritance, and in making official the usages and customs that originated in the steppes. This code no doubt expressed the spirit of the Mongol nomadic society at the beginning of the thirteenth century: henceforward no Mongol could ignore or defy the law. The *jasaγ* did not run counter to nomadic practices; it overturned neither hierarchical foundations, the prerogatives of the *noyans*, the dominance of certain prestigious clans, nor familial relationships among individuals linked by blood or descent. In the rigidity of its framework, however, it welded together peoples who shared a common way of life, spoke related languages and harked back to similar traditions.

## Expeditions into the Taiga

The steppe peoples were almost all now under the sway of Genghis Khan, but certain Turco-Mongol nomadic or semi-nomadic groups from the north of what is now Mongolia still retained their independence. These were forest dwellers who bought or bartered skins, game and certain manufactured articles from the pastoral people. One of the most important of these tribes of hunter-gatherers was the Oirat; they were related to the Buryat who today constitute a recognized Siberian minority group. The Oirat lived to the west of the vast Lake Baikal, in the enormous forests of conifers that fringe the Arctic regions, the habitat of fur-bearing animals (bear and ermine) and certain cold-climate cervids (the maral or Siberian stag and musk deer). The Oirat hunted them and also lived on edible berries which they found among the mosses and the lichens. 'They did not live, as did other Mongols, under felt tents,' wrote one Persian chronicler. 'They had hardly any livestock, but lived by hunting in their immense forests, and they professed great scorn for pastoral people. Their only shelters were huts made of branches and covered with birch bark. In winter, they hunted on the snow by attaching snowshoes to their feet and holding a pole in their hands which they dug into the snow, as a boatman dips a pole into the water.'

The Oirat represented no real threat to the steppe herders, but they could be of use to Genghis Khan in his conquests, by providing him with men, game, wood, or furs. The khan ordered that his brother Jochi Qasar force the Oirat into submission. Returning from his mission, Jochi brought with him several tribal chiefs bearing some very welcome gifts: skins of black sable; otter, beaver and ermine furs; and hunting birds. One of the Oirat chiefs, Qutuqa Beki, offered to put himself immediately at the khan's disposal, undertaking to lead his own men in the khan's service. Satisfied at having thus quickly secured an allegiance, Genghis Khan showed his gratitude: he offered to the two sons of his new and opportune ally two royal-born princesses, one of whom was his own granddaughter, daughter of his son Tolui. This matrimonial alliance put the seal on the collaboration of the forest Mongols of the 'country of Sibir'.

Jochi Qasar then turned his horses' heads westwards, towards the territory of the Turkish tribes, the Kirghiz, who lived as nomads around the course of the upper Yenisey. This region of high altitude and wild forests sheltered fur-bearing animals and herds of semi-domesticated reindeer from which various groups of people obtained milk, meat, skins and antlers.

The Kirghiz were ready to fall under the yoke of the khan, but other forest dwellers, such as the Tumed of the Irkul mountains, refused to accept his sovereignty. Temüjin took offence at this and charged Boroγul with bringing them under control by means of an operation which resembled the war against the Naiman. In the heart of this deep forest, enormous tree trunks encircled by brambles and tangled undergrowth formed a jungle which only the hunter-gatherers could penetrate without becoming lost. Boroɣul's men struggled to make progress: time and again they had to dismount and call a halt so that they might get their bearings. A suffocating dampness filled the air and myriads of insects pestered man and beast alike. Everywhere slippery, worm-eaten tree stumps concealed treacherous quagmires. The horses pressed on with the greatest of difficulty through this dank and dark vegetation, so thick that light scarcely made its way through it. Boroɣul and his men were soon surprised by an ambush. Archers hiding in thickets and under cliffs assailed them on all sides. Boroɣul almost immediately received several hits and these proved fatal. Two of his officers, the *noyan* Qorchi and the Oirat chief Qutuqa Beki, who had recently joined forces with Genghis Khan, were captured by the Tumed.

When he heard of this disaster, Genghis Khan was all for setting out immediately to avenge the defeat. Alert perhaps to the dangers of such a mission, Muqali and Bo'urchu dissuaded him, suggesting that he send Dörbei Doɣshin (Dörbei the Terrible) instead. The captain went about his reprisal mission with great skill and cunning: using the paths of wild animals out of the way of the enemy scouts, he was able to spring upon the Tumed while they were at rest, overcome them easily, and liberate the prisoners. The khan then offered Qutuqa Beki, his unfortunate ally, a prize concubine: the queen of the Tumed, Botoqui Tarɣun (the 'Great Lady').

Having now rid themselves of the last rebel groups, the Mongols could congratulate themselves: the entire northern Siberian flank had been pacified: the steppe had conquered the forest. From now on, Mongol expansionism was to focus on more distant horizons.

## Occult Powers

Genghis Khan now appeared to enjoy undivided rule over men who obeyed him with respect on their lips and fear in their bellies. Nevertheless, there were still some who, sensing that they had the protection of Heaven, dared to defy authority. These men who behaved in such a free and easy manner, combining impudence with imprudence, were the shamans who surrounded the khan.

Regarding the religion of the Mongols of Genghis Khan's era, opinion remains divided on various points. For the essence of it we shall rely here on the work of the Turcologist Jean-Paul Roux, who has ferreted out the secrets of the myths and rites, gods and demons, and astrology and cosmogony of the Turco-Mongols before the introduction of Lamaist Buddhism and of Islam.

The first descriptions of the religious universe of the Altaic peoples (Turco-Mongols and Tungus) tell both of a cosmobiological work of nature and of supernature, as well as of the shamanist practices which were grafted onto this. The Turco-Mongols believed that vital energies support the universe, a conception in which they made a distinction between an upper world and a lower world (and later on an intermediate zone of tenure). The first is ruled by Tenggeri, the Eternal and Divine Sky. The distributor of energy, he is to be seen in cataclysmic phenomena, in messages carried by animals that manifest themselves in supernatural forms, and in 'signs of destiny'. Tenggeri can spurn the pleadings of one who intercedes with him; he can bring death. He even has the power to channel his energy and convert it into secondary forces. He is both the guardian of the universal order and the primary cause of a 'Great All'. The lower world comprises four elements: first, complementing the 'Blue Sky', there is the brown earth, the nourishing mother and source of fertility. Then there is water, linked to the sky by rain as intermediary: it is an element of purity but not of purification. Perhaps because they often occur near mountain summits, and therefore close to the sky, river sources were often held to be sacred. Lastly, there is the purifying fire, and wood, which feeds fire.

There were many other divine manifestations. The Mongols accorded great importance, as we have seen, to the cult of mountains, worshipped as the supports of heaven, symbols of ascent and natural features pointing towards Tenggeri. Similarly, a tree possessed divine power because it plunged its roots into the nourishing earth while also raising its branches towards the sky. And there were innumerable other things which believers had sometimes to cleave to, through rites of incantation, or to turn away from, through other rites of deprecation: rocks, ancestral or totemic animals, statuettes, and other props for the soul, connected with invisible beneficent or maleficent forces.

These complex beliefs, which were current among all Altaic peoples, must no doubt have evolved in various ways according to the era and the populations in which they were rooted. The Altaic 'religion', with its cult of natural forces, deified animals and mountain worship, was a form of cosmic mysticism that is in many ways reminiscent of Japanese Shintō rites. This archaic religion, lacking scriptures and dogma alike, hard to make out in this shifting and nebulous environment of forest and steppe, seems to have had features in common with all religions: the cult of nature, idolatry, zoolatry, polytheism, a cult of ancestors, the oneness of a celestial god, divination by means of objects, all were superimposed on top of one another. As Mircea Eliade has written about the religious life of primitive peoples, 'it cannot be reduced to animalism, or totemism, or to a cult of ancestors, but . . . includes and recognizes supreme beings.'

Within this cosmogonic vision, man fits harmoniously into one of those everyday microcosms which make up the cells of the Great All. The niche he finds and the role he plays are the function of a certain number of practices intended to create a balance between the individual and the cosmos. To achieve this, it is necessary to have intermediaries, intercessors: the shamans. Shamanism is such a fundamental element of the Altaic religion that the term has for a long time been used to define the entire religion, and equally to designate, sometimes pejoratively, religious phenomena that are encountered in other parts of the world. Shamanism is still practised by various Siberian ethnic minorities, and in Korea its adherents, known as *mudang*, probably number around 100,000 men and women. 'Shaman' is a word of Tungusic origin denoting an individual 'transported', 'thrown into confusion', someone who goes through periods of ecstasy and possession. He may be a member of a tribal community, a hunter, shepherd, or blacksmith; he may come from a family of shamans: his skills are noticed and recognized and in due course he is designated a shaman by the elders. Once he has been chosen by the clan, he delivers himself into their service.

When a shaman dies, the tribe has to find a replacement for him. This search relies as much on collective knowledge and recognition as on any individual's personal gifts. It is a matter of finding among the old shaman's peers one or more people who are 'inhabited'. The signs which allow the clan to discover the name of the person who will be called to fulfil that role are many and complex: strange or premonitory dreams, nightmares, a tendency towards an isolated lifestyle or unintelligible speech. The 'symptoms' of shamanism observed in central Asia, Siberia and Korea include a wide variety of manifestations: prostration, fear of light, falling rocks, gesticulations or 'Arctic hysteria' (*piblokto*). Somnambulism, autism, hysteria and certain signs of mental derangement are closely associated with the phenomenon. It is thus by way of certain ill-defined psychosomatic disturbances that the clan may recognize a 'shamanist vocation'.

Then the apprenticeship begins. Gradually the shaman is brought into communication with the supernatural, with a view to defending the clan's interests: he has to learn to 'negotiate' with the powers of the invisible in order to work for the banishment of epidemics, of animal diseases or of a run of bad luck. To do so, he has to become transported into the realm of the celestial or subterranean spirits in an initiatory voyage that sometimes involves a declamatory speech or theatrical monologue portraying a stay in the world beyond. To effect this voyage, the shaman puts on magical accoutrements, often a coat decorated with metal plates, ritual embroideries and the tails or claws of animals that are charged with cosmogonic or sexual significance, or that are symbolic of the art of hunting. Then he goes into a trance, to the accompaniment of the ceaseless and deafening sound of drums hammered with curved mallets, the frenzied ringing of bells of all kinds and the humming of jew's harps. Foaming at the mouth, his eyes turned up to leave only the whites exposed, and uttering throaty, high-pitched whistles, low moans or animal cries, the shaman, like a bear in a cage, is seized by wild body movements that are almost cataleptic; at last he 'changes worlds'; he 'rises to heaven' where he encounters phantoms, spirits, divine animals and other inhabitants of the invisible world, all of which communicate extraordinary faculties to him. Shamans do have a charisma that can be quite disturbing, conferred on them by their therapeutic and priestly powers and their gifts of divination and appeasement. In a world where superstitions, prohibitions and purifications played such an important role, it was unthinkable that ordinary men, be they tribal chiefs or khans, would not live in fear of shamans.

**The Shamans against the Khan**
These men who were in some form of communication with the world beyond, with the dead, and with occult forces and who, it was claimed, could even make hail, wind and lightning were feared, flattered and respected. In the khan's headquarters they were regarded as indispensable, and all the taking of auspices fell to them to perform: the reading of human entrails, divination using bones or arrows, and scapulimancy (foretelling the future by examining the shoulder blades of sheep). By the very fact of their nomadic life, Mongol shamans could not anchor their powers to any fixed or recognized cult places; nevertheless, their power was great: purifications, offerings and funerals all passed through their and only their hands.

In Genghis Khan's circle there lived just such a shaman of prestige and importance: Teb Tenggeri, the 'Very Celestial' Kököchü. He was the son of Münglig, whom Yesügei in his last agony had begged to look after the orphans he was leaving behind. Although Münglig had rather neglected to fulfil his friend's dying wish, he had still apparently retained considerable affection for Temüjin. Kököchü, the fourth of Münglig's seven sons, had become one of the most influential of shamans. It was he who had organized the ceremonies of the great *quriltai*. He was very ambitious and displayed an impudent arrogance towards the highest court dignitaries. One day he went so far as to give the khan's brother, Jochi Qasar, a thrashing. Whether some political rivalry was the cause or whether this was some mere drunken brawl is not known. But from this time on Kököchü was at odds with the house of Genghis Khan.

Jochi Qasar, the Tiger, famous for his strength and bravery, presented himself at his brother's tent to beg that amends be made. Much to everyone's surprise, Genghis Khan merely reproached him for his baseness and cowardice. Jochi Qasar, reduced to tears, departed and remained out of his older brother's sight for three days. Was the khan reluctant to take direct action in response to the slight which had been dealt to one of his closest relatives, and thus to him? Or did he genuinely find his brother's conduct pusillanimous and deserving of condemnation? We do not know, but the matter was to have some most unfortunate consequences.

Indeed, the shaman went to see the khan and mutter confidences to him: Jochi Qasar, he said, was plotting against Genghis Khan and setting himself up in direct rivalry against him. That same night guards came to arrest Jochi Qasar. But the khan's brother had followers and friends, who lost no time in putting his case to Hö'elün and alerting her that this arbitrary step had been taken. Hö'elün's anger was terrible to behold. Her first concern was to safeguard family unity and harmony, which this action had put under threat. Like a cat defending her kittens, she sharpened her claws: forcing her way into the khan's tent, she demanded the immediate release of Jochi Qasar and furiously admonished Genghis Khan. Then she went to see the prisoner and had his belt and his cap, which had been torn from him as a sign of his loss of status, restored to him.

The matter did not end there. Kököchü renewed his assertions about conspiracy and in the end the khan dismissed his brother from favour by depriving him of part of his tribal apanage. From that day onward, Hö'elün became visibly weaker and she spent the last days of her life consumed with sorrow at seeing her family rocked by rivalries. Did Genghis Khan really believe that Jochi Qasar wanted to oust him? And was he trying, by removing several thousand men from his brother's command, to clip the wings of the sparrow-hawk that threatened one day to eclipse the eagle? Or was he only pretending to believe in his brother's treachery, as subsequent events seem to show?

For Kököchü, a true Iago of the steppes, was playing a dangerous game. He had flattered his master, warned him of webs of intrigue that were being spun, and doubtless fomented a few of his own. In so doing, the great shaman seems to have risen rapidly in the Mongol sovereign's regard. The khan always exercised great care to protect the interests of his house, yet the case of Kököchü seemed to show a weakness on his part, some chink in his armour. Perhaps he was simply afraid of this man with his unpredictable designs. Or perhaps he feared the occult and maleficent threats of a world peopled by gods and devils that lurked behind the shaman's presence and that he alone knew how to summon and tame. We do not know what was in the khan's mind.

Here was an affair in which the unity of the clan and the khan's personal prestige and authority were at stake, and here again it was a woman who stepped in to break the deadlock. This time the woman was Börte, Genghis Khan's wife. Bitterly she reproached her husband for his cowardice in abandoning his brother Jochi Qasar and equally for standing by while another of his brothers, his youngest, Temüge, was also suffering at the hands of the great shaman. The latter had, in fact, managed to appropriate some of Temüge's servants for his own use. When Temüge, bent on retrieving what was rightfully his own, had gone to demand their return, Kököchü's six brothers had pushed him to the ground and made him beg the shaman's pardon for his insolence! So it was Börte who took it upon herself to open the khan's eyes to the shaman's shameful manoeuvres and to insist that this destructive influence on the reigning family be brought to a halt: 'How is it that Kököchü and his brothers have been allowed to perpetrate such insolent deeds?' she demanded accusingly. 'Recently they beat Jochi Qasar. Today they have forced Temüge to his knees before them! What have we come to? . . . How can you sit and calmly watch the treatment that is inflicted on your brothers?'

These arguments at last convinced the khan that he must regain the reins of power which Kököchü was trying to wrest from him. He told Temüge that he had *carte blanche* to take whatever steps he thought fit with regard to the great shaman. Doubtless he preferred to leave the matter to Temüge rather than deal with it directly himself. At the sovereign's command, Teb Tenggeri presented himself before Genghis Khan.

Temüge then proposed that the shaman take his quarrels elsewhere and leave the imperial tent in peace. He did not have time to answer. Some of Temüge's men leapt on the great priest, broke his spine, and threw his body 'near the place where the carts stood', that is to say, on a field strewn with debris.

When it became known that the great shaman had been assassinated, his family rose up in arms, with Münglig at their head. Grooms were abused, blows were exchanged, and daggers drawn. Genghis himself was jostled. He tried to struggle free and called for assistance from his 'quiver-bearers' who were posted outside his tent. The great khan locked in conflict with the brothers of the great shaman he had just had slain: here was a scene worthy of Shakespeare, lacking for nothing in the aggressiveness or vulgarity of its high-ranking characters!

The body of Kököchü, the 'Very Celestial', lay for three days inside the tent, guarded by the khan's police. During this time, the chronicle says, 'the body rose up out of itself by its orifice of ventilation', a phrase which suggests that Kököchü perhaps did not die immediately but lay in the throes of death for several days before his soul departed for the Eternal Heaven, which presumably then granted it admittance.

Thus abruptly was settled a rivalry of interests that lay concealed beneath a more obvious clash between the temporal power of the khan and the spiritual power of the shaman and his entourage. It was right that the 'Very Celestial' Kököchü should be accorded this funeral oration by Genghis Khan: 'Kököchü beat and slandered our brothers; therefore Tenggeri, removing his divine protection from him, has taken away his life as he has taken away his body.' These words were chosen with consummate cunning, for they gave the listeners to understand that the great shaman had died because he had lost his heavenly mandate.

This ugly business was brought to an end that was as sudden and brutal as it was treacherous, and with it expired also any desire on anyone's part to usurp the khan's power. The supreme khanate now had to follow a course that involved some tasks of rather petty policy. The khan reproved Münglig for having failed to bring up his seven sons properly and for not having restrained their impudence in challenging the royal authority. Nevertheless he pardoned all those involved. First stern repression and reprisal, then mercy! Genghis Khan designated a replacement for the late shaman, proving that temporal power could sometimes intercede between Heaven and its augurs. He chose Üsün, and gave him a white courser and accorded him the place of honour befitting a great religious dignitary. This time Genghis Khan took the right decision: Üsün Beki was a genuine old sage!

# 9
# Shadows over China

*In days gone by was built the Great Wall*
*To fix and bound the homeland of the barbarians;*
*Then towers were built and topped with torches.*
*The torch signals burned always, day and night,*
*The long campaigns went on, knowing no end.*
*There was fighting on the plains, men were killed, men died.*
*The horses of the dead neighed and cried pity to heaven.*
*The crows picked at the entrails of the dead,*
*Then flew away and perched on the branches of tinder-dry trees.*
*The soldier fled across the mud and the grass,*
*The general stood helpless, his efforts all in vain.*

**Li Bai (701–762)**

At the beginning of the thirteenth century, Genghis Khan decided to launch a new offensive, this time against China. The conquest of this huge country was an ambition that was perfectly in line with his apparently unquenchable thirst for power. More prosaically, it was also within range of his cavalry. Before embarking on this project, which, if it succeeded, would propel him onward into a formidable process of expansion, Genghis Khan took stock of his forces. He was by now uncontested master of several tribal federations that were all united under his banner. The peoples of steppe and taiga alike bowed to his will: the vast majority, that is, of the true Mongols, together with some Turks and even some peoples of Tungus stock.

How did things stand, prior to the Chinese campaign, in the *ulus* (population, assemblage of peoples) under the great khan's control, this shifting nation that was entirely subordinated to his authority and that of his appointees? Historians of Mongol military campaigns (Martin, Liddell Hart, Haenisch) estimate that, at the outset of the invasion of China, Genghis Khan's army numbered 110,000 men and that this number grew during the course of subsequent conquests to between 130,000 and 200,000 men. We might make the (somewhat far-fetched) comparison between

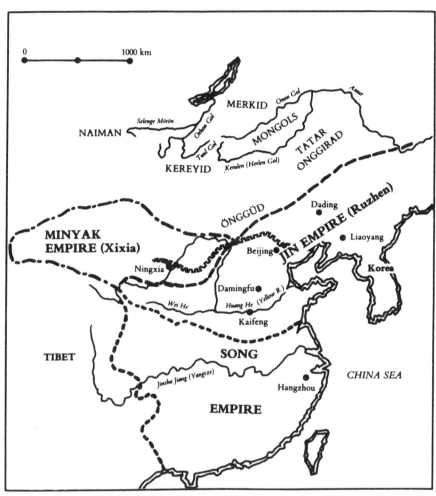

Map 4.    China at the Beginning of the Thirteenth Century

these numbers and the present Mongolian People's Republic, which, with a population of about 1.8 million towards the end of the 1980s, maintains an army in peacetime of 45,000 soldiers, to which may be added 15,000 special militiamen, border guards and territorials. Were a conflict to break out, this army could mobilize 120,000 soldiers, or one for every fifteen inhabitants, quite an impressive ratio, even for a modern nation. Certainly the ancient Mongol context is quite different from that of contemporary Mongolia; even so, going on these figures, one may estimate that Genghis Khan was in command of perhaps a million nomadic Mongols. To our eyes, the effective forces of the Mongol army seem inadequate for an undertaking of that size, the conquest of such vast territories as northern China, the Turkish and Arab–Persian kingdoms of high Asia and southern Russia. And yet it must be remembered that this strength was very considerable for the time, especially by European standards. Philip Augustus, in 1214, at the Battle of Bouvines, had a mere 1,300 horsemen at his disposal. Besides, the Mongol army was not meant to serve as a force of occupation; instead it comprised essentially shock troops. On the other hand, it should be pointed out that in China, as well as in the Middle East, Genghis Khan's army nearly always numbered fewer men than the enemy could muster.

## The Chinese Tripod
China, as we have seen, was at that time divided into three distinct states: in the northwest was the Minyak empire (peopled by the Xixia or Tangut); in the north was the Jin empire of the Ruzhen; lastly, there was the Song empire in the south.

The Minyak empire of the Xixia, which comprised twenty-two partly agricultural, partly pastoral provinces, extended, beyond the Great Wall, into the Ordos (in Chinese, Hetao) region, a vast plateau situated within the great loop of the Huang He, in the area of present-day Ningxia and Gansu provinces. Little is known about the origins of the Minyak empire, except that it emerged at the end of the tenth century as a sort of Chinese dominion. The Xixia or Tangut (related to the Tibetans and the Qiang) had served the Chinese emperors of the Tang dynasty, who had accorded them a territory under their protection. Allies of the Chinese under the Five Dynasties (907–960) and then under the Song (960–1279), they claimed their independence when the Chinese bowed under the pressure from invaders from the north, the Khitan. In 1038, the Minyak state became independent, and ten emperors in succession ruled from the capital at Irgai (later Ningxia). At the time of Genghis Khan, the Minyak state was under threat, despite its army of some 150,000 men, because it was surrounded by more important powers.

The second state was ruled by the Ruzhen (or Jurchen), an Altaic people of Tungus stock who came from Manchuria. It extended from the Amur river to the southern part of the Huang He basin, a wide swath of land over 2,000 kilometres long, occupying all of Manchuria, present-day Inner Mongolia and the northern Chinese provinces of Shandong, Hebei, Shanxi and northern Shaanxi. With the exception of the purely Chinese regions, this enormous empire was conterminous with that of the Khitan (or Khitai) who, from 904 to 1125, had installed the Liao dynasty there. The Khitan came from a proto-Mongol federation and were originally nomads who had adopted a settled way of life. They had been driven out by their Ruzhen vassals, who were allied with the Song dynasty of southern China. Under the leadership of one of their princes, they had had to go as far afield as Ili, in central Asia (east of Lake Balkhash), where they founded a new empire, that of the western Liao, or Qara-Khitai; some of them, however, remained behind in subservience to the new conquerors.

The Ruzhen, who were related to the Manchu, founded the Jin dynasty. Though they retained the specific characteristics of their ancient tribal system, they became Sinicized and adopted the administrative and judicial institutions of the Tang and the Song rulers. The Ruzhen aristocracy ruled over a diverse collection of peoples (a Chinese majority, Khitan and Bohai; peoples with a way of life ranging from nomadic to more or less sedentary). Throwing off their position as subordinates to the Chinese, they seized the reins of power, though they did not practise a policy of racial discrimination as did subsequent governing powers. The Ruzhen administration was, it seems, cosmopolitan and therefore multilingual. Harking back to their old seasonal migrations, the Ruzhen retained the different capitals that had already been in existence under their Khitan predecessors. The economy of this northern empire was based largely on cereal production and on barter with the steppe nomads, the Xixia and the Song, who were none the less obliged to pay tribute to their overlord neighbours in order to guarantee their goodwill. The Ruzhen had also set up in the frontier zones a number of agro-military colonies, often run on a day-to-day basis by prisoners of war who had been reduced to virtual slavery. At the same time, the confiscation of the most fertile Chinese land in the cause of maximizing the profits of the feudal Ruzhen empire quickly brought about a serious crisis. Chinese owners and farmers hired their services as agricultural workers to the occupying power, which inevitably provoked deep antagonism between the Ruzhen overlords and the exploited Chinese workers.

The empire of the Ruzhen, which maintained diplomatic and commercial relations with the Song Chinese, the Minyak empire, and Korea, now freed of its ties of allegiance with China, must have numbered nearly 50 million inhabitants. But the colossus had feet of clay, for it was constantly being undermined by one Chinese revolt after another, or by uprisings among the Khitan against the occupying rule, and also by a self-interested and unscrupulous aristocracy. Its five capitals — Zhongdu (Beijing), Bianjing (Kaifeng), Datong, Liaoyang, and Dading — were in themselves proof of the disruptive nature of the centrifugal forces within the empire that threatened its very existence.

The third leg of the Chinese tripod covered the whole of southern China, except for the mountainous borders of Sichuan, Guizhou and Yunnan, where ethnic minorities and the Thai contained Chinese expansion. Cut off from its northern part and governed by a prince who had fled the Ruzhen invaders, Song China stretched south from the river basins of the Huai He and the lower Huang He. Irrigated rice cultivation prevailed in this part of China, unlike in the north, where it was colder and where wheat and millet were grown. The Song empire attained a level of political and cultural organization that was in advance of nearly every other country in the world. It had entered upon an entirely new phase of development, far removed from the pluralist and secular feudalism which had been its previous condition.

This evolution of Chinese society in the Song era brought about a radical transformation. While the ruling Confucian bureaucracy continued to keep the merchant classes at arm's length, these latter, with their activities, their entrepreneurial spirit and, before long, their wealth, were gradually drawing closer to the levers of economic control and thus to political power. This new class of trader-middlemen, however, took time to emerge: it had not yet reached the point where, as in Italy or northern Europe, it could control institutions such as 'free cities' or 'communes', for the Chinese government was highly *dirigiste* in nature. China undoubtedly experienced rapid development, as a result of technical innovations and some great scientific discoveries that were well ahead of their time: the compass, printing and gunpowder (navigation, cartography, artillery, etc.).

Favoured by a relatively peaceful political situation, the economic impetus was accompanied by a strong upsurge in population growth: according to the demograper Zhang Jiaju, in 1125, China under the Song numbered about 60 million inhabitants. Soon after Bianjing (Kaifeng) had been abandoned to the Ruzhen invaders, just at the time when somewhere in some encampment of tents Genghis Khan was being born, the new Chinese capital, Hangzhou (Hangchow), already had over 500,000 souls living in it! 'It is without doubt the largest city in the world,' wrote Odoric of Pordenone at the turn of the thirteenth century. 'It is said one would travel a hundred miles to go round it and within this great circumference there is not a single open or uninhabited space . . . It has twelve main gates and outside each, eight miles away, is a large city, larger than the city of Venice.' A hundred years later, when Marco Polo visited it, the city had reached a million inhabitants, a fantastic number for that time, and the Venetian was duly surprised by the amount of urban traffic:

> In the main streets of the city you meet an infinite succession of these carriages passing to and fro. They are long, covered vehicles, fitted with curtains and cushions, and affording room for six persons; and they are in constant request for ladies and gentlemen going on parties of pleasure. In these they drive to certain gardens, where they are entertained by the owners in pavilions erected on purpose, and there they divert themselves the livelong day, with their ladies, returning home in the evening in those same carriages.

Hangzhou, on the banks of the Jinsha Jiang (Yangtze), was characteristic of the new urban civilization that was beginning to take shape. There were in this gigantic metropolis ten large markets that had a great deal of custom, wooden buildings overhanging modest artisans' shops, popular theatres, cabarets and 'houses of ill repute' that did a roaring trade not only among traders and officials but also among boatmen and porters, not to mention thieves, beggars, and dropouts of every hue. On the fringes of the marketplaces, where bridges crossed the canals, and around the places of culture lived and worked the Chinese community, seething with life: sellers of ravioli and of confectionery drawing their custom from among the poorer classes, storytellers, acrobats, mimics imitating bird calls for the amusement of passers-by, singers with and without talent, and pimps soliciting idlers on behalf of streetwalkers and brothel girls. People mingled indiscriminately, spied, and intrigued, closely watched by a police force that was always on the scene. In this great cacophony of Chinese urban life, everything was for sale and for everything there was a buyer. The port was always busy with sampans loaded with food and provisions that plied their trade all along the coast, and there were ocean-going junks filled with spices, silk or tea, capable of carrying 600 passengers, that set sail for distant ports — in Japan, the Philippines, Malaya, India, the Middle East, and even Madagascar or Africa.

Imperial China, which underwent such a marked upswing in economic and commercial development and which permitted the emergence of an urban 'bourgeoisie', also enjoyed a rich and thriving cultural life. Scholars engaged in great debates; educated civil servants conducted lively discussions within their own cliques and circles, touching on the finer points of politics as well as of history, archaeology, literature and painting.

But this glowing picture of China under the Song also had its dark side: officialdom was undermined by corruption and nepotism; bribery and embezzlement were the rule at all levels of the administration of the mandarins, a state of affairs which treasury problems only abetted and compounded; speculators and wheeler-dealers found easy pickings in the treasury while taking cover behind the imperial bureaucrats. The administration was vastly overmanned and badly paid and tended to throw prudence to the winds as far as expenditure of public funds was concerned; the court too had got into the habit of splashing money around with lavish carelessness. This situation was so acute for so long that when nomads started to make incursions along the northern frontier the entire government tended to skid badly out of control. Like the Jin dynasty, the Song, despite their large population, their ubiquitous armies and above all their excellence in so many fields, were largely unaware of the storm that was to sweep over them.

### The War against the Minyak Empire
The Persian historian Rashīd al-Dīn would have it that it was around 1205 that Genghis Khan attacked the Minyak (or Tangut) empire, known to the Chinese as Xixia. The chronology of these first stages in the conflict is, however, not known for certain, and it is probable that the campaign did not get properly under way until shortly after the great *quriltai* of 1206.

The war that was about to break out largely overran the territories of northeast China. Though it had been ravaged by Mongol expeditions from the thirteenth century onwards, the Minyak empire to a great extent remained an unknown quantity. Chinese annalists say that the Xixia, a people of Tibeto-Burmese stock related to the Qiang, had adopted the institutions of the Tang Chinese. This dynasty, who ruled from 618 to 907 over a powerful and unified China, had almost managed to assert their influence beyond their own borders: apart from Tibet, the Tang exercised protectorates in central Asia (Anxi, Mengchi, Kunling) and kept in their hold the states of Sogdiana and Tukharistan, north of Afghanistan, until the Arabs inflicted a decisive defeat on China at the battle of Talas (751). Reduced to satellite status by its powerful Chinese neighbour, the Minyak state continued to exist as a Sinicized dominion until it obtained its independence in the eleventh century. The astonishing religious sculptures carved in the grottos at Dunhuang between the fifth and the tenth century attest to the vigour of Buddhism in the region over a long period.

Having been China's faithful allies for some time, the Xixia sovereigns were eventually granted by the Chinese the privilege of imperial titles and the use of dynastic Chinese names (Li, Zhao). The founder of the Minyak empire, the emperor Li Yuanhao (died *c.* 1048), ordered his associates Yu Qi and Yelü Renrong to invent a Xixia script inspired by those of the Chinese and the Khitan. The result was a graphic system of some 6,000 characters — some having a phonetic, others a semantic, value — based on and similar to Chinese pictograms, and permitting the printing of Buddhist scriptures. The Xixia emperors, installed in their capitals at Lingzhou and Ningxia, at first maintained turbulent relations with the Chinese power, but in due course signed a treaty of good neighbourliness with the Chinese leaders and this gave their economy a tremendous stimulus. Straddling the caravan routes of high Asia, the Minyak empire prospered, thanks to its trade in products that were much in demand (silver and silk, but especially tea, salt and armour). In addition to its status as a trading nation, the Minyak empire enjoyed the benefits of an advanced agriculture that was practised in alluvial zones and in lands around oases; in the arid regions, economic activity was confined to nomadic or semi-nomadic pastoralism which was a necessary concomitant to participating in the caravan trade.

It was this settled state, Sinicized but still retaining many of its original qualities, that Genghis Khan planned to invade — for what reasons nobody knows. We do know that some Naiman or Kereyid princes had been granted political asylum by the Xixia of the Minyak empire, and it is possible that from this safe haven some of them may have tried to spread anti-Mongol propaganda or to hatch plots to damage or overthrow the Mongol federations. Equally, it is feasible that the khan, in devising his first expansionist schemes, set out deliberately to break a weak and peripheral link in the Chinese chain.

In 1205 or 1206, the khan sent mounted troops out against the Minyak empire, under the command of a Khitan general, Yelü Aqa, and they launched themselves on the widely scattered Xixia armies. Squadrons first demolished the forts of Digili and then attacked the fortified city of Ginglos (which has not been identified) and pillaged the entire surrounding region: they burst into farm granaries, they took men and women captive, they fell upon the herds of animals, and from the caravan trains they seized thousands of camels and dromedaries that were being sent to Mongolia. These light-haired camels, later described by Marco Polo, had been rare in the region until that time, and were highly prized, partly for their usefulness as pack animals in drier regions.

Hard on the heels of these Mongol raids which ravaged the western part of the country, political trouble erupted within the innermost circle of the Xixia court. At the beginning of the year 1206, a *coup d'état* toppled the sovereign from power and installed in his place his cousin, who lost no time in seeking the recognition of the Jin empire of the Ruzhen, hoping thus to obtain diplomatic, even military, support. The Mongols' conquest of the Minyak empire nevertheless took several years of hard fighting and three military expeditions (1206, 1207 and 1209).

The Minyak forces numbered about 150,000 soldiers, divided into battle corps: strictly speaking, these were supposed to consist of Xixia troops, but they also included Tibetans, Uighur and Chinese. When Genghis's troops fought in open country, they could force their opponents — who were only on foot — into fairly easy retreat. But when they came up against the Minyak fortified cities, well-defended and well-supplied, the nomads simply had to mark time, since they did not then have siege equipment.

It is claimed that to take Wulahai, a town surrounded by apparently impregnable ramparts, the Mongols had recourse to an extraordinary stratagem: they entered into negotiations with the besieged generals, promising that they would immediately lift the siege if the generals undertook to hand over all the cats and all the birds in the city. Astonished by this demand, but glad to have got off so lightly, the Xixia defenders organized a gigantic hunt within their walls to round up all the cats and winged creatures: these, in their hundreds, were shut in wicker cages for delivery to the Mongols. The latter prepared bits of oakum and carefully attached some to the tails of the cats and the claws of the birds. Then they set fire to the oakum and let the little creatures go, a few at a time. Terrified, the animals instinctively raced for cover to their usual homes and perches; many died in agony in some corner of a granary or stable, while the fires caught and spread in countless different places around the city, rapidly throwing the town into confusion. Taking advantage of the destruction of the fire-ravaged defences, the assailants poured into the city, which by now had been reduced to a state of panic.

This peculiar tactic was used again in the Manchurian campaign and has been the subject of various accounts which confirm that animals were indeed used in the course of battles: in addition to using homing pigeons to convey messages, the Chinese are known to have made use sometimes of dogs, cattle or other animals, which they released into the enemy ranks, having first covered them with burning pitch and tied flaming pikes to their flanks with various devices.

In 1209, after several victorious but indecisive operations, the Mongols were still not in control of the two Xixia capitals, Ningxia and Lingzhou, whose high walls were an effective defence against the nomads' cavalry. The invaders then had the idea of diverting part of the Huang He by building a dike, so as to drain dry the foot of Ningxia's city ramparts. Thousands of prisoners were pressed into the hard labour of constructing the earthworks, but the Mongols lacked experienced engineers and the right equipment and were unable to drain the arm of the river that protected one side of the city. Indeed, as the autumn rains grew heavier and more frequent, they had to suffer the ignominy of watching their own camp become flooded.

Chinese annals tell us that the Minyak monarch was able in the end to secure the retreat of the invader by proposing an honourable peace to the khan. Under the terms of the treaty, he agreed to accept the khan's nominal suzerainty; offered him one of his daughters, famed for her beauty; and in addition yielded up a booty consisting of numerous camels and their load of fabrics (probably *kesi*, tapestries decorated in iridescent hues, of Coptic origin, introduced into central Asia by the Uighur Turks). The Xixia empire judged that it was in its own interests to accept reasonable peace terms in order to stop nomadic incursions from ruining its trading economy.

For Genghis Khan, it was a victory without any real glory. Nevertheless, the signing of a peace treaty saved him for a time from having to deal with the Minyak attempts at resistance and allowed him to draw appreciably closer to the rest of China. Moreover, in 1207, part of Tibet swore allegiance to the Mongol khan.

## Preparations for War

Mongol raids into Xixia territory had seriously disrupted the caravan trade that plied various roads along the Silk Route, which was defended poorly and only intermittently along its length. The experience of these raids had taught Genghis Khan that attacking a highly organized state that boasted a number of citadels was a distinctly more difficult enterprise than launching short, sharp swoops. Armed conflict with China was going to require spying out means of communication, sending out patrols and gleaning information from collaborators. There would be times when his troops would engage with the enemy in long and uncertain battles and get stuck without means of retreat. Strategies that worked well on the steppes would very likely seem feeble and ineffectual when used against China, with its vast size, population, and resources. But the khan had already committed himself to a policy of aggression and had no alternative but to continue along that road, for 'once the saddle is on, it is time to mount the horse'.

Genghis Khan took steps to ensure that he had the support of all the Mongol federations, each of which would supply its share of mounted fighting men, and he organized a programme of lightweight logistics, using mainly waggons to transport supplies and war materiel. The training of men in the art of mounted combat had to be stepped up, and military equipment had to be assembled and meticulously maintained; over and above that, the horses had to be prepared: for Genghis's troops they represented the equivalent of armoured vehicles in a modern army; they alone lent the fighting forces their legendary mobility and speed, for the nomads used virtually no infantrymen.

The army of Genghis Khan, as we have already observed, was already divided into decimal units. Well trained in manoeuvring and backed by the experience of the great hunts that were organized every year, the cavalry was now further divided into three sections: *jegün yar* (left flank), *bara yun* (right flank) and *qoel* (centre). Their orders would be transmitted either by the shouted commands of their officers or by the showing of small flags. War-trained from many intertribal strikes and pillaging

175

expeditions, this cavalry now constituted a formidable fighting force, no doubt without parallel at that time.

As for the warriors' equipment, Pian del Carpini described this in these terms:

> Moreover, they must have at least these implements of war: two or three bows or one very good one and at least three large quivers full of arrows. And one hatchet. And ropes for towing vehicles. The wealthier soliders also have sharp-pointed swords with one cutting edge, and slightly curved in shape. And they have horses with protective coverings, and wear greaves and indeed protective helmets and leather cuirasses. Some of the cuirasses, like the horses' harnesses, are of leather and they are made thus: some have thongs made from cowhide or the skin of another animal, measuring about the width of a hand, which are stuck together with pitch, three or four at a time, and tied with laces or cords. The straps at the upper end are attached to the lower edge, while the laces of the next thongs are tied to the middle, and so on. Whenever the wearer bends over, the lower pieces slide up next to those above and thus double or triple the protection afforded to the body by the leather.[1]

This comes close to a description of chain-mail or of Japanese armour, which was composed of hinged metal plates that covered the warrior with protective flexible scales; unlike heavy body armour, it allowed the wearer freedom and speed of movement. In addition the horsemen wore metal helmets lined with leather.

Medieval observers all noted that Genghis Khan's cavalry were often provided with a long lance with a hook on the end or with a lasso fixed to a rod, both of which were designed to unhorse their opponents. Some fighting men also carried battle-axes. Incidentally, the bow used by the nomads, admiringly described by Meng Hong and by Western explorers, was far superior to the famous English model used at the battle of Crécy (1346). It had double curvature, a pull of 80 kilos, and a range, as a number of travellers testified, of between 200 and 300 metres; it could fire a dozen arrows per minute. According to Pian del Carpini and Marco Polo, these arrows, which had eagle feathers at their base, could pierce armour. This bow remained superior for a long time to musket, even rifle, fire, which was inaccurate and slow: at the battle of Friedland (1807), Napoleon clashed with Kalmyk Mongol archers enlisted by the tsar! The horses were usually covered with a cuirass of leather pieces which protected their flanks and chests from the impact of lances or arrows; Chinese and Persian paintings generally depict the horses wearing this protective gear.

This, then, was the Mongol army, ready to be unleashed against the Chinese lines. Mobilization was carried out with all address and rigour. Under the supervision of the *noyans*, grooms and nomadic shepherds became true warriors as soon as a campaign was embarked on. Scouts, recruited from among border tribes, and prisoners accompanied by interpreters, would already have furnished information on access roads, fords and bridges; on the state of fortresses; and on the organization of enemy troops.

For weeks on end, when evening came and while the women, like shadows, were going about their daily tasks, men crouched in their tents would talk passionately about the conquest of China, the subject that was on everybody's lips in all the encampments. The oldest ones, who had taken part in all the skirmishes and battles waged against the Merkid or the Naiman, could form a picture of what awaited them beyond the Great Wall. Each of them could call to mind memories of bold dashes on moonless nights, of snow muffling the sound of men struggling and panting, of real or imaginary fights — tales of intoxicating excitement for teller and listener alike. Seasoned warriors would explain, using gestures to demonstrate, why it was necessary to aim low, for the throat of the enemy, if one wanted to strike him in the face with a stroke of the sword, for every horseman when threatened instinctively lowers his head. They would go on to describe the best way to slide a sword tip into flesh so as to turn a slash into a deep wound. But most of the men, unconcerned about the dangers they might face, were interested only in the spoils to be had in the course of this glorious, exciting escapade. The great *ulus* of Genghis Khan was ready, not only in body but also in spirit, to burst upon the countryside and the towns of their giant neighbour, China.

### The Campaign against the Jin Empire
It will be remembered that in his youth Genghis Khan had for a time been a vassal of the Jin kingdom: he was made use of with To'oril as leader of the Mongol mercenaries and on the Jin ruler's behalf carried out operations against Tatar tribes. To'oril had received the Chinese title of king (*wang*) and Genghis Khan the more modest designation of 'cohort

leader', which the Ruzhen sovereign, with feigned munificence, had bestowed on them. In 1208, the Jin monarch vacated the throne and Genghis Khan then considered himself freed of his allegiance thereto.

The new sovereign at Zhongdu (Beijing), the prince of Wei, was a grotesque character, lacking in authority, who readily allowed himself to be put under the thumb of his staff. When the Chinese embassy, headed by one Yunzi, came, as custom demanded, to announce the name of the new Jin monarch to Genghis Khan, there was a to-do — as the *Yuan Shi* relates: 'The reigning emperor sent an ambassador called Yunzi to receive the customary tribute from Genghis . . . But Genghis poured scorn on the envoy, calling him stupid, and accordingly omitted to perform the traditional ceremonies of welcome.'

It is claimed that the official history of the Yuan conceals the circumstances of a diplomatic scandal. In reality, when Yunzi informed the Mongol khan of the name of his sovereign, Genghis made it clear that he thought the prince of Wei an imbecile, refused to perform the traditional prostration on the ground (kowtow) and, adding insult to injury, spat in the direction of the south, which was where the court at Beijing was installed. Then he put his feet in the stirrups and rode off, leaving the members of the embassy of the new Jin ruler confused and humiliated. In outrage, Yunzi hastened home to his country; there he submitted his report to the sovereign and urged him to send a punitive expedition against those barbarians who had made the occupants of the throne lose face. But the Jin ruler was weak and commanded little respect; he knew very well that it was no use going to ask a tiger for its skin. He declared the matter closed, judging that the incident was, in any case, too insignificant to qualify as a *casus belli*.

The Jin sovereign embarked on his reign in a state of feeble indolence. Genghis Khan, on the other hand, had adopted the adage, 'In everything preparation guarantees success, just as lack of foresight brings failure.' In March 1211, he convened another *quriltai* in order to take a reading of the alliances and forces on which he could count for the invasion of China. From the farthest steppes and the most distant forests, tribal clan chiefs came to renew their oaths of allegiance. There were Mongols among them, and Turks too. In his tent on the banks of the river Kerulen, he received a string of princes and princelings who settled for several days in the imperial yurt. One of these tribal chiefs was the Ïduq Qut (ruler of the Uighur Turks, who had taken up residence in the Turfan area); another was Arslan, chief of the Qarluγ, who lived south of Lake Balkhash.

The allegiance of these princes was a matter of some importance because their territories controlled the roads of the Silk Route. It was thanks to these roads and the trade they carried that China was able to maintain diplomatic and commercial relations with the Arab–Persian and European West; along this route, which connected one caravanserai or oasis with the next, the caravans brought merchandise that was much prized in China: carpets, muslins, armour, and sabre blades hardened and wrought to perfection by the steelsmiths of the Middle East. At a single stroke, Genghis Khan would be able to seize control of the trade with western Asia and lay his hands upon miracles of workmanship hitherto unknown in Mongolia. If the Mongols had access to these regions, with the assistance of new allies and so-called Turco-Mongol traders, the khan would be able clearly to see — and to hear — what was going on in the world outside, among settled peoples.

The *quriltai* of 1211 gave Genghis Khan two essential assurances: the first was the unconditional support of his entire assemblage of vassals; the second, rear protection, by virtue of his alliance with the Qarluγ. It was the guarantee of not having to fight on two fronts simultaneously that was to precipitate the offensive against northern China.

Genghis Khan and his headquarters were well aware that the power of the Jin dynasty was rocked by factions. As early as 1204, the chief of a Nestorian Turkish tribe, the Önggüd, which was charged with guarding a section of the northern Chinese frontier, had begun talks with the Mongols, presumably with the aim of setting in train serious secret negotiations that would have advantages for both sides. In 1206, in the Liaodong Bandao peninsula northeast of Beijing, a war broke out between the Ruzhen rulers and the Jin dynasty. This affair made the great khan realize that it required just one rough shock to destabilize the Ruzhen state and thus the Chinese tripod.

To the great khan, China represented a huge domain for hunting and fighting and therefore a very rich prize. Armed with information from travellers, deserters, and the Önggüd chiefs who served as Jin border guards, Genghis Khan no doubt instantly understood, with the certainty of his predatory instinct, that a great opportunity now presented itself: despite its wealth, China was at that moment a country where peasants, who detested the Ruzhen occupants, were burrowing for safety into their homes; where poorly paid mercenary troops were scurrying from their ranks like rabbits; and where, finally, the weak and unstable rulers had but a single thought — to save their own skins.

Genghis Khan gave the court in Beijing to understand that it was a personal account he wanted to settle with them: he made out that he was intent on extracting payment in blood from the Jin rulers who, in some long-ago border conflict, had seized two of his 'uncles', Ambaγai and Ökin Baraqaγ, and, with the help of the Tatars, had put them to death by nailing them to a wooden ass.

Before embarking on the campaign, the khan obeyed custom and asked the Sky God for protection. Once more, he went to the slopes of Mount Burqan Qaldun to perform his ritual devotions: he unfastened his belt, which he then hung around the back of his neck, and took off his fur cap, gestures which demonstrated that he renounced his authority, and presented himself naked before Tenggeri, the Blue Sky. Then, prostrating himself on the ground three times, he declared: 'O Eternal Tenggeri, I have taken up arms to avenge the blood of my uncles Ökin Baraqaγ and Ambaγai, whom the Golden kings [Jin] shamefully put to death. If you will favour me, reach me your arm in help from on high, and ordain that here on the earth below men and spirits unite to assist me.'

The die was cast. The Chinese campaign was about to commence. However, 'He who mounts on the back of a tiger does not so easily get down again.' The Ruzhen, with a population in the region of 50 million, were able to field an army of 500,000 men, a quarter of whom were cavalrymen recruited mainly from nomadic mercenaries — Önggüd, Solon, Mukri and even Khitan or Ruzhen — the remainder being infantry regiments composed mainly of Chinese. Furthermore, Jin China was protected by small forts equipped with antisiege gear, not to mention the gigantic line of defence which was the Great Wall.

The cavalry mobilized by Genghis Khan probably numbered somewhat over 100,000 men. The khan took personal command of the 'centre'. Accompanied by Jebe, Sübetei, and the princes Tolui and Jochi Qasar, Muqali became leader of the left wing. Chagatai, Ögödei, Bo'orji and Jochi Qasar were familiar faces taking part in the invasion, but there were also some newcomers: Chaγan, a Xixia adopted by the khan, and two Khitan, the brothers Yelü Aqa and Yelü Tukha.

The army seems to have gone into action about March 1211, just after the *quriltai* (Chinese sources diverge on this point: the *Yuan Shi* and the *Xin Yuan Shi* [*New History of the Yuan*] suggest March, while the *Mengwuer Shi* [*History of the Mongols*] gives a later date). Information on the routes taken by the Mongol invaders is vague. Apparently the great khan's army assembled north of the Kerulen and crossed the frozen river before

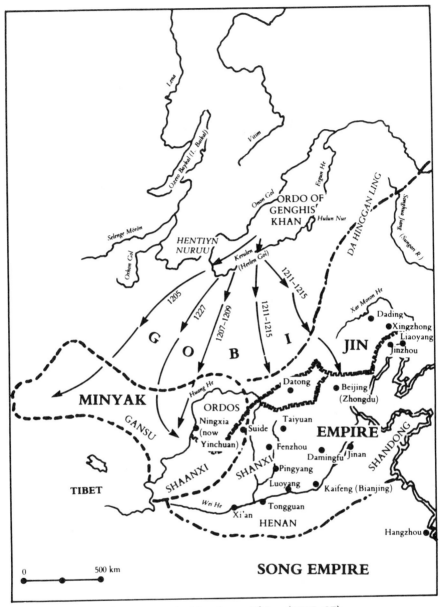

Map 5.   Mongol Invasions in Northern China (1205–27)

'Beijing/Peking' means 'northern capital'. Under the Jin dynasty, the Chinese empire extended further north than it does today, and so the name was applied to Dading (and will appear thus in some texts). Its application to Dading in this book has been avoided to obviate confusion. 'Zhongdu' — 'central metropolis' — is the site of present-day Beijing. The name 'Beijing' has been applied in this book to present-day Beijing or any earlier city on the same site.

dividing into two corps: one, commanded by the khan, advanced to the upper reaches of the Luan, while the other, under the banner of the princes, made its way via the Tuul Gol to the Khorio Gol. After 800 kilometres the troops split into regiments that were drawn up at regular intervals so as to avoid using up the scarce water supplies that were to be found in this region of semidesert. Squads of scouts spied out the route, sought out sources of drinking water, found and marked sheltered sites and difficult stretches of terrain, and took prisoners. Waggons filled with provisions, small field tents, and military equipment followed the troops. At last, two months after their departure, the Mongols reached the frontier zone held by the Önggüd.

## To the Gates of Beijing

The Mongols had no trouble in eliminating the first small forts and the villages nearest the border; the Ruzhen, meanwhile, kept their troops in reserve. At the beginning of the summer of 1211, after some successes of no great strategic importance, the invaders halted their advance and seemed to be marking time, although no counteroffensive from the Ruzhen side appeared to be forthcoming. No doubt secret discussions took place between the Mongols and the Önggüd chief, Ala Quy Tegin, for he suddenly turned traitor to the Beijing side and went over to the enemy. Swiftly moving into action agàin, Genghis Khan, smoothly and without striking a blow, took the slope that protected the northwestern side of Beijing.

The imperial capital was thunderstruck. Sino-Ruzhen troops were hastily despatched to form a buffer between the city and the nomads. But the fortresses of Fengli, Wusha, Huan and Fuzhou, in the far north of Hebei, quickly fell into Mongol hands. The Jin command sent fresh troops up to the vicinity of the Great Wall, under the leadership of the prince-generals Wan Nü and Hu Sha. The Jin dynasty could no longer be in any doubt that the nomads were at the threshold of the empire, this time not to carry out their usual raids, but to invade it. Military reports confirmed the approach of enemy columns, complete with numerous extra horses, waggons loaded with supplies, and herds of animals. It was clear that there was some central coordination and that all the Mongol troops were complying with directions in a disciplined manner.

It was on the slopes of the enormous plateau that is present-day Inner Mongolia, where the land sweeps down towards the vast Chinese plain, that the first confrontation took place. This was the battle of Ye Hu Ling (the Summits of the Wild Foxes) and the site north of the Huang He. The imperial troops of the Ruzhen Chinese lost a great number of soldiers: less than ten years later, crossing the site to go and meet Genghis Khan, the Taoist Chinese pilgrim Chang Chun observed:. 'We saw a battlefield covered with whitened human bones.'

The Jin infantry was far superior to that of the invaders, but their cavalry a great deal inferior. The generals chose to bide their time, hoping that a substantial rescue force could be mounted in Manchuria to take the Mongols from the rear. But the operation moved forward only slowly and this, combined with the indecision within the Jin command and difficulties in communication, favoured the khan's advance. To descend into the plain, the Mongols, who were massed in the north of Hebei and Shanxi, had a choice of three access routes: the first went via a defile across the river Yang; the other two followed approximately the course of the Sanggan He. The Jin command had the walls of some of the forts strengthened so that garrisons could be disposed there instead, but Jebe and Yelü Tukha were too fast for them and, seizing several defensive units, fell upon Weining. One officer, Liu Bolin, escaped from this citadel by means of a rope and turned up at the camp of Jebe, where he set about obtaining the surrender of the regional Khitan troops.

Chinese sources are very vague about the various operations that occurred that year in the north of Jin China. Skirmishes led on to major battles, and reverses were often followed by crushing defeats. At Jin headquarters, there appears to have been a difference of opinion: one group was for acting immediately to stop the ever-threatening enemy in its tracks; others thought it preferable to wait until troops could be concentrated in sufficient numbers to form an 'iron curtain' against the enemy. But, whichever view they took, they were all staggered by the apparent ubiquitousness of the Mongol columns spilling down off the arid plateaux where their devastating cavalry had been shaped and honed.

Shortly afterwards Genghis Khan received another surrender: that of the Khitan Shimo Mingan. Then prince Hu Sha was crushed and forced to seek refuge with his decimated troops in the western capital, the city of Datong, then called Xijing. Hu Sha, afraid he might be trapped there, forced a way through the screen of Mongol lines and made a desperate attempt to escape, but was pursued by Genghis's troops. Meanwhile, Jebe met and joined forces with the great khan, while Genghis's three sons were left carrying out actions north of the Great Wall, where they managed to break down the defences of several cities. Having ravaged some villages and a few poorly fortified cities, and succeeded in picking their way through pieces of wall that were unattended, the massed Mongol forces assembled together in the region of Beijing, probably in the winter of 1211–1212. In six months of fighting, the entire Jin territory backing onto present-day Inner Mongolia appears to have been abandoned to its fate by the ruling dynasty.

In the course of the Chinese campaigns, whole regions had succumbed to and been sacked by the invaders. Millet and *gaoliang* crops and orchards were laid waste; farms, grain stores and stables were plundered. Men who had escaped mobilization wandered about in search of shelter and formed small gangs of raiders. Refugees from combat zones camped below city walls where they could find neither food nor lodging. Wherever Genghis's troops passed, they left piles of ruins. The Mongols were accustomed to wide open spaces and did not linger for long within the walls of conquered cities. All they cared about was booty and prisoners: they wrenched peasants away from their lands and turned them forcibly into their labourers, and they did violence to the women. Whole villages suddenly found themselves out on the roads, carrying their starving children and with their few belongings stuffed into small bundles.

The Chinese soldiers were ill-prepared, paid only irregularly, and badly fed, and the long marches hither and thither exhausted them. The songs and poems that we have dating from the time of the nomads' invasions are invariably long laments out of the mouths of people who have known nothing else but defeat. Lü You wrote: 'The Wall was built, with cries of pain and sadness; the moon and the Milky Way seem low in comparison with it. But if all the white bones of the dead had been left piled up there, they would reach the same height as the Great Wall.'

When Genghis Khan was within sight of the city of Beijing, he realized that he would not be able to take it: the place was encircled by three high walls which were defended by the best of the imperial troops. He decided instead to go foraging in the surrounding countryside, pillaging villages, stealing horses and grabbing whatever was easy booty. After six months of war, his troops needed a breathing space. It was the middle of winter and the animals would be short of food unless reserves of fodder were appropriated from the villages all around.

Jebe was therefore sent to the region of Liaodong, northeast of Beijing, along the coastal plain. Crossing over Shanhaiguan (the Pass between

Mountain and Sea), he soon reached the city of Liaoyang (then called Dongjing, the eastern capital) and succeeded in seizing it, having crossed the frozen Liao He river. In order to take the fortified city, Jebe had recourse to a trick that the Mongols used several times: he made it look as if he had to beat a headlong retreat before the enemy defences, and abandoned his camp a little way from the town; reassured that Jebe was out of the way, the Jin inhabitants and troops went out, as expected, on an expedition of plunder. The Mongol general, however, after a remarkable ride during which he was in the saddle for 24 hours without a break, burst into the town in the middle of the night, while its people were preoccupied with celebrating the lunar New Year. Everyone, soldiers and civilians alike, was busy feasting, the gates open as in peacetime, and the guard posts entirely deserted. Jebe had no difficulty in taking the garrison by surprise. It was 4 February 1212.

**The Khitan Uprising**
There were squalls blowing through Beijing; the wind was invariably icy and heralded the snows that were soon to bury the whole of northern China in a shroud; the Mongols carried out further raids in the countryside of Shandong around the lower Huang He and farther north beyond Beijing, and then settled into winter quarters. Certain forts held out against Mongol attacks: Genghis Khan did not press the matter, for he knew that his lack of siege weapons and of technical personnel constituted a weakness. Tolui, the khan's youngest son, took a number of fortified positions. But the Mongols' surge had lost some of its impetus, and the gallop of its horses had slowed gradually to a trot. Slowly, the invaders retreated northwards, leaving behind whole societies whom, at every level, Mongol murder and mayhem had shattered and scarred.

In the spring of 1212 the Jin suffered another catastrophic blow: a descendant of the old imperial Liao family, one Yelü Liuge, who came from the Khitan dynasty that had been conquered by the Jin Ruzhen, turned rebel. This occurred in the extreme north of the imperial territory (present-day Jilin), not far from the old Khitan capital. Together with another Khitan, Yedi, he gathered some troops together: soon the rebels numbered more than 100,000 soldiers.

The military revolt came to the attention of the Mongols via their messengers, and was of much interest to them. Genghis Khan acted straight away: he sent his lieutenant Alchin to take stock of the newly arisen situation. The rebels came face to face with the Mongol envoys on the banks of the Liao and decided that it would be prudent for them to swear their allegiance to the great khan. A treaty was signed, and sealed with oaths and the ritual sacrifice of animals. Troops sent by the Jin to quell the revolt arrived too late: the Khitan, with the Mongols' help, routed them. This defeat was seriously disturbing to the Jin, since the territories around the approaches to the Korean peninsula had now been snatched out of their hands, and along with them the support of a significant division of the army.

Following the rebellion of Yelü Liuge and of Shimo Mingan, and the treachery of the Önggüd, the Ruzhen began to have grave doubts about the loyalty of foreign mercenaries. It became clear to them that any new crack in the Jin edifice could split the entire structure open. At the court at Beijing passions raged and plots were hatched. Captains were roundly criticized but the worst of the abuse was hurled at the generals. Nevertheless, although they had been beaten, mocked and insulted, the military still held all the cards.

By 1213 the situation was little changed. The Mongols were entrenched in northern China and laid waste cultivated land and villages, without, however, succeeding in wresting firm control of the key strongholds of the country, of its imposing fortified cities where the civil and military administrators had their headquarters, or of its government ensconced behind the stone ramparts of the imperial capital. The nomads were efficient raiders and took numerous prisoners, but they remained unable to impose a real military occupation on China. To do so, they would need to keep garrisons and gain at least a small hold on the levers of administration. The truth was that at this time the conquering nomads held only a small part of the immense territory that belonged to the Jin empire.

## The Battle of the Passes
In this same year, 1213, Genghis Khan's army, which seemed to have retreated to the plateau heights of the interior, started to move down again towards the Chinese plains. The khan took possession early on of a stronghold which commanded the most direct road towards the Great Wall.

This huge line of defence, 6,000 kilometres long, was a complex of fortifications with double, sometimes triple, walls; forts; operational bases; and salients climbing up to the crest of the wall. The height of the walls varied from 7 to 8 metres, and here and there watchtowers, barracks, magazines and casemates for the use of soldiers had been incorporated into the structure. The approaches to the forts were protected by *chevaux de frise* made out of spikes or stakes. Each watchtower was linked with the next by means of a visual signalling system (coded flags, smoke by day, fires by night) or by sound (the beating of drums). In the space of only a few hours it was possible to transmit messages up to a range of 500 kilometres.

Perhaps by using trickery, but certainly also with the help of collaborators and rebels, Genghis Khan managed to clear the gates of the Great Wall with his cavalry. The first test he faced was the capture of Huailai, a small straggling village that had a rather sparse garrison, but it was fortified, and it straddled the approach roads to the Jin capital. It was Tolui who took the village, although it is not known whether he did so by simply storming it or by trickery and the help of accomplices.

Having crushed one section of the Sino-Ruzhen army, the nomads advanced through a narrow defile, Nankou, which was overshadowed by steep hills, topped at long intervals by guard posts. Negotiating the 22-kilometre length of this strategic pass was an extremely hazardous challenge. Nevertheless Jebe showed fine initiative: setting out with his riders on what purported to be a reconnaissance, he pretended suddenly to have lost heart and turned back. This old soldier's trick worked again on this occasion: the Jin troops, coming out of their entrenched positions, set off in pursuit of the runaways and fell into the most classic of ambushes. The defence posts they vacated were seized by the Mongols, who then forced a passage through to the site at Longhu Tai (The Plateau of the Dragon and the Tiger). From there, it was only 30 kilometres to Beijing.

At the same time, other army corps were riding across the Rehe and Shanxi. The first obstacle, quickly overcome, was the citadel of Datong where they set free Önggüd prisoners held there, including the son and widow of Ala Quy Tegin, who had been assassinated by an anti-Mongol breakaway group. Beijing was now surrounded, threatened and only a moment away from being entirely at the Mongols' mercy. None of the passes had presented any real obstacle to the invader, since all the garrisons which had been posted around them had fallen without being able to offer effective resistance. With the exception of the Juyongguan gate, the Great Wall itself had not been stormed.

Even today one cannot help but be amazed by the tactical skill of Genghis Khan, who rarely failed to take the enemy by surprise and subjugate him on his own ground. Chinese sources shed little light on the dearth of initiative in Ruzhen strategy and the incompetence of the Jin leaders, but there is no doubt whatever that the Sino-Ruzhen losses were terrible. The Chinese historian Wang Guowei even goes so far as to suggest that the Jin suffered so many losses right from the beginning of the conflict that they were later unable to muster sufficient soldiers to fight in important engagements in the field. This claim seems rather extreme, since a little later the Jin authorities did raise a significant number of new troops.

The prime reasons for the Jin rulers' defeats had to do, above all, with the tragic inexperience of their supreme command, its indecisiveness and its lack of speed. There were some capable men amongst the higher-ranking Ruzhen officers — those, for example, who had conquered the Song of the south — but these were not in evidence in 1211. Moreover, the Ruzhen apparently underutilized their mounted archers in most of the engagements with the nomads, who, for their part, made this the key tactic of their operations. There were times, too, when the coordination between the Jin cavalry and infantry was quite badly managed and one saw cavalry colliding with infantry in tragic confusion, most notably during the battle lost by Hu Sha near the upper reaches of the Yang He.

Once they had attained power, the Ruzhen, these ancient nomadic Tungus peoples, whose determination had made it possible for them to conquer the Chinese, acted like nearly all other conquerors: they foundered in self-indulgence and the pleasures of court life. Their leaders certainly failed to ponder the Chinese saying, 'The force of an arrow shot from a mighty bow weakens and dies as the arrow falls to ground.'

The Jin empire had been thrown into serious crisis and it was necessary to find people to blame. Heads rolled at every defeat. Every council of ministers turned into an arena in which robes ran red with stab wounds. As so often, the sword in the end won out against the sceptre. A general, Wenyan Hu Sha, organized a conspiracy and seized power, killing the legitimate ruler in the process. In the place of the weak prince of Wei, a new man mounted the steps of the throne in August–September 1213: Utubu.

# 10
# Operation Great Wall

*The grass grows thick on the tomb of Yue Fei. In the dismal light of autumn, the stone beasts there seem menacing. The ruler and his ministers, withdrawing south of the river, were too hasty in abandoning the rich grain fields. The old men of the central plain long to see the imperial standards again. But alas, the hero is dead, it is too late. The country, deprived of its mainstay, has split down the middle. Do not recite my verses by the lake in the West; neither water nor mountain will rise above their sadness.*

**Zhao Mengfu, 1254–1322**

## The Mongol Hordes

Genghis Khan lost no time in reacting to the news of the revolt at the palace which had just toppled the Jin dynasty: with three army corps behind him, he mounted an expedition which was to deliver a decisive blow to the new government of the emperor Utubu. Since he was still not in a position to occupy the imperial capital, Beijing, the khan deployed beneath its walls a cordon of troops, in order to prevent possible reinforcements from going in or out. Then he embarked on a journey south of Hebei and Shandong, in the direction of the Huang He, the Yellow River.

The Yellow River, that great life-giving waterway and cradle of Chinese civilization, had, for thousands of years, carried down rich alluvial deposits, which men had always been very eager to turn to productive use. A chequered pattern of fields created by hard-working Chinese peasants stretched away as far as the eye could see. On these brownish soils, farmers raised pigs and poultry and grew millet, sorghum, sesame and soya beans — so long as they were not crushed by taxes and the sudden river floods did not sweep away their harvest or even, at times, their villages. A large population lived crammed together in the

*189*

Huang He basin, unlike in the north, where planters had virgin lands to clear.

This patchwork of a landscape, domesticated and humanized, came as a surprise to the nomads. To them, the land their horses now trampled seemed to have been violated, and the men who lived on it no better than livestock in pens. Few of them had any understanding of the sedentary life. The armed columns of Genghis Khan were in the habit of plundering the land and thundering through in such a way that any cultivated soils they passed over would be rapidly returned to their natural state. Irreversible destruction and systematic pillage were all they knew and understood: how, then, were these nomads from the wide open spaces, here at the beginning of the thirteenth century, to muster respect for the way of life and property of the Chinese and the Sinicized Ruzhen, these people of whose history, language and customs they knew nothing and who, dug in behind their walls, were single-mindedly bent on riddling them with arrows? The invaders were on land they had conquered, which is as much as to say they were on enemy territory. They had come for no other purpose than pillage. For months, excited by the infectious sound and fury of battle, they had been living side by side with death. Death was everywhere and they themselves dealt it out in a free and easy manner, sometimes out of necessity, sometimes with pleasure or in a drunken frenzy, for death prowled about, waiting and watching, as if aware that, subconsciously, men were trying to exorcize it.

More often than not, rumours preceded the invaders' onslaught. Deserting Chinese soldiers and the wounded would appear in the villages, looking for food or shelter. Recruiting officers raked through cities and even entire districts to force peasants to enrol. For the latter, the war was but another item in a long catalogue of calamities. Their lands were scarcely defended at all, since the generals had their sights set on other strategic objectives. The result was this tragic exodus of agricultural peasants leaving their villages against their will, wandering here and there with their offspring, camping at the foot of external walls of cities that were protected by garrisons, in the hope of some illusory protection.

Having passed Beijing, the invaders soon reached the south of Hebei and then the province of Shandong, where the mighty Huang He divides into many channels which shift position periodically so that the river is barely navigable. The khan and his men approached the city of Jinan, a commercial centre surrounded by lakes, springs, and forested hills and thus a country resort for the nobility. The Mongols reached a low-lying region where the land was intersected by streams, which were difficult to cross as there were no bridges. So they wandered at random, bursting into villages and taking people prisoner. The peasants, who were unable to lay their hands on any weapons, let themselves be rounded up like sheep and were grateful if their poor farms were left alone and their wives and daughters not abducted. The nomads used them as porters and labourers. The prisoners were made to repair bridges and carts and to feed the animals. Throughout the whole of the summer of 1213, the nomad hordes swept through entire regions, sowing the seeds of death and destruction.

Nor was that the worst of it. When the Mongols had insufficient numbers to mount an attack against a fortified village, or when they lacked the technical means of forcing the heavy wooden gates that protected the towns, they used the massed prisoners as a sort of enormous shield: herded in front of the warriors, the unfortunate captives were pushed forward towards the fort gates, or the ramparts of the fortified towns, and there, using axes, rams, ladders, boar-spears or just clubs, they were forced to batter away at the outer defences. Those who refused or resisted were cut down. And so the whole huge mob of them, reduced to a state of stupefaction, obeyed the criminal orders of the conquerors, and each individual became a link in the chain that bound them all together in the tragic episode of these 'suicide squads'. Standing on the walls of citadels taken by storm, Chinese soldiers, sometimes under Ruzhen command, first attempted to dissuade the attackers from approaching, failing which they simply massacred them. More often than not, the opposing sides were within call and could clearly see and recognize each other. Under siege, the Chinese would find themselves letting fly their arrows against their compatriots — the inhabitants of a nearby village, perhaps, or even of their own — under the impatient gaze of the Mongols, who stood by and waited until the time was right for them to go into the attack themselves, when they would ride roughshod over the remains of their hostages up to the defensive walls. The Mongols' way had a terrible efficiency about it: to make the best use of friendly forces and to decimate those of the adversary.

All through the summer of 1213, the provinces of Shaanxi, Hebei and Shandong witnessed a mass exodus of people fleeing the combat zones. There were thousands of them, driven out by the Mongols — dispossessed villagers, minor officials, craftsmen ruined by the disruption to their trade and deserters — all trudging along the roads. Fleeing soldiers left behind their weapons but kept their cuirasses of felt or leather to protect them from the chill of the nights. Some officials travelled by vehicle with their families, followed by coolies carrying bamboo poles over their shoulders from which were slung whatever valuables they were able to take with them. Barefooted, straw-hatted peasant families straggled along and behind them came carts filled with baskets for winnowing and other uses, and jars. Men, women and children in their thousands, dressed in rags and tatters, stunned and exhausted by hunger and thirst, had become vagrants in their own country. All around, the countryside lay rotten and dead.

This was a black period in China's history, when the nation was invaded, stripped bare and ravaged by enemies who were not only primitive but also quite without mercy. And yet, had not China already suffered repeatedly from barbarian attacks over the centuries? In the seventh century, lamenting the atrocities of war, the poet Zhang Wei wrote:

> *They say that the emperor and his ministers*
> *Are now sending our troops to pacify the barbarians.*
> *Certainly it is a wonderful thing to have peace along our borders,*
> *But must all the men in China be dispersed to that end?*

Echoing his sentiments some six centuries later, Zhao Mengfu, a painter and poet of the Yuan dynasty, wrote:

> *Slung from saddles, skulls jangle together, crying.*
> *There are officers whose backs bear eighty wounds;*
> *Torn flags envelop the corpses lying at the side of the road.*
> *The survivors, resigned to dying, mourn the fall of the citadel that now lies empty;*
> *In the victory bulletins, there will be one name only, that of the general.*

## Beijing Sacked

At first the Mongols did not launch frontal assaults on the large cities that were defended by élite troops. They confined themselves to destroying settlements, foraging in grain stores and setting fire to small towns. While the khan was riding across the great northern plain which is an extension of the Mongolian steppes, his sons Ögödei, Jochi and Chagatai, leading the troops that formed the right wing of the invading army, were going down the western fringes of Hebei on the way to Henan north of the Huang He. Suddenly they branched off towards southern Shanxi and came out into the fertile valley of the river Fen. The small provincial villages of Pingyang, Fenzhou and Xingzhou fell one by one into their hands. The large city of Taiyuan, built on the banks of the Fen He and protected as it was by massive ditches, was nevertheless also captured and its inhabitants scattered to the winds. A third army division, commanded by Jochi Qasar, Genghis Khan's brother, left the Beijing area and, crossing the famous Shanhaiguan pass (the Pass between Mountain and Sea), ascended towards the Rehe: this division laid waste what is today Manchuria, up to the banks of the Amur, the Ruzhen's original territory.

It is surprising to note the apparent ease with which the nomad invaders on this occasion took possession of Chinese towns protected by defensive structures and earthworks. One might have thought that the Sino-Ruzhen garrisons would have been able to repulse some of the attacks and also inflict considerable losses on the Mongols. Evidently the Jin leaders made a tragic mistake. They relied to excess on the strategy of pulling back from the combat lines, and they gained a false sense of security from lurking behind their fortifications. It was a fatal combination: the Mongols, refraining from launching direct assaults on citadels which they could not take by storm, had found another way of wreaking havoc. They skirted around the cities and vented their fury on the countryside, inflicting on it the worst possible damage — a scorched earth policy. They laid waste to farms, plundered granaries for fodder for their horses, set houses on fire, ripped up dikes and choked up irrigation canals to drown or desiccate cultivated land, and, in the end, wiped out completely the grain reserves of the districts through which they passed, rendering barren the life-giving earth and thus suffocating the villages. To destroy the land of an essentially agricultural country was, in the short term, tantamount to snuffing out the cities and trapping their citizens 'like fish at the bottom of a cooking pot'. In a way, it was like taking the fish out of water to die; and all this happened seven centuries before Mao Zedong.

Indeed, it seems that the Jin leaders were not always aware of what was going on. Some of their generals certainly defended themselves against the invaders, but many instead apparently sought to conserve their troops; except on some rare occasions, the Jin armies passively suffered the assaults mounted against them. Furthermore, there was at no point an outstanding political or military figure who emerged to face up to Genghis Khan and his captains. The Chinese people, who had largely been mobilized by and within the troops of the Ruzhen occupying power, seem to have refused to defend the Ruzhen. Bowed under the yoke of a foreign dynasty which had split China in two, the people had evidently decided that the best attitude to adopt was one of 'wait and see'; consciously or unconsciously they must have been hoping that the Jin rulers would meet their downfall at the hands of the Mongols. From this stemmed their reluctance to fight on behalf of the foreign dynasty that reigned in Beijing. Yet we should do well to avoid glib conclusions and remember the proverb which says that 'behind every praying mantis on the trail of a cicada there is an oriole on the look-out'.

For as China was yielding itself up, unresisting, to the enemy, the vice on the nation was slowly but surely being screwed ever tighter. While one Mongol division, commanded by the khan's brother, Jochi Qasar, was advancing up the coast of the gulf of Bo Hai towards Manchuria to attack the Ruzhen from the rear, the khan's own troops were concentrating in front of the Jin capital. It was April 1214. Several of Genghis Khan's generals wanted to launch an immediate assault on the great imperial city, but the sovereign considered that he did not have the wherewithal to take the city yet and chose to play for time. He even went so far as to enter into discussions with the authorities with a view to negotiating his own retreat. This was a clever move, since the Ruzhen sovereign, shut in his capital with no hope of rescue, was readily persuaded to accept the khan's terms. Utubu had no military reserves, he was cut off from the Manchu northwest by the presence of Muqali's columns of men, and the ravaged countryside all around was incapable of yielding the slightest quantity of fresh provisions; he therefore had no alternative but to throw himself on Genghis's mercy. Accordingly, he accepted the demands of the conquerors, which included an enormous booty: gold, silver and silk in inordinate amounts.

Nor was this all that Genghis Khan demanded: he also wanted horses — stallions from the imperial stables — a thousand of the city's most vigorous young men and the most attractive of its girls. Lastly, the khan asked for and duly received a personal gift: a royal princess, Jiguo, the youngest daughter of Utubu's predecessor. Heavily loaded with this profusion of treasures, the Mongol sovereign withdrew towards the north and made his camp on the borders of the Chinese empire, not far from his familiar steppes. He left behind him columns of soldiers charged with the task of churning up the land.

In Beijing itself there was a pervasive feeling that the regime was gasping its last. Ministers, advisers and military leaders all accused their ruler of cowardice and an intolerable lack of drive. A crisis had been reached: the booty handed over to the enemy had been colossal and the treasury's chests were empty. Utubu sensed the storm coming. Was he merely anxious to put as much distance as he could between himself and the invaders camped to the north, or did he fear a military revolt? Whichever concern was uppermost in his mind, he left the Beijing court a few weeks after the Mongols' retreat, in June 1214, and took refuge in Kaifeng, farther south: the city was protected by the raging waters of the Huang He; there he would have time to raise new troops. The fact that the Jin authorities retreated so precipitately is further proof, if any were still needed, of the weakness of a ruling dynasty that could abandon the north completely and without a second thought.

The next year was to see the fall of the imperial city of Beijing before the Mongol attack. Set upon by thousands of soldiers bent on destruction, the capital was set on fire. Its agony lasted a whole month. The defenders of Beijing, then called Zhongdu (Central Metropolis), were aware that they were being offered up as sacrifices in a rearguard action. Utubu had entrusted the defence of the city to the imperial prince Shu Zong and to two generals, the prince Fu Xing and Moran Jinzhong. Situated in the middle of a narrow plain commanding all the access routes to China proper, the city was also at a point where different types of landscape converged: they reflected the country's diversity — the steppe expanses of the northwest; in the northeast the great plain of Manchuria, with its continental climate; and in the south the warmer regions of the great plains.

At this time, in the year 1215, Beijing corresponded approximately to what is now called the 'Outer City' (or 'Chinese City'). It had formidable ramparts 43 kilometres in length, punctuated at intervals by a dozen monumental gates; behind them, several hundred thousand inhabitants were crammed into districts that, for the most part, had the character of villages. In the heart of the city were the imperial palace, the chancery, other administrative buildings both civil and military, and barracks, in the midst of residential quarters shaded by parks famed for their variety of species and for the beauty of their floral displays. The city was overflowing with shops selling porcelain, lacquers and spices, with restaurants and tea-houses, and coolies' humble dwellings, all of which breathed life and soul into the place. That life and soul, however, were soon to be blotted out of existence in a terrifying orgy of destruction.

When he heard that the Jin had abandoned the imperial city, Genghis

Khan returned to the south in January 1215. He erected his tent at Longhu Tai and distributed his troops around the edges of the starving city. In March, the khan renewed his peace offer to the Jin authorities. At the same time, however, the city's leaders, although under siege, had managed to slip through the Mongol lines some troops who had orders to recover what supplies they could; moreover, the Jin sovereign, from his refuge at Kaifeng, had ordered soldiers and food reserves to be sent to the beleaguered city. The military governor of the southeastern part of Hebei, Li Ying, got together a convoy which was to join other help being sent from Chending: together, they had a strength of 39,000 soldiers, each of whom was compelled to carry about 30 kilos of provisions, in addition to those which were transported by waggon.

Seeing that initiatives were being taken to save the city, Genghis Khan apparently revoked his offers of peace and despatched detachments to meet the enemy forces. Li Ying's troops were taken by surprise by the Mongols commanded by Shimo Mingan and Shen Sa and suffered a severe defeat. According to Chinese sources, 3,000 Mongols set upon 39,000 Jin soldiers, whose leader was drunk and incapable of enforcing the slightest discipline among his men. Li Ying was captured and 1,000 waggons full of provisions fell into Mongol hands. The government of Kaifeng, who were contemplating sending a second rescue mission, now changed their minds and resignedly abandoned Beijing to its fate. In May the Mongols, who had been joined by some Chinese troops, won some further successes.

Within the city, the lack of food soon caused frightful famine and, so it was said, ghastly scenes of cannibalism. The generals who were in command of the town clashed violently over whether they should make a desperate bid to get out and die by the sword or stay and starve to death. Prince Fu Xing chose to commit suicide, but his equally ill-starred companion succeeded in slipping out, along with a few intimates, at the other side of the besieged city, leaving behind the imperial princesses whom he had sworn he would rescue. Having forced his way through the enemy lines, probably by night, he arrived at Kaifeng, where he was executed.

Now that their commander had chosen that shameful course of action and fled, the officers capitulated and sent emissaries to the attackers outside the walls. At last, in June 1215, the enormous gates of the ramparts of the imperial city were opened: Beijing was offering itself, exhausted and worn down by defeat and despair, to vulgar barbarians who came from the remotest steppes. Genghis Khan himself, however, had not waited for the siege to end before moving northwards once more, perhaps because of the great heatwaves that descend on the Beijing plain at that season. And when the capital did surrender, he made not the slightest move to retrace his steps. Besides, what was there for him to do there? His part of the booty — and the same applied to princes, officers and every simple fighting man — would be scrupulously reserved for him, as was the custom. Why go back just to witness the confused spectacle of a vanquished city being sacked?

Although the city had capitulated, the conquerors made no attempt to check their violent instincts. Accompanied by Turco-Mongol auxiliary troops and Khitan and Chinese who had thrown in their lot with the victors, the Mongols immediately set about killing: thousands of inhabitants were put to the sword because they refused to give up their possessions, or because they ran for cover into their houses and were unable to understand what was shouted at them by some drunken soldier, or simply because they were the losers in the conflict . . . Men armed with axes, sabres, and maces ran about the streets in bands, charging into shops that had been ripped apart to winkle out any last supplies of food or wine that might be left there. Everywhere — in the alleys, in the villas of the well-off, in the offices of the mandarins — were strewn utensils, broken jars, and lacquered folding-screens, all jumbled together with dirt and rubbish. Half-naked men jumped from their horses and, swearing copiously, argued over who should have this or that piece of silk cloth, jade jewellery, trimmed hanging, or even some rag doll or a mirror — and all the while art treasures lay unnoticed in the dust. Old men had their throats cut when they tried to defend their children from the looters' vengeance, and women were tossed onto waggons already filled with an odd collection of miscellaneous objects. Some parts of the devastated city looked like a market that had been blown apart by an explosion.

Soon, however, the victors had to withdraw because the stench of bodies left unburied had become lethal. Stray dogs and rats in their thousands came sniffing around swollen corpses wedged underneath heaps of rubbish and rotting rapidly in the unbearable June heat. Hundreds of thousands of Beijing's people survived in the ruins or in the suburbs beyond the walls, camping on waste ground or on debris close to sources of water, polluted though it all was. The whole town had been engulfed in boundless misery; yet each person thought there was refuge or consolation to be found in the company of his fellows. Disaster, like

joy, is best shared. It was not long before people started moving to and
fro, in a more or less organized fashion, between the city and the outlying
districts, to find wood, ropes and straw in order gradually to patch up
what had been damaged or lost. And it was not long, either, before the
wailing and the weeping began to die down: the Chinese people had, after
all, already experienced many a misfortune, famine or war.

Nevertheless, for a month whole districts continued to burn. Going
through the ruins of Beijing a few months later, a diplomatic delegation
sent to Genghis Khan from the Khwārezm observed with horror that
there were mounds of human bones to be seen in certain parts of the town
and that the earth where several dwellings had stood was still stained
with the blood of the victims. Epidemics continued to rage through the
city and several of the envoys from Khwārezm were taken ill, probably
with typhus.

Apprised of the surrender of Beijing to his ally Shimo Mingan, Genghis
Khan sent his adoptive brother, Shigi-Qutuqu, and two of his guard
officers, Önggür and Arqai Qasar, to draw up an inventory of the riches
in the imperial treasure. The imperial official, however, offered the
khan's envoys only a few scraps of the treasure: the two officers of the
Mongol guard accepted what was offered, but Shigi-Qutuqu rejected it,
saying that he could not take for himself what by right belonged to his
sovereign. Genghis was kept informed of these matters by his entourage
and was full of praise for the loyalty of his adoptive brother while at the
same time sharply reprimanding the two officers for their disloyalty and
selfishness. The khan's demand for absolute obedience to himself, his
keenly developed sense of his own prerogatives, and his unquenchable
thirst for undivided power: these traits are all very much in character
with the Genghis we know. He still had a long way to go before his lust
for power would be satisfied.

**A Reign Doomed to Die**
Always alert to political advantage, the khan immediately sought to
exploit his troops' military success in obtaining the surrender of Beijing.
Hardly wasting a moment, he sent a new expedition against Utubu, who
had taken refuge in Henan. He himself, however, remained in the north
and did not take part in the expedition.

Members of the Jin ruling class who had moved to Kaifeng were
rendered helpless. There were no longer any communications with the
Manchu northeast and other villages in Hebei were surrendering to the

invaders. Jin power had contracted and was now confined to the interior of China; the territorial borders were not in its control any more. The fact that the court had fled had dealt a severe blow to imperial prestige. Here and there uprisings began to break out and certain provincial army generals took advantage of the situation to dissociate themselves from the Jin leadership.

In April 1215, while the Mongols were laying siege to Beijing, the Jin rulers were suddenly brought up against a severe famine which was sweeping through Henan and driving tens of thousands of people from their homes and their land. Soldiers fleeing from the Mongols went southwards, followed by their families, pulling carts filled with their possessions and anything else they could pick up in villages along the way. It is said that this tragic exodus involved a million refugees. The imperial authorities, anxious to avoid having all these unfortunates turn up at the gates of the capital, adopted drastic measures in an attempt to accommodate them on the land in Shandong, a good distance away from Kaifeng. But the provincial officials who were given the task of requisitioning the land and running the refugee camps were tainted with corruption. Bribery, falsification of documents and misuse of public funds were common practices, which combined to reduce many of the peasant population to misery. It was not long before armed revolts began to disturb the traditional peace of the countryside. Troops were sent out to quell the uprisings, and at the hands of these imperial soldiers no fewer than 30,000 insurgents met their deaths. Nevertheless, the peasants' revolt continued. The court at Kaifeng was obliged to have soldiers drafted in from Manchuria who, because of the Mongol invasion, had to travel by sea. The uprising, known as the revolt of the Redcoats, attained a massive scale and was not put down until 1223.

Seeing advantage to themselves in the troubles that were shaking the Ruzhen throne, the Xixia of the Minyak empire now reared their heads; they joined the battle and attacked all the Jin positions, achieving a number of victories in Gansu as well as in Shaanxi. The Jin rulers despatched troops to halt the Xixia advance and these in the end won a victory over an army of 80,000 men.

Battling against the Mongols, the Xixia and the internal rebellions simultaneously was a particularly wearying experience that tested the Jin rulers to their limits. Chinese documents from that time testify to the tremendous mass levies that had to be organized to enlist all the able-bodied men still to be found in the villages and on the land. Recruiting officers patrolled the provinces with their guards, enrolling agricultural labourers and vagrants wherever they could be found to serve under the imperial banner. Gradually armed corps took shape and these were deployed like a collar around Kaifeng, some to the north of the Huang He, others to the south. The soldiers were allowed to take their families with them: it was hoped that this might make them less inclined to desert. But these hastily assembled troops had no cavalry and little training.

In Kaifeng, the Jin regime held out, reluctant to admit the possibility of defeat. There was talk at the court of eventually retaking Beijing and of the rewards that might accrue to those who thus distinguished themselves. But each new military reverse only intensified personal animosity and rivalry and undermined the defence system which was already handicapped by the soldiers' lack of experience and preparation. All around the emperor Utubu, Jin territory was shrinking like leather.

Soon after the fall of Beijing, the Mongol invaders called a halt to major offensives — until the end of the warm season — because men and animals were in need of recuperation. But when July came, in the year 1215, Genghis Khan mobilized his troops once more. Four army corps headed off southwards. They included some Khitan and Chinese, in ever increasing numbers. The first column, led by a Qongqotat, Tolun Sherbi, was charged with invading western Hebei. The second, comprising Chinese only, advanced into the extreme east of the province to seize Pingzhou. The third corps penetrated Shanxi and the last — 10,000 Mongols commanded by Samuqa — had orders to advance up to the walls of Xi'an, across the Ordos plateau, in Xixia territory.

Thanks to his alliance with the Minyak sovereign, Genghis Khan was able to join forces with Xixia horsemen and his troops were therefore free to cross their territory. The invading army did not number a great many men, but the khan was anxious to test the Jin defences. At the same time he sent to Kaifeng one of his lieutenants, A-la-Qian, who was to enter into talks with Utubu's court: Genghis Khan demanded not only that all the cities of Hebei and Shandong capitulate but also that Utubu abandon his imperial title and retain only that of king of Henan. Memories of the 1213–1214 invasion, of the sack of Beijing, and of the attendant turmoil were still vividly alive; nevertheless, the imperial court at Kaifeng was courageous enough to turn the khan's demands down flat. And so the war went on.

In September 1215, the town of Pingzhou fell, and the Chinese who were fighting alongside the Mongols, under the command of Shi Tianni, now joined the army corps led by Tolun Sherbi. Together the two generals scored a number of new successes, before going on to lay siege to Damingfu: the town fell when Shi Tianni stormed it, but he paid for this victory with his life. Advancing further into the province of Shandong, the invaders then came to the shores of Dongping Hu, a lake southwest of Jinan, but they were unable to cross the Huang He. Meng Gugang, one of the bravest Jin generals, was waiting for them and repulsed them. This seemed to be the signal for the invading armies to go on the rampage and fan out in all directions throughout the whole area, sparing neither man nor beast and seizing several more towns. At last, at the beginning of 1216, in the middle of winter, both armies headed north again.

In the province of Shanxi, the third corps of Mongol cavalry took some small towns, but Taiyuan continued to hold out. The Redcoats' rebellion was spreading along the northern bank of the Huang He: the countryside was blackened by fire and red with the blood of the victims. The peasants were always in the front line of sacrifice in all Chinese wars: now, as ever, their suffering was immeasurable. When the Mongol columns retreated northwards, however, the Jin generals launched a counteroffensive: during the summer of 1216, they succeeded in reoccupying several districts in Shanxi and Hebei. With much toil and trouble, fields were brought under cultivation again, devastated cities were enclosed once more by new walls rising from the ruins of the old, and operational bases were reinforced.

Farther west, the Mongol army led by Samuqa and Xixia reinforcements from the Minyak empire crossed the Huang He, probably by requisitioning some junks. The cavalry rode down the eastern edge of Shaanxi as far as Suide and then on to Yan'an. In autumn 1216, the Mongols crossed the Wei He near Tongguan, a citadel of strategic importance, situated at the confluence of the Wei He and the Huang He. Samuqa tried to take possession of this famous fortress and failed. He therefore pressed on hurriedly southwards, skirting along the edges of the neighbouring province of Henan. Jin troops rose to meet him, but he forced a way through, only to be caught in a trap some kilometres west of the imperial capital, Kaifeng. In mid-December, under attack on many fronts, Samuqa was forced to fall back to a position between the Huang He and the Luo He, though in the process he fought and won some pitched battles. In January 1217, when the countryside was hard with the winter's ice, his army of horsemen crossed the frozen Huang He and reached the gates of Pinyang.

Meanwhile the Jin rulers were not idle. They sent couriers into the enemy camp to spread the news that all men who had been forcibly enlisted by the Mongols would receive a pardon if they deserted. Documents of the period report that, out of Samuqa's 60,000 men, more than a sixth broke ranks and rejoined the Jin side to collect the promised rewards. Samuqa now had to pull back abruptly, and at the same time the Xixia regiments turned and headed back towards Minyak territory.

Nevertheless, Samuqa had fulfilled his mission. With an army numbering about 40,000 men, he had succeeded in forcing open all the routes into enemy territory and insinuating himself within the Jin military dispositions, not to mention challenging Utubu just a few leagues from his own throne. He had defied and beaten forces far superior to his own, even if he could sometimes count on the support of Xixia or Chinese reinforcements, of *tijun* (auxiliaries enlisted by the Khitan), of Xi or of other nomads drawn from the farthest corners of the empire. From November 1216 to January 1217, he had conducted a lightning campaign, covering 1,200 kilometres in 60 days, crossing mountains and fighting all the while.

The Mongol campaigns had severely shaken the Jin court and threatened Utubu's very throne. They demonstrated that large-scale operations combined with raids penetrating deep into enemy country could drive the Kaifeng court into a purely defensive corner. On the other hand, they also showed that cavalry charges, for all their efficacy in the countryside, were quite useless in gaining possession of large fortified towns.

## Muqali in Manchuria

The first of the Mongol incursions into Manchuria, that huge region in northeastern China, took place in November 1214, prior to the siege of Beijing. The territory, which has an area of some million square kilometres and which now belongs to China, formed a connecting link between Siberia, China and the Korean peninsula. In shape it is a long corridor, bounded in the west by the Da Hinggan Ling range and in the east by the Xiao Hinggan Ling and the Pacific Ocean. Great grassy plains sweep across the region to the fringes of the taiga; its people are herders, foresters and fishermen. It was through this area that the Ruzhen, founders of the Jin dynasty, entered China.

Genghis Khan, having found an ally on the northeastern side of China, did not at first trouble himself to invade Manchuria, although it was potentially a vast reservoir of horses. The few nomadic or semi-nomadic tribes who lived there — Solon, Nonni or Mukri — were too few in number to offer any resistance to the Mongols. But in 1213, when Beijing sent soldiers to put down the rebellion led by Yelü Liuge, the khan emerged as a threat to the northeastern part of the Jin empire. Yelü Liuge, a Khitan, alarmed at the strength of the imperial forces, asked Genghis Khan for help and received a speedy response in the form of 3,000 horsemen, sent to his aid under the leadership of Anchar. These numbers were few enough, but with their help the Khitan managed to repulse General Hu Sha. To show his gratitude for Genghis's military support, Yelü Liuge sent the khan all the goods he had seized from his defeated adversaries. Responding in kind to this act of loyalty, the khan authorized the Khitan to adopt the title of king of Liao. As soon as he was so elevated, he installed his wife on the throne and set about organizing his new kingdom: he created a civil administration and appointed a commander-in-chief, whom he was, however, obliged to make answerable to a Mongol military adviser.

The Beijing authorities tried by various means to remove the recalcitrant general from the Mongols' influence. In vain. Thereafter, the Jin rulers decided to resort to strong-arm tactics and charged General Puxian Wan Nü with the task of crushing this crowned upstart who was in the pay of Genghis Khan. Further, they demanded that he avenge the defeat suffered by Hu Sha, which had had disastrous consequences, since some of the fortified towns in Manchuria situated at the mouth of the Yalu He, near the frontier with Korea, had fallen into Mongol hands. But in the confrontation with Yelü Liuge, Wannu came off worst. Fearing demotion or arrest because of his defeat, and that a murder he had committed might, in spite of his efforts, become known to the Kaifeng court, Wannu turned rebel. In February 1215 he proclaimed his independence from the Jin empire and went on to occupy a territory which he declared his kingdom and which was recognized as such by the Mukri tribe. Ignoring his revolt, the Jin rulers sent him new instructions. Wannu made short work of these and formed an army; he spent the next few months ravaging the peninsula of Liaodong Bandao. His winning streak did not last long: at the beginning of 1216, he had to retreat beyond the Yalu He to a part of Korea that was subject to the Jin empire.

Meanwhile, Yelü Liuge, the rebel general who had rather more luck on his side, took advantage of the difficulties of the Jin rulers, who were undergoing repeated Mongol attacks. Picking up the territorial remnants his unfortunate rival had had to abandon, he gained control of part of the present-day Manchu provinces of Liaoning and Jilin. His followers then pressed him to proclaim himself emperor, but the turncoat general insisted on remaining loyal to Genghis Khan: 'I have sworn to be the vassal of Genghis Khan. I cannot break my oath. To crown myself emperor of the East would be contrary to the will of Heaven, and to oppose the will of Heaven is a grave crime.'

Yelü Liuge was well aware that his recently acquired power rested solely on an unconditional alliance with Genghis Khan: to make this allegiance binding, he presented himself before the khan in December 1215. He was received most warmly — the luggage he had brought with him contained impressive quantities of silk and precious metals — whereupon he offered the khan his own son as a servant at the Mongol court. Genghis Khan enquired about the latest census of the population in southern Manchuria — three million inhabitants — which gave him an idea of its armed forces. Then Yelü Liuge denounced a Mongol envoy who had abducted the wife of the vanquished general Wan Nü. The khan despatched some guards to bring the offender to him, bound hand and foot. The abductor got wind of this move and took Yelü Liuge's rival, Yelü Sibu, into his confidence. The latter put it about that the khan's ally, Yelü Liuge, had died, and then had 300 Mongols who had accompanied the rebel Khitan into Mongolia executed. Three of them, however, managed to warn their master. Yelü Sibu was compelled to flee; he took Yelü Liuge's wife captive and shortly afterwards proclaimed himself king of Liao.

This act of violence against the ally whom Genghis Khan had taken under his wing turned the situation in Manchuria upside down. Just when he thought that he could, with Yelü Liuge's help, take control of this region, he was suddenly driven into a situation requiring that he send forces there. Accordingly, he despatched not only Muqali but also his brother, Jochi Qasar, to the region; one travelled along the valley of the Songhua Jiang (Sungari river), the other took a more southerly route, via the river basins of the Luan He and Laoha He. This new expedition was bound to weaken the Jin dynasty, already on the defensive, by cutting off an enormous chunk of its northern territory. Yet again, Genghis Khan had drawn up his plans to perfection: Utubu's court had just taken in the monarch who was on the run from the besieged city of Beijing, and morale among the Jin imperial troops was very low.

The two Mongol armies had moved off late in the year 1214. The first, commanded by Jochi Qasar, had set off from its position at Qagan Nur, heading north, seized Linhuang and other towns without sustaining any losses, and advanced towards the Songhua Jiang, in the direction of the modern town of Harbin. From the valley of this tributary of the Amur they had marched into the territory of the Solon, to whom they bluntly said: 'Pay tribute or prepare for war!' Terrified, the Solon rushed to make every facility available to Jochi Qasar's cavalry. Two clans had the duty of escorting them onto their territory, and the khan's brother was given as a gift a princess whose dowry contained a marvellous tent of panther skins. This is more or less the sum of what is known about Jochi Qasar's journey, except that, having pacified some of the Manchu territories, he returned to the area of the Kerulen.

For his part, General Muqali, accompanied by several officers (Möngke Buqa, Üyer, Shimo Yexian, and the Chinese Shi Tianni and Shi Tianxiang), had led his horsemen away in the direction of Dading. As usual, the Mongols began by taking small posts which they could use as operational bases in their efforts to put a stranglehold on the large and impregnable fortresses: their activities centred on the area of the rivers Laoha He and Xar Moron. By January 1215, Muqali had already brought the western part of Liaoning under control. A few weeks later, General Aodun dug himself in the northern capital, Dading, which was situated on the upper reaches of the Laoha He, northeast of Beijing. Despite a revolt by some Khitan soldiers, which disadvantaged the garrison quite severely, the Mongols' violent attacks achieved nothing, and Muqali did not succeed in taking the town. Aodun was assassinated by one of his officers in the course of a second uprising. Nevertheless, the defenders stood their ground firmly. Exasperated by this desperate resistance, Muqali gave up his frontal assaults in favour of a blockade of the Jin capital.

Just at this moment, the Mongols had a remarkable stroke of luck: the court at Kaifeng sent a man to Dading to replace General Aodun. Since Muqali's troops were camped south of the town, the officer was obliged to take a detour to reach his post. He embarked on a ship, which took him to the north of the gulf of Liaodong Wan, from where he hoped to continue his voyage up the river Xiaoling. On the way, a Turkish general in Muqali's service, one Shimo Yexian, lured him into an ambush and had him put to death. Then he perpetrated a daring trick: he got hold of the official documents of the dead man and donned his clothes as a disguise, then, since he passed for the officer who was to succeed Aodun, he installed himself in his place. Once he arrived in Dading, his luck continued to hold: he asked to be taken to see the commander of the citadel, who also fell into the trap, putting himself at the service of his putative superior. Explaining that Muqali was in the process of pulling his troops back, Shimo Yexian promptly had the guard posts removed and the other defence dispositions dismantled. At nightfall he sent a message to Muqali and sat back patiently to await developments.

Muqali had no trouble at all in taking the city of Dading, now that its defences had been undermined by his colleague. The commander, realizing that he had been tricked, took refuge inside the Forbidden City — each of the five Jin capitals had such a district, which was the emperor's seat — and braved the Mongols. Muqali was for burying him alive at all costs. In the end the officer was saved by Shimo Yexian, who persuaded his superior to take him into his service. The capture of Dading meant that a great deal of booty fell to the Mongols, particularly weapons, with which they were able to arm several thousand men. The occupation of the northern capital took place around March 1215, three months before the fall of Beijing.

At the beginning of spring 1215, Muqali was still occupied in launching a number of attacks against the Jin, and his efforts were nearly always rewarded with success. At the end of May, he received orders from Genghis Khan to go northeast of Hebei to lend support to Tolun Sherbi. After Muqali's departure, there continued to be fighting around Guangning, Xingzhong and the Liaodong Bandao peninsula, which the Mongols won. The whole region southwest of the present town of Shenyang was the subject of engagements that were often very violent and which are reported at length by Chinese annalists in the *Yuan Shi* and *Mengwuer Shi*.

The battle for Jinzhou, not far from the gulf of Liaodong Wan, involved a whole series of armed encounters. When the gates of the city were at last opened, probably in September 1216, Muqali and his lieutenants were able to take stock of their victory: tens of thousands of Jin soldiers or men allied to the Ruzhen had been killed or captured. Wherever the horsemen rode, wreaking violence, they served to consolidate the nomads' power. Muqali apparently did not as a rule trouble about taking prisoners unless they could be of use to his people: thus he had all the inhabitants of Yizhou and Guangning massacred, with the exception of stonemasons, carpenters and actors. It is interesting to note here the Mongols' early fascination with comedians: such actors were able to find work readily in the theatres in China under the Yuan (1276–1368), the dynasty founded by Genghis Khan's descendants.

By now in control of the right bank of the Liao He, Muqali crossed the river to add to his conquests the peninsula of Liaodong Bandao, which protruded like a wedge into the gulf of Bo Hai, at the border with the province of Shandong. His lieutenants, joined by the Khitan Yelü Liuge, pressed forward with their horsemen to the tip of this tongue of land, a place called Lüshun. By the end of 1216, Muqali had conquered almost the whole of Manchuria, of which he became viceroy. The present-day provinces of Liaoning and Jilin, the extreme north of Korea, and part of Heilongjiang south of the Amur had all fallen into Mongol hands.

The king of Korea agreed to recognize Mongol sovereignty over this region, but was profoundly shocked by the rough manners of the khan's envoys: they had entered the royal palace without laying down their sabres and bows and had gone so far as to touch his royal hands! Nevertheless the Korean sovereign paid a tribute to Genghis Khan, a symbolic one, in fact, because the Mongol emissaries actually paid the entire amount to the last penny: lengths of silk and cotton and, rather unexpectedly, 100,000 sheets of rice paper of the largest size. One additional point worth noting is that, on leaving the kingdom of Korea, the Mongol general left behind him forty men whose task was to learn the Korean language!

It cannot be said that, by 1217, Genghis Khan truly occupied China, but he had certainly brought it to its knees. It was then that he said to a Jin plenipotentiary with respect to Utubu: 'The current situation can be compared with a hunt. We have taken all the deer and the other animals. Only one rabbit is left. Let us leave him alone!'

### China Makes its Mark

The invasion of the Jin empire was a shock wave of frightful brutality, and it left China deeply scarred and bruised. Ten years of attacks by Mongol marauders, raids by nomads and bloody massacres were deeply etched into the memory of the Chinese people. And yet this wave of terror sweeping over China marked the beginnings, small and tentative though they were, of change among some nomad leaders. Men from the steppes had temporarily turned into men of war and in the process they had discovered Chinese civilization. The sight of such a densely populated country, so different from the open spaces to which they were accustomed, of a cultivated landscape and of booming cities: all this could not fail to surprise and impress the men from the north.

The nomads' superior officers made use of indigenous collaborators who, willingly or unwillingly, supplied a wide range of information on the geography of the country or on craft techniques, and who travelled alongside the invaders, interpreting, teaching them new words, and instructing them in new ideas. The Mongol invaders were constantly forging links with Khitan, Turks and other people who were of nomadic origin but had become Sinicized over many generations, a fact demonstrated by the significant number of military men and civil administrators whom they won over to their side. It is therefore hard to conceive how some Mongol leaders, at least, could have failed to be influenced by what they saw in imperial China. One factor in the relationship between the two nations must have been the great fascination that China exercised on the northern nomads: crossing the Great Wall to strip China of its riches was, after all, a sure sign that they recognized the superiority of Chinese civilization.

Of course we do not know what perception the nomads had of this country with its centuries-old culture. We can only guess at the astonishment of their princes and their *noyans* and at the curiosity of their companions-in-arms. One relationship, however, has been handed down to posterity: that between a highly cultured aristocrat, Yelü Chucai, and Genghis Khan.

The exact circumstances which brought these two apparently opposing personalities together are not fully known. It is very likely that, just after the sack of Beijing in 1215, the conquerors would have trawled through the thousands of prisoners taken within barracks, offices of the imperial administration and craft workshops. Amongst them they would have found one Yelü Chucai. As his name indicates, he came from a family in the Khitan aristocracy and had served the Jin dynasty. His ancestors were nomads who had long ago taken to a settled life and become entirely Sinicized; in the tenth and eleventh centuries they had belonged to the ruling class, under the Khitan Liao dynasty, before they were chased from power by the Ruzhen. Yelü Chucai's family had collaborated with the occupying rulers and he himself had been appointed to a sought-after post, that of adviser to King Utubu. Here was a man who had the most intimate and up-to-date knowledge of political realities and who had kept company with the highest-ranking members of the regime.

As was said earlier, Genghis Khan, to hide his greed for booty and power, had let it be understood that he was invading China to avenge his ancestors who had been put to death by the Jin authorities. When Yelü

Chucai was brought before him, the khan told him that he would rise to triumph and avenge the Khitan who had been dispossessed of their power by the Ruzhen of the Jin dynasty in 1122. Far from being grateful for this opportunity, Yelü Chucai replied that for three generations his family had served the Jin dynasty with total loyalty, and that he would find it difficult to change his attitude simply because he had a change of master. Luckily, his proud response pleased Genghis Khan, who was very dedicated to the notion of loyalty, even when it showed itself in an opponent: Yelü Chucai, with his great height and the long beard that lent him an air of nobility, made a very strong impression on the khan, and the Khitan's extreme candour had also worked in his favour.

The two men were both of Mongol stock and it was no doubt their common origin which accounted for the cordiality of the relationship which was struck up between these two very different personalities. One of them, who had probably had pastoralists among his distant ancestors, had become superbly cultured and risen to the highest echelons of society where great things awaited him. The other, a horse breeder of old and son of a minor nobleman, had also ascended the ladder of power, though by markedly different means, to say the least. The bond that was formed between the two men held them together for the rest of their lives.

So in 1215, when he was about 60 years old, Genghis Khan took Yelü Chucai in as a valued member of the court that accompanied him from one location to another in the Mongolian steppes. King Utubu's former adviser was a practitioner of an art that must have filled the khan with amazement: scapulimancy. This was an extremely ancient form of divination that was well known in China under the Shang dynasty, fifteen centuries before the birth of Christ, but probably also as long ago as Neolithic times, and it was found, too, among the ancient Turco-Mongol peoples. Rubrouck and Rashīd al-Dīn mention its occurrence among the Khitan. It consisted in removing the shoulder-blade of a sheep, goat or even a freshly killed deer, scraping it carefully and then placing it in a flame, whilst at the same time 'thinking intensely' about the problem that had been posed. The *daluchi* (scapulimancer) would then interpret the cracks in the bone caused by the heat, according to a code which he alone knew. The Chinese of the Shang dynasty had frequently employed this divinatory practice, using either long bones or tortoise carapaces. Often the soothsayer would inscribe with a dagger the question to which he hoped to get a reply. It is very probable that Yelü Chucai demonstrated his alleged gifts as a seer in the khan's court. He had, as well, some medical knowledge which impressed the Mongols, since it is claimed that he successfully treated the wounds of several injured people who were thought to be past saving, and that he was able to stop an epidemic in its tracks.

Yelü Chucai was indubitably a true intellectual and a supremely learned man, with a strong personality to boot, and his long years of political experience, gained in the inner recesses of the Jin court, had opened the way for him to enter the khan's court and sit at the steps of the throne. The dominant position he attained at court gave him influence and he used it to temper the barbarism of Temüjin and his lieutenants. 'Far from destroying towns,' he said, 'we must knock down their fortifications and then encourage them to develop, for they are sources of wealth.' Yelü Chucai was well ahead of his time in stating firmly that it was better to tax people than violently oppress them. It is hard to understand how such a man could agree to serve the great khan. Perhaps he felt bound to do so in order to protect his life or that of his people, ever at risk from the whims of their capricious masters. Or perhaps he hoped to convince the Mongol ruler of the justice of a morality that he had not been able to instil within the Jin dynasty, and so make himself the apostle of a kind of 'barbarian reformation'.

Doubtless the Chinese sources that tell of the meeting between the Mongol khan and the wary aristocrat, which by all accounts Yelü Chucai was, are not altogether free of certain embellishments. Utubu's ex-adviser played a role that was both ambiguous and incomprehensible: he was a Khitan; he became a collaborator of the Ruzhen, apparently in line with family tradition; and then he took on the guise of a sort of critic of Genghis Khan, conqueror of his former masters. It may be that he was following in the footsteps of 'Master Kong' — Confucius — a reformer who spent a good part of his life seeking a sovereign who would grant him a principality in which he could practise the virtues of his teachings. Be that as it may, Yelü Chucai continued, after the death of Genghis Khan, to guide and instruct Ögödei, the great khan's successor, in all aspects of political administration. Certainly, Yelü Chucai did not invariably succeed — far from it — in restraining the Mongol prince's excessive brutality when waging war, but at least he seems to have made him see that there must be limits and that the nomads simply could not systematically wipe out all settled nations.

As master of northern China and its 50 million subjects, the great khan adopted some methods of administration which were based on what he saw in use in that country. Scribes, chancery secretaries and interpreters who worked at the great khan's *ordo* played an increasingly important role within the ruler's travelling court. The expansion of the Mongol empire made it necessary to employ corps of messengers and civilian officials. In the course of the Mongols' victories, a steady stream of booty flowed in convoys of waggons back to Mongolia, where 'offices' full of accountants, treasury officials and other experts were kept busy valuing and distributing this sudden wealth. Most of these bureaucrats were Uighur, Khitan or Chinese. All of them had, to varying degrees, developed their skills while Chinese civilization prevailed in the land. Gradually they became indispensable adjuncts to the Mongol court and formed the core of the future administration of the dynasty of Genghis Khan.

# 11
# Darkness in the Lands of the Thousand and One Nights

*After the Mongols' invasion, the world seemed as tangled as the hair of an Ethiopian. Men were like wolves.*

Sa'dī (1213–1292)

## At the Foot of the Roof of the World

The war in China had been going on for five years. It was to drag on until 1234. Genghis Khan and his command headquarters, however, had left as long ago as January 1217, leaving behind him his faithful companion-in-arms, Muqali, who was in charge of operations in northern China, with the title of viceroy of Manchuria. Muqali was a tireless horseman and he set about organizing his regiments, incorporating in them more and more Chinese and Khitan warriors whom he drew from the vast well of Chinese people. He was still engaged in this process at the time of his death in 1223. The Jin rulers got involved in a score of futile battles, in which their efforts were frustrated and their strength drained, as though they had been sucked into quicksand. This prolonged war was destroying their forces and at the same time contracting their territory around the imperial city of Kaifeng. The Ruzhen dynasty continued to administer Henan and some districts of Shaanxi, Shandong and Shanxi, although a large part of these provinces henceforth slipped out from under their control.

Genghis Khan had reason to return to his camp on the banks of the Kerulen: some major events were taking place in central Asia. It will be

213

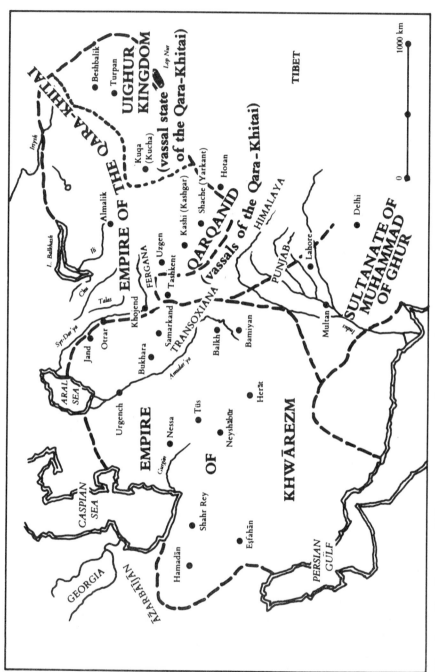

Map 6.   The Empire of Khwārezm prior to the Mongol Invasion

214

remembered that in 1122 the Khitan who ruled northern China had been driven out by the Ruzhen, founders of the Jin dynasty. The majority of the Khitan had come to terms with the new occupying power until the time of the Mongol invasion, and some had even gone over to the enemy, perhaps in the hope of thus regaining the reins of power. But a minority had fled westwards where they had founded an empire, that of the Qara-Khitai, between Lake Balkhash and Lake Issyk-Koul and along the course of the rivers Ili, Chu and Talas, a zone of alluvial plains and lakes, which corresponds with the southern part of Soviet Kazakhstan. The Naiman Güchülüg had found a place of asylum there and even become the son-in-law of the Gür Qan, the chief of the Qara-Khitai. He had not, however, come to this place alone: along with him had come several thousand armed men — Naiman and Merkid — and he was hardly there when he started conspiring against his weak and elderly protector.

In 1210, Güchülüg established some secret contacts with the shah of Khwārezm, the neighbouring empire. Soon afterwards, his new ally, Mohammed, invaded part of the Qara-Khitai empire, but was forced back by a counteroffensive which posed a severe threat to Samarkand. At the same time, Güchülüg mounted a revolt against his father-in-law. With his band of followers, he entered Fergana, took Uzgen, and advanced towards the Qara-Khitai capital, Balasaghun. The Gür Qan reacted speedily against his son-in-law, but had to submit at the Khwārezm front. Simultaneously a rebellion broke out among the Turks in the capital, directed at the lords of the Qara-Khitai empire. Taking advantage of the confusion, Güchülüg seized power in 1211 and put his father-in-law under house arrest, while pretending to continue to recognize him as Gür Qan. It does seem, in fact, that the old man was treated with respect until his death in 1223.

But the usurper of the Qara-Khitai empire, a nomad through and through, was hardly the sort to appeal to the settled Turks who formed the majority group in his new empire. His political blunders, along with the religious persecution that he organized, set off a whole series of disturbances. Güchülüg, who was a Nestorian Christian, wanted, in effect, to force the Moslems in the cities of Hotan and Kashi (formerly called Kashgar) to renounce their faith and to embrace Nestorianism or Buddhism, which seems to have been his wife's religion. The imam of Hotan was crucified at the very door of the Koranic school.

A little later, Güchülüg ordered the assassination of the king of Yining (Gulja), who had paid homage to Genghis Khan. It was thus that he was now to come up against Genghis Khan. The widow and son of the prince of Gulja fended off the usurper for a time and then called on the khan for assistance. The opportunity was doubly advantageous for the khan: at the same time as ridding himself of a nuisance, he could come promptly and gallantly to the aid of a kingdom which was favourably disposed towards him.

Genghis Khan sent his lieutenant Jebe to assist the widow and child. Then the Mongol leader himself set off in the direction of the plateau of the Pamirs, keeping along the line of the Mountains of Heaven (Tian or Tien Shan), and soon reached Gulja. Güchülüg meanwhile had fled farther south to the Kashi (Kashgar) area, leaving some of his territories to receive the Mongols under Jebe as true liberators. Jebe's attitude, unlike that of other Mongols with regard to settled peoples, was that people and their goods and chattels must be treated with scrupulous respect, and for this he earned the admiration of all. Soon afterwards, some of Jebe's men caught up with Güchülüg at the foot of the Pamirs and there put him to death. The last of his friends and followers were wiped out by the Mongols, who took only a matter of weeks to occupy the whole Qara-Khitai empire. In 1218, all of western Turkestan came within the ambit of Genghis Khan's domination.

One wonders if it is true that, as has been claimed, the great khan was jealous of Jebe's success. Perhaps it was a fear that this conquering general, whose exploits on the slopes of the Pamirs had covered him in glory, might turn rebel that made him send Jebe a message advising him to avoid the pride which had been the downfall of the *tayang* of the Naiman before he lost his son Güchülüg. But instead Jebe proved himself totally loyal: he had sent to the imperial camp a thousand horses, all with white-speckled muzzles, similar to the animal which, many years before, he had killed with a single arrow while locked in battle with Genghis Khan. This episode, even though it has probably been elaborately embroidered, once again underlines Genghis Khan's mistrust and jealousy and his desire for nothing short of absolute power. But here was the khan's lieutenant, with thoughts of carving out a personal kingdom the furthest thing from his mind, smoothing the way for the khan to gain an empire that was at the foot of the roof of the world.

**Murder of an Ambassador**
The annexation of the Qara-Khitai empire brought the Mongols of the time into direct contact with the Islamic world, which they had hitherto

known only via intermediaries such as the merchants, artisans, or diplomats who passed their way in caravans.

Neighbouring the Qara-Khitai empire to the west was Khwārezm. This state had grown up from the little kingdom of Chorasmia, which had long since broken free from Persia. Bounded by the lower Amudar'ya and the Pamir range in the east, and the Aral'skoye More (Aral Sea) and the Caspian Sea in the west, Khwārezm at that time extended into northeastern Iran and most of present-day Afghanistan, and encompassed part of the Soviet republics of Turkmeniya, Uzbekistan, Tadzikistan, Kirgiziya and Kazakhstan. In 1212, following a *coup d'état*, Shah Mohammed installed himself in Samarkand. A minor incident was soon to involve Khwārezm in a disastrous conflict.

A camel caravan arrived from Samarkand bringing to the Mongol khan's court bales of common calico and silk — much prized by the nomads, since they themselves did no weaving — and the sellers asked an exorbitant price for the load. Their unscrupulousness annoyed the khan, who showed the caravaneers some very fine Chinese cloths, in an attempt to convince them that there were connoisseurs to be found in the steppes too; for good measure he also confiscated the bales offered by the Samarkand merchant with the highest asking price. The other traders took fright at this and agreed to offer their merchandise at the price the khan specified. At this, the khan's haughtiness came into play, and with extravagant generosity he paid the caravaneers, gave back the cloth he had confiscated and invited the traders to be his guests.

Not long afterwards, Genghis Khan decided to send the shah of Khwārezm a lavish present: jade objects, ivory, gold bars and pieces of felt made from immaculately white camel hair. Three hundred caravaneers had the task of escorting the load and among them were some Mongol noblemen and three men from Bukhara and Otrar who bore an ambiguous missive:

I know your power and the vast extent of your empire. I have the greatest desire to live in peace with you. I shall regard you as my son. For your part, you must know that I have conquered northern China and subdued all the tribes of the north. You know that my country is a swarm of warriors, a mine of silver, and that I have no need to covet further domains. We have an equal interest in encouraging trade between our subjects.

This message simply evoked Mohammed's mistrust. His reaction was to confine himself to sending back the khan's emissaries without providing them with a reply. This was a none too subtle way of playing the judge who refuses an application for a hearing. Genghis nevertheless made further overtures to the shah. In 1218, he sent a second caravan — 500 camels, so it is said, although the figure seems unconvincingly high, given that the animals were rare in Mongolia until after the conquest of the Middle East. The beasts were loaded with packsaddles of beaver and sable fur and were escorted by Moslem merchants. The leader of the caravan was an official representative of the Mongol court, one Uquna by name.

The caravan passed through the steppes and the sands of the Silk Route before coming to the frontier town of Otrar. There, for reasons that are barely known, the governor of the town had about a hundred cameleers put to death and their merchandise confiscated. As for Genghis's ambassador, his special function afforded him no protection for he was one of those assassinated by the Khwārezmians. The news of the murder took several weeks to reach Mongolia. The great khan is said to have shed some tears on hearing it. Had he simply been following the advice of Yelü Chucai and trying to establish neighbourly relations with Khwārezm in order to further the development of trade? Possibly. In any case, the Khwārezmians' treachery could not go unpunished. The khan had to respond in person.

Just as he had done before going to war against China, the khan set out to invoke Tenggeri and to ask the Eternal Blue Heaven to endow him with some of its divine power. Then, in a last-ditch attempt at reconciliation, he sent an ambassador to Mohammed. But the khan's emissary, a Moslem, was executed and his men subjected to the humiliation of being sent back to his court with their heads shaven. Furthermore, the governor of the frontier town of Otrar, who had been responsible for the massacre of the caravaneers, was confirmed in office. From then on, all attempts at diplomacy were discarded. Genghis Khan decided to 'pursue politics by other means'. Those 'other means' found expression in the use of his horsemen, who had to date been his most effective instrument of policy.

Arab and Persian chroniclers offer rather contradictory versions of the origins of this conflict. Juwaynī and Nasawī imply that the Otrar incident arose out of an independent initiative on the part of the governor and that the shah had no alternative but to back him. Ibn al-Athir, however, places the blame firmly at the door of Shah Mohammed himself.

## Conquest of the West

During the summer of 1219, tens of thousands of nomadic horsemen gathered at Genghis Khan's headquarters. According to the Mongolist Barthold, the khan assembled between one and two *tuγ*, that is, some 150,000 to 200,000 horsemen, trained to the peak of their powers by the war in China; many of them were former fighting men who had since been given additional responsibilities. At this time, the khan could actually mobilize at least 50,000 more men than he had used to conquer China, a fact which suggests that the Mongol army now included increasing numbers of Turkish mercenaries.

Shortly before he was to set off at the head of his mighty army, one of Genghis's wives, Yesüi, pressed him to make arrangements for his succession before he went on his campaign. In a speech of lyrical eloquence, the young woman evoked the perils of war and the possibility that her husband might not come back alive. At the same time, she urged him to reply to the question that all those close to him were asking: who would be his successor?

For every creature is mortal, every being is ephemeral. If your body, now like a mighty tree, should one day lean and fall to the ground, what would become of your people, they who resemble stalks of hemp or a flight of birds? Which of your four noble sons do you recognize as your heir? The question I ask you now is being asked also by your sons, your brothers, and your subjects. We need to know what your wishes are.

According to *The Secret History*, Genghis Khan admitted that his wife's advice was sound:

You are only a woman but you have just spoken wise words to me, words that neither my brothers nor my sons, neither Bo'urchu nor Muqali has ever dared to utter in my hearing. Yes, I have neglected to think of that, as if I myself had quite peacefully succeeded my predecessors, or as if I were never going to die.

The great khan therefore sent for his four sons, his brothers, his captains and some of his most faithful friends, and they assembled in his tent. Then, to open the debate on the succession, he asked the opinion of his oldest son, Jochi. Before the latter could even open his mouth,

*219*

Chagatai took his father to task, saying that Jochi had no right to express an opinion since he had been conceived among the Merkid who had abducted Börte. His voice rising with passion, he threw out the word 'bastard'. Jochi paled at the insult and hurled himself at Chagatai. The two men faced each other, fists raised, seething with a hostility that was, one surmises, the more savage for being so long repressed. People rushed to separate them; the khan, seated in his place of honour, remained impassive. An old servant of the khan, Kököchü, ventured to speak up and tell the two rivals what he thought of them: he reminded them of the days of heroic struggle when there was nothing but misery in the camp where they lived, when the steppes were in the grip of clan anarchy, when Börte, their mother, 'took the morsel of food out of her own mouth to feed [them]'. He appealed to their sense of motherly love, to their generosity. Genghis Khan added further pleas and reproofs: *The Secret History* paints the picture of Chagatai unable to check his tears before his father's admonitions and reports that the two brothers left it to their third brother, Ögödei, to express his view. Ögödei had a reputation for fairness, balance and generosity. Jochi found the proposition acceptable: it disposed rather cheaply of his birthright, but, given the doubts about the legitimacy of his birth, he had virtually no alternative.

It was thus that Ögödei was finally designated heir apparent. The portrait we have of him shows him to have been a sturdy man with an air of severity. He had a very flat nose and narrow eyes and looked quite unlike his father. He was said to have been the favourite son. He was endowed with good sense as well as with intelligence and had a mild temperament. He also had a great liking for the bottle. Ögödei promised his father solemnly that he would strive to deserve his trust. Tolui, the youngest son, declared that he would support his brother to the best of his ability and remind him of his duties.

So the question of the succession was temporarily resolved. But Genghis Khan had made a further decision: 'Mother Earth is vast,' he said to his sons, 'the rivers and streams are many. I shall divide up my empire in such a way that each of you will have his own separate government and all of your tribes shall have distinct zones of pasture land.'

That done, Genghis Khan's army could launch itself forward into the conquest of the lands of Islam.

**A Lightning War**

The khan set off with his four sons and the best of his captains: Sübetei,

Toguchar and Jebe, who commanded the vanguard. In an unprecedented move, he took with him one of his wives, Qulan ('she-ass'), supposedly a woman of great charm who had won her way into her master's heart. This may have been the reason for the favour but it is also possible that Qulan seized the opportunity of plotting to gain the upper hand over Yesüi.

The shah of Khwārezm, Mohammed, had made an error: he had scattered his forces over a huge area. Part of his army was based in the heart of Khwārezm proper, the Khiva-Urgench area, south of the Aral Sea. Another part was concentrated around Samarkand and Bukhara. Still another division had advanced to the borders of the empire, into the Fergana and along the course of the Syr-Dar'ya river. The Mongol army was like a powerful battering ram: compared with this, Mohammed's position was weak indeed. In numbers alone he had a considerable edge over the Mongols, but locally, whenever it came to a clash, he was disadvantaged.

In 1219, when the Mongols were preparing to invade western Asia, they seem to have been quite well supplied with military equipment, at least in certain corps of the army. The Chinese campaign had given them the chance to seize siege machinery and, more important still, to enlist Chinese or Khitan technicians who were capable of using it or of passing on their know-how to the nomads. The Chinese had been manufacturing gunpowder weapons since the tenth century. These included mortars, which were not used until 1280, as well as tubes firing incendiary bombs: these caused such a din and gave off such quantities of spiralling smoke that they were bound to cause panic among the enemy. The Mongols also used older types of engine that dated back at least 1,000 years: siege crossbows mounted on massive trestles, which could fire enormous arrows a distance of '200 long paces', and catapults which could fling stones with great force. While the siege was in progress, sappers would tunnel underneath walls, with the protection of movable towers (*lin*) equipped, like fire engines, with retractable ladders. Besides these siege engines, which were known as 'cloud ladders', battering rams and bombards (small-bore mortars) firing metal balls (*tiehuopao*) must certainly have put in an appearance during sieges, as well as fire rockets (*feihuo*), capable of setting fire to the combustible parts of fortifications.

The Mongols' first objective was the town of Otrar, a walled city under the command of Inalchiq Qayir-Khan, the governor who had killed the khan's emissary. Certain that he would be executed if the battle was lost, the man fought shoulder to shoulder with his beleaguered troops and strove with the last drop of his energy. The Persian chroniclers say that the siege of the city, which began in September 1219, lasted for over a month, and that once the city had been taken the governor shut himself up in the citadel along with his remaining forces. In the end, when he no longer had any arrows to fire, Inalchiq collected bricks to hurl at his assailants. When he was overcome, he was taken, with his limbs tied with leather thongs, before the great khan, who ordered that he suffer an exemplary punishment, of a kind that was apparently characteristic of the Mongols: molten silver was poured into his ears and eye-sockets.

The second Mongol army corps, led by Jochi, reached Khwārezm via the left bank of the Syr-Dar'ya and immediately laid siege to the citadel of Sighnaq. As usual, the Mongols demanded unconditional surrender. When the enemy refused, Jochi's warriors launched a furious assault which continued throughout a whole bloody week. In the end, the assailants won control of the town and slashed open the throats and bodies of all its inhabitants. Next it was the turn of the city of Jand, on the Syr-Dar'ya, north of the Kyzylkum desert.

Meanwhile, other Mongol riders, led by Alaq-Noyan, were attacking Banākat, north of Khojend and west of Tashkent. The Turkish mercenaries who were defending its walls fought for three days and then begged to be allowed to surrender. But no one was spared once the Mongols gained entry into a place. There again all the inhabitants were rounded up. Craftsmen were allocated to combat units or placed in camps prior to being sent to Mongolia, while the women were distributed among different clans. The rest of the population were taken into various Mongol units where they could be useful as hostages or simply serve as a human screen between the assailants and the besieged.

The next city in the line of attack was Khojend, in the Fergana area. Its commander, Temür Malik, had a reputation as a skilled tactician and a man of courage. He shut himself inside a citadel that had been built on the riverside, along with 1,000 élite troops, all determined to fight like lions. The Persian chronicles claim that the citadel was so advantageously sited that the enemy had to mobilize 20,000 warriors and 50,000 prisoners in the attack, though no doubt those figures have been much inflated in the telling. The Mongols had their prisoners build a bridge of boats across the whole width of the river, upriver from the fortified castle. Then the prisoners carried stones to sink the footbridge which was cordoned off by moored boats; this effectively dammed the river and allowed the foot of the fortress walls to be drained. Temür Malik saw these preparations going on and took clever countermeasures: he too had boats at his disposal and he used them to hinder the labourers trying to dam the river and the men who were guarding them. But what could 1,000 men do against the mighty Mongol army? Temür Malik gathered together a few of his bravest and trustiest supporters and managed to board boats on the Syr Dar'ya; drifting with the current, he succeeded in finding a place to land on the bank and, with enemy squadrons in hot pursuit, reached the shah's camp safe and sound.

While his men were picking off the western cities of Khwārezm one by one, the khan and his son Tolui were entering Transoxiana, a region situated between the Syr Dar'ya and the Amudar'ya. They took the city of Nūr by means of a ruse: dressed in the clothes of caravaneers, Mongol warriors managed to pass for runaways and got into the suburbs without being spotted by the sentries. When they reached the foot of the town proper, they forced their way through; the authorities, seeing that the game was up, capitulated, and had to pay a tribute of 1,500 dinars into the bargain. The town's inhabitants were driven out and the place looted. The invading army went on its way, the booty piled high on its carts.

At the beginning of February 1220, the Mongols came within sight of Bukhara, then one of the finest cities in Khwārezm, even in the entire west. It was situated at the westernmost point of the great oasis of Zeravshan, at the edge of the Kyzylkum (the desert of Red Sands) and had been the seat of the Samanid — Iranians converted to Islam — and later of Qarqanid and Qara-Khitai (Turkish) dynasties. The intellectual and religious life of the place was intense and pilgrims came from far afield to gather at the Friday mosque, over the tomb of Ismael the Samanid. Bukhara, famed for carpet weaving, was a commercial centre with clients as far away as Asia Minor and Egypt. Around the town there was a multitude of irrigation canals (*ariq, östang*) and of underground channels (*kārīz*) which distributed the health-giving waters. These waters were brought in via a system of reservoirs, floodgates and dams, and were used to wash the wool and to dilute the dyes used in carpet-making. It took Genghis Khan's army less than a month to add Bukhara to their list of conquests.

When the Mongols attacked, the large garrison of Seljuk Turk soldiers tried to break out, but failed disastrously: all the mercenaries were hunted down in the outskirts of the city and their numbers decimated. In mid-February, Genghis let his prisoners loose on the gates to break them down and, using ballistae, managed to force the defences. Shortly afterwards, he personally entered the city. The last of the fighters still shut inside the citadel were executed and the inhabitants of Bukhara were lined up and made to leave. Any whom the Mongols found hiding in the recesses of the city were stabbed on the spot.

All the Persian chronicles report that the sack of Bukhara was a sacrilege of monstrous proportions and that the Mongols displayed the most terrible contempt for the vanquished and for their religion and culture. We are told that the Mongol horsemen profaned holy places and threw sacred Koranic books into the dirt, while the khan himself burst into the great mosque, believing it to be the shah's palace. The faithful who were worshipping there recoiled in terror as Genghis rode in, shouting to his officers as he did so that it was time the beasts were given some fodder. Hundreds of citizens chose to commit suicide rather than submit to the outrages of the invaders, and men killed their own wives so as not to deliver them up to the lust of the enemy. The *qāḍī* Ṣadr al-Dīn, the imam Rukn al-Dīn, and many other notables of Bukhara were among those who died by their own hands.

Juwaynī immortalized this massacre through Genghis Khan's words: 'I tell you I am the scourge of Allah, and if you had not been great sinners Allah would not have brought my wrath upon your heads.' And the Arab Ibn al-Athir, in his description of the Mongol invasion which he relates in *al-Kāmil fi'l-ta'rīkh*, translated under the title *The Perfect History*, evokes the pathos of the scenes that unfolded at Bukhara: 'It was an appalling day; nothing was to be heard save the sobbing of men, women and children, separated forever as the Mongol troops callously parcelled out the population among themselves.' The tragedy ended in an enormous conflagration. For dozens of years afterwards, the city of Bukhara lay lifeless. The thousands of corpses, too numerous for burial, exuded disease, and so drove away the living. Peasants from the surrounding region sought refuge farther away. Animals, abandoned to their fate, perished. The irrigation canals were destroyed, the fields, left untended, lay bare except for a covering of blown sand. Of Bukhara, its palaces and its mosques, nothing remained except for the ruins that had not been burned to the ground.

### Khwārezm: A Bloody Holocaust

Genghis Khan now moved on. To the west lay Bukhara, still in its death throes. He followed the course of the Zeravshan to march on Samarkand.

Behind his carts trudged the prisoners, forced to work as labourers and helping, against their will, to destroy their own country. Samarkand — the Maracanda of old — was a city laden with history; it had once been the capital of Sogdiana; captured by Alexander in 329 BC, then occupied by the Arabs in AD 712, it experienced a considerable impetus under the Samanid. It was situated at the heart of an oasis and owed its prosperity to a superb system of irrigation.

Like most medieval cities, including neighbouring Bukhara, the city of Samarkand was divided into quarters. Beside the citadel was the official and administrative quarter, with palaces and offices, libraries and religious buildings made of brick and often decorated with the coloured ceramics that were famous throughout the East. Further out were clustered together scores of stalls, thronged with gold- and silversmiths, saddlers, coppersmiths and tanners, all in a fever of activity. Whole streets were given over to dealers in earthenware, to sword-cutlers who produced sabres of the finest quality, and to carvers and cabinet-makers who made articles that were sold as far afield as the most distant Mediterranean ports: the products included steel blades, coats of mail, painted and varnished ceramics, objects of precious inlaid wood and elegantly carved ewers. Even paper was made, using techniques imported from China. Gardens and orchards produced delicate flowers and fruits which were dried or preserved with aromatic spices. Pistachio nuts, dates, 'apples of paradise' (oranges) and melons, according to season, were piled up in profusion on the market stalls of Samarkand. Some traders sent the best melons as far as Baghdad, arranged 'in lead boxes lined with snow' to keep them fresh until they reached their distant destination.

The city of Samarkand was at that time surrounded by ramparts that had recently been erected. The garrison included a great many mercenaries. Few indeed of Samarkand's inhabitants can have imagined that their city would suffer the fate that had befallen their neighbour, Bukhara, 250 kilometres to the west, just a few months before. The Chinese Taoist monk Chang Chun, who passed through the city a year later, noted that

Samarkand is a city of canals. Since it never rains in summer or autumn, the inhabitants have diverted two water courses towards the town and distributed the water along all the streets, so that each dwelling has a sufficient quantity. Before the defeat of the shah of

Khwārezm, Samarkand had a population of more than 100,000 families
. . . Most of the fields and gardens belong to Moslems, but they have
been obliged to recruit Chinese, Khitai and Tangut [Xixia] to carry
out their work and manage their properties. The dwellings of Chinese
workers are scattered throughout the town.

Four monumental gates formed openings in the walls of this famed city
of Khwārezm. One of them, the gate of China (or of the East), evoked the
ancient and fundamental importance of that country in commercial
exchanges, which had for centuries taken place between the Far East and
the East along various itineraries on the Silk Route.

In the spring of 1220, Genghis Khan and his troops arrived in front of
the walls of Samarkand. Seeing how strong its external defences were,
the khan decided to wait for reinforcements: meanwhile he prepared his
battle plan down to the last detail and deployed a curtain of troops around
the circumference of the city. When Ögödei and Chagatai had joined his
lines, driving thousands of Khwārezmian prisoners in front of them, he
called a council of war, where it was decided that the best course of
action would be to trick the enemy into a false impression of the strength
of the Mongols' effective forces. Thousands of prisoners were assembled:
their turbans and their own clothes were taken from them and they were
dressed instead as nomads. Then, closely guarded by Genghis Khan's
officers, the unfortunate prisoners advanced towards the walls of
Samarkand, preceded by Mongol banners. The besieged town's
mercenaries surged forward to charge the attackers. Once again, the
nomads had in mind the old tactic whereby 'out of any thirty-six
stratagems you may devise, by far the best one is to flee'. The flight that
now took place was, however, staged to deceive: the Mongols allowed
the disguised prisoners to fall into the hands of the adversary and then,
suddenly revealing themselves for who they were, they fell upon the
enemy, slashing about them with sabre and axe until they forced their
stunned opponents into a disorderly retreat. After this severe thrashing,
the Turkish mercenaries deserted on the fifth day of the siege of the city.
It was hardly surprising: their pay was erratic, and they were cut off from
the mainstream of the population, from whom they differed in customs
and language; when they had abandoned Samarkand, the town became
defenceless and had to capitulate.

The town's notables went out to the Mongols' front line to confer with
their leaders: they were given a formal promise that all those who

evacuated the city would be spared. Once the inhabitants had cleared the town, it was sacked. A few hundred recalcitrant citizens wanted to hold out to the end: their reward was to be put to the sword, while part of the town went up in flames. As for the Turkish mercenaries who thought they could escape with their lives by surrendering, they were simply treated like criminals, and one Persian chronicler claims that 30,000 of them were mercilessly massacred. About 50,000 citizens were able to buy their freedom by paying a collective ransom of 200,000 dinars. Those who were too poor to pay were enlisted into the Mongol troops, where they served as labourers and workmen, while the most skilled of the artisans were deported to Mongolia, entire convoys of them at a time. It is said that when the remaining people of Samarkand returned to live in their former dwellings, there were so few of them that they could not even repopulate one quarter of the town.

The conquering nomads then headed northwards, gaining control of new territories in Khwārezm as they did so. The khan's troops had only to follow the course of the Amudar'ya, between the deserts of Kyzylkum and Karakum. Within a few months, they were at least 500 kilometres northwest of Bukhara, at the head of the delta of the river that flows into the Aral Sea.

Like the other cities that fell prey to the Mongols, Urgench had an oasis economy. It was the capital of Khwārezm and the centre for a great deal of commercial activity; its bazaars selling herbs and spices, calico and weapons were the outward manifestation of its prosperity. Here too it was Turkish mercenaries who were responsible for defending the town. But here, whether it was because they retained a special loyalty for the shah or because they were shrewd enough not to trust the Mongols, the soldiers were determined to defend themselves, and in this they had the support of the civilian population. Provisions, weapons and water were carefully stockpiled against the possibility of a long and difficult siege.

Genghis Khan charged three of his sons, Chagatai, Jochi and Ögödei, with the task of taking possession of the capital of Khwārezm. They were accompanied by captains who had taken part in numerous other battles: Qada'an, Tolun Sherbi and Bo'urchu. It is estimated that they had about 50,000 horsemen at their disposal. It appears that the khan promised to bestow Khwārezm on Jochi. The khan's son, fighting therefore on his own behalf, clearly wished to avoid unnecessary destruction, knowing that everything that escaped conflagration would belong to him. As was their practice, the Mongols sent emissaries to the besieged city, demanding unconditional surrender. The authorities of Khwārezm rejected this 'offer' and so the Mongols duly decided to lay siege to the town.

The Mongols' prisoners were sent out for a period of several days all over the region to find mulberry trees: since the attackers had no stones to insert in their catapults, they had the tree trunks sawn into large chunks, which were then carried to the foot of the city's walls. Meanwhile, labourers, under fire from the town's archers, were filling in the moat. After about twelve days, sappers advanced, under cover from siege engines, to hollow out the brickwork and thus nibble away at the defences.

All these preparations took a long time and the Mongol high command began to grow impatient. At this point Jochi again contrived a quarrel with Chagatai. Each blamed the other for the slow progress of the siege. The former wanted to wait for as long as it took to complete the preparations properly. The latter was more headstrong and was all for pushing ahead as soon as possible. Both sons set about marshalling support for their own policy among the officers. What they were unable to do by sheer force of authority, they tried to do by persuasion. The rumbling dispute had a disastrous effect on headquarters, however, and eventually Genghis Khan himself came to hear about it. Once again, he found a way of imposing his views: he brought Ögödei in over the heads of the warring brothers and under his guidance order was restored.

As soon as Ögödei had taken charge of the situation, the siege of the Khwārezmian capital was intensified. Once they had broken down the walls of some of the outwork bastions, Mongol commandos were able to force a way in. The defenders had not the slightest intention of surrendering and fought with an unparalleled ferocity born of desperation and a clear awareness of what would happen to them if they were defeated. Both sides used naphtha to set fire to houses that provided shelter for squads of fighting men. Battle was waged street by street and house by house. On staircases in houses blackened by fire, men were chased, cornered, and stabbed and slashed to death. For the nomadic horsemen accustomed to fighting on the move and to sweeping cavalry charges on a grand scale, this urban 'guerrilla warfare' seemed rather unnatural. The battles were draining and wasteful, both of bodies and of souls. Everywhere alleys and streets in Urgench were engulfed in flames from the burning naphtha; houses collapsed and their inhabitants fled. Bodies littered the streets. Mongols, Persians and Turks were united in death.

Having taken that part of the town which was situated on one of the banks of the Amudar'ya, the Mongols still had to reach the other bank. A bridge that had been thrown across the middle of the river was the scene of a tragedy of enormous proportions. The Khwārezmians succeeded in repulsing the enemy, and the Mongol troops lost more than 3,000 men in the fighting.

A ruined town can provide its defenders with excellent bastions and strongholds. From within the rubble of Urgench, the Khwārezmians continued to hold out, with the support of the civilian population, whose sufferings were terrible. In the end, Ögödei decided to set fire to all the quarters occupied by the Turkish mercenaries. The beleaguered soldiers were forced to pull back, but the cost of the action was frightful, as hundreds of men and women were burnt to death. After seven days of constant attacks and while the fires still raged all around, Ögödei's troops realized that members of the town's council were indicating that they wished to parley. One city notable, 'Alī al-Dīn Khayyātī, begged Jochi to show mercy towards the last of the brave men who continued to defend their capital: 'We have seen the fullness of your wrath; now show us the measure of your pity.'

But Jochi had waited long enough and was in no mood to stop now. He refused to make even the slightest move towards peace. He had lost countless warriors and now the desire for victory possessed him. At once it became clear that the battle survivors were condemned to death or to exile in some distant corner of central Asia, where they would, as sure as fate, be reduced to slavery. By April 1221, Urgench, proud capital of Shah Mohammed, had ceased to exist.

In his description of the Mongol invasion, *The Perfect History*, the Arab historian Ibn al-Athir writes:

Everyone fought, men, women, children, and they went on fighting until they [the Mongols] had taken the entire town, killed all the inhabitants, and pillaged everything that was to be found there. Then they opened the dam, and the waters of the Jayhūn [Amudar'ya] submerged the town and destroyed it completely. . . . Those who escaped from the Tatar were drowned or buried under the rubble. And then nothing remained but ruins and waves.

### Death on the Caspian

Mongol chronicles suggest that Genghis Khan was deeply vexed by the Pyrrhic victory of the capture of the Khwārezmian capital: the siege of

Urgench had lasted six months and Mongol losses had been much heavier than usual. For this he blamed the imperial princes who had been in charge of operations and who, contrary to his orders, had seized the whole of the booty in the town without reserving part of it for their father.

The khan sat brooding in the camp to which he had withdrawn, and for three days refused to receive Chagatai and Ögödei. The khan's companions-in-arms at last persuaded him to look upon his sons more kindly; they must also have talked the matter over with the princes, because these two soon presented themselves before the khan to make their excuses. When they entered the tent, the khan exploded in anger. Three officers of his personal guard, all quiver-bearers, namely Qongtaγar, Chormaghun and Qongqai, eventually succeeded in calming their master by explaining that his sons lacked active battle experience and that a few campaigns in the West would soon make real captains of them. To toughen them up, one of them suggested casually, why not send them against the caliphate of Baghdad?

Jochi had not presented himself before the khan. He and his *ordo* had set up camp on the steppes which were soon to be part of his inheritance. But relations with his father apparently remained strained. We do not know whether he made the decision to make himself scarce and keep out of Chagatai's way, or whether his brother and rival somehow contrived to push him aside and have him thrown into disgrace.

This was a time of drama and crisis for Shah Mohammed. His capital had been taken, large numbers of his troops had been crushed by the Mongol avalanche, and everything around him lay dead and bare. Hoping to create an obstacle to Genghis Khan's advance, he had put a scorched earth policy into operation in his own country; it had proved disastrous. Having crossed the desert of the Black Sands (Peski Karakum), he headed purposefully southward until he came to Neyshābūr, a town situated at the foot of the Kūh-e-Binālūd mountains, in Khorāsān. He was assailed on all sides by messengers bringing bad news. Since it was now impossible for him to assemble his troops, he resolved to march towards the northwestern part of his empire.

Genghis Khan, however, now more than ever determined to capture the shah, sent after him three of his best captains, Toguchar, his son-in-law; Sübetei; and Jebe, along with 20,000 horsemen. The Mongols had orders to take the shah prisoner and to leave fortified places unmolested if they surrendered without striking a blow and refrained from showing any warlike intentions. In spite of these instructions, Toguchar found it impossible to resist the temptations of plunder. When Genghis Khan heard of this, he stripped Toguchar of his command and downgraded him to a simple soldier, under the supervision of a trusted officer; he was inclined to have the man beheaded for his disobedience, but his daughter's reproofs and entreaties eventually won him over.

The mounted columns led by Jebe and Sübetei came down from Transoxiana, crossed the Amudar'ya and arrived in Balkh. They had no boats and so used the old technique described by Pian del Carpini:

When, moreover, they come to rivers, they cross them by this means, even if they are wide: the officers take a round, light sheet of leather. Around the edges of the circle they attach numerous rings, into which they insert a cord. This they draw tight around the circumference so that the circle forms a kind of womb-like shape. The hollow rounded border is stuffed with clothes and other things. Then they place saddles and other rigid objects in the middle. The men then sit in the middle and tie their horse's tail to the improvised boat. Then they make one man swim along in front with a horse, guiding it. Sometimes they use two oars and with these they row across the water and thus they cross the river. They drive the horses through the water and one man swims beside one horse, guiding it, and all the other horses follow him.[1]

It took the horsemen of Jebe and his companion-in-arms only a few days to achieve a lightning strike of 700 kilometres and arrive within sight of Neyshābūr, which Shah Mohammed had just left. They took possession of the nearby town of Ṭūs — almost on the site of present-day Mashhad, the holy Iranian city — and from here the two Mongol generals sent out 'arrow-messengers' in all directions to make enquiries about the whereabouts of the sovereign of Khwārezm and to see if they could pick up his tracks. Wherever there was a road that the shah might have had no option but to take, patrols were posted at the exits and at junctions with other roads. Collaborators were obtained through bribery and informers mobilized. The fugitive's scent was picked up quite quickly in the region of Qom, and then at the foot of the Elburz mountains which rise to the south of the Caspian Sea. The Mongol riders were at his heels. As they followed in pursuit, other towns fell into their hands: Dāmghān, Semnān and Amol, on the Caspian coast. Then, all at once, the mounted columns involved in this manhunt arrived outside Shahr Rey, near Tehrān. The

Genghis Khan

city was at that time famed for its skilled potters who produced exquisitely refined miniatures. For the inhabitants of Shahr Rey, the surprise was total. They had believed the invaders to be in the region of Urgench or Samarkand, more than 1,000 kilometres away. Shahr Rey's suburbs and bazaar certainly felt the impact of the shah's pursuers, but the town escaped being destroyed.

The next sighting of Mohammed was at Rasht, southwest of the Caspian, at the eastern edge of Āẕarbāïjān. He was camped there with his troops, but his officers were unable to control their men, who were deserting en misse. The shah's son was, however, able to assemble some sparse forces to attempt a counteroffensive. Nevertheless, the Khwārezmian camp was in a state of utter chaos, with orders being countermanded as fast as they were issued. By launching an attack, they had hoped to take the Mongols by surprise, but the attempt turned to failure as the enemy rose up in their thousands against them. Once again Mohammed was forced to flee. This time he headed for Hamadān, in the direction of the Tigris. Then, doubling back, he headed north. He reached the Caspian shore, thinking that he had at last found a refuge. Not for long: the enemy riders soon burst upon the scene. Running under a furious hail of arrows, he just succeeded in reaching some boatmen, who took him along the coast to the island of Abeskum, near the entrance to the bay of Gorgān. It was there that his strength finally failed him and, in January 1221, he ended his life.

Shah Mohammed had succeeded in controlling one of the largest empires of the Middle East and central Asia. But within ten years the Khwārezm empire had collapsed like a castle of sand. Medieval Arab and Persian chronicles give graphic accounts of the khan's wild fury as he locked horns with the shah. Their epic tone also evokes the greed of the ambitious rival princes, which counted for more than political motives. Nevertheless the khan's devouring ambition does not in itself explain the conquest of Khwārezm; there were other factors to be discerned in it, including the wish to expand economically and to seek new territories which could be bequeathed to his numerous heirs. Being a statesman of exceptional gifts himself, Genghis Khan was shrewd enough to make a very accurate appraisal of his opponent's weaknesses and of the vulnerability of his empire. The Khwārezm empire was headed by an intolerant and incompetent leader; its adherence to Islam had failed dismally to weld the people together; and it was riven by a destabilizing feudalism: all these factors made it ripe prey for Mongol expansionism.

After occupation by the Golden Horde for a century and a half, Khwārezm fell partly into the hands of Tamerlane's descendants and subsequently of the Uzbek of the 'Arabshāh dynasty until the end of the seventeenth century, only to come again under the thumb of the heirs of a neighbouring branch of the family of Genghis Khan. The history of this state is like a harlequinade, a tragicomedy of buffoonery, deception and constant change. It was no more capable of resisting external assaults than it was of containing the internal stresses and strains that threatened to rip it asunder.

# 12
# Islam in Flames

*From the days of the Prophet – may Allah bless him! – until our own times, the Moslems have not had to suffer such evils and such woes. Those infidels, the Tatar, have already seized the lands of Transoxiana and reduced them to ruins; then their throng crossed the river [Amudar'ya] and occupied Khorāsān where they inflicted the same [ravages]; then they marched on Rey and the lands of the Jabal and Āzarbāijān.*

**Ibn al-Athir (1160–1233)**

## Interlude in Transoxiana

While his generals were hot on the trail of Shah Mohammed, the khan himself paused in his campaign of conquest. In the middle of 1220, he decided to set up summer quarters in Transoxiana, in the Nasaf oasis. It was there that the Mongol nomads — along with Turkish auxiliaries, of whom there were increasing numbers in Genghis Khan's ranks — spent some time regaining their strength. The army had been in the field for over a year.

Thousands of nomads spread out over a vast area and erected their tents in accordance with the traditional rules of clan hierarchy. Prisoners were set to tasks of many different kinds: guarding the livestock, collecting fuel, and tanning lamb skins ready to make into warm garments for the forthcoming winter. The most important job was the tending of domestic animals, for, though they were in distant lands where there were wheat, buckwheat, aubergines and apricots growing in plenty, the Mongols had still not abandoned their customary eating habits; the wine they carried off from local warehouses was a welcome luxury, but mares' milk continued to be their staple drink.

The Mongols were interested to compare the local horses, of which they had captured thousands, with the much smaller *taki* of the steppes which they knew so well. Saddles were tried out and the indigenous methods of treating leather with alum were examined. The booty had also included hundreds of camels, which had come to be greatly prized by the Mongols, who used them as pack animals on their journeys through the arid regions of high Asia. The camel, living frugally on grass and spiny or woody vegetation, seemed heaven-sent to the stock-rearers of dry lands, to whom it had been a valued aid for centuries. Not only that, but it was soon discovered that this noisy, braying beast also yielded several litres of milk per day. Depending on its state of health and the difficulty of the terrain, the animal can cover between 30 and 50 kilometres a day and its sedateness and even temper are legendary. Its stomach has five pouches and this is what permits the animal to store up calories and thus to regulate its water requirement and its temperature even in conditions of intense heat: it can lose up to 25 or 30 per cent of its body weight without suffering any ill effects. The Mongols were also very eager to learn what they could from the cameleers about the care and training of the animals: the nomads saw how the beasts were housed, how their tails were tied up in such a way that their excrement would not soil the cameleers' clothes and how to treat ulcers on the camels' shoulders or humps by cutting off the gangrenous parts.

In the evening, summer life on the pastures of Transoxiana was rather like that in the camps of the high plateaux of Mongolia: the men gathered around fires of *argol*, the fuel that the nomads of high Asia also used. The Tibetans and Mongols, living as they did in the mountains, the steppes or the desert, hardly ever had access to trees and so they used for fuel the substance of which they had plenty to hand: the dried dung of domesticated animals. Father Huc, who lived in these inhospitable regions at the end of the nineteenth century, showed a kind of childlike keenness for the continual search for *argol*, essential to secure his own heat and food:

Everyone threw a sack over his shoulder and we all went out side by side to look for dung. Those who never lived the nomadic life may find it hard to believe that this occupation can actually be rather enjoyable. Thus, when one is lucky enough to find, hidden under a clump of grass, a dung-pat which is a good size and has just the right degree of dryness, one's heart leaps up in a little tremor of joy, one of those sudden feelings that bring a moment of happiness.

Around the camp fires, lit with a flint, a knife blade and a pad of tow, men enjoyed games of knucklebone and played with the dogs. Off to one side, some of the men might be amorously caressing a beautiful Persian prisoner. These were rare moments of relaxation and often they would call to mind the men's wives and children whom they had left behind on the steppe. They were moments of sadness too, for there were brothers and companions-in-arms who had died on this foreign soil which the nomads had still, after a year's fighting, not succeeded in occupying on a permanent basis.

Sometimes wrestling contests were arranged in which different clans would compete against each other. As a preliminary, they would execute various arm movements, not unlike those that the wrestlers in the steppes today still perform. Then the contestants would weigh each other up. With naked torsos, each would circle round the other, seeking the hold that would throw the opponent off his balance; then, with a lunge, a wrestler would throw his opponent to the sand, to the sound of loud cheering. Sometimes, too, people would break out in a real fit of violence. The cause might be a stolen knife or a woman, or there might be no reason at all, but insults would be snapped out like whip cracks, and there would be streams of abuse, full of obscenities and totally devoid of reasoned argument. And then suddenly the scuffle would turn into a major riot. Out would come the cudgels and the sabres and men would lash about them at random, smashing teeth and cutting throats. Around them stood onlookers, shouting and barracking, but never daring to interfere: custom forbade it, and so did the *jasay*.

But these disturbances never lasted long and when they died down life would resume its normal course. In the camps there would be feasting on goats cooked on white-hot stones and gorging on strongly-flavoured boiled mutton offal. The weather was warm enough for these meals to be eaten outdoors. Besides, there is a saying that 'dust can be wiped away and butter can be licked away'. The food would be accompanied by wine fermented from dates or wine made from grapes, served from gourds; these had been obtained by barter or simply stolen. Vessels would be filled and refilled to the brim, for the wine warmed the heart and heightened the sense of euphoria. On some evenings, a clan chief or even a humble servant might find himself cast in the role of bard to the camp. Mixing dialects and accents according to his mood, he would declaim a piece of epic poetry or sing an obscene song about pining lovers. Standing there in his pitch-covered clothes, he would improvise a rhapsody, filling the calm night sky of Transoxiana with magical sound; and his listeners, these small, squat men with their dark skins, would be silent, transfixed.

Wherever the Mongols went on their long journeys, they were accompanied by music — songs of praise, epic chants, lullabies, love songs, or melodies composed on the spur of the moment. Some of these are still current today, especially those produced from throat or larynx — known as diphonic chants: in this form the singer can produce two melodies at once, in the same way as a bagpiper can play a high-pitched tune and a deep drone at the same time. It has been claimed that these extraordinary chants — which originated mainly in eastern Mongolia and certain parts of Siberia — evolved out of a wish to imitate the tumultuous roaring of torrents, the murmur of the wind in the dunes and perhaps the cries of certain taiga birds.

For its part, the instrumental music of the time relied on drums, jew's harps, flutes and vielles (medieval precursors of the viol). In one very old legend, the Mongols are credited with the invention of the violin: a nomad, with a young and lovely wife, was a passionate equestrian who would ride off on journeys that lasted for days on end. Put out by his constant absences, the horseman's wife hamstrung his horse to stop her husband from going away. Maddened with grief, the man wept over his companion and eased its death by caressing it gently. Then, taking hold of the hairs of its long tail, he made them vibrate delicately so that they produced sounds that expressed his terrible anguish and that of his horse. Since then, the scroll of the Mongolian violin (*quγur*) has invariably been decorated with a horse's head. This musical instrument has four strings stretched over a long fingerboard and the head of the bow is passed underneath the strings. The resonating chamber is made of wood, covered with a skin. Apparently, this instrument, the *shanaγan-quγur*, was originally nothing more than a *koumiss* ladle fitted with strings.

The bards accompanied themselves on the vielle when they were improvising musical poems or recitatives in which all their heroes were brought to life. Rather like European troubadours in the Middle Ages, some of the bards combined the roles of court jester, wandering minstrel and servant: they were summoned to feasts and weddings. No doubt Genghis Khan, during his Afghan sojourn, heard epic songs composed to celebrate his victories. Seven centuries later, there are still pieces of music in circulation which evoke the exploits of the great khan.

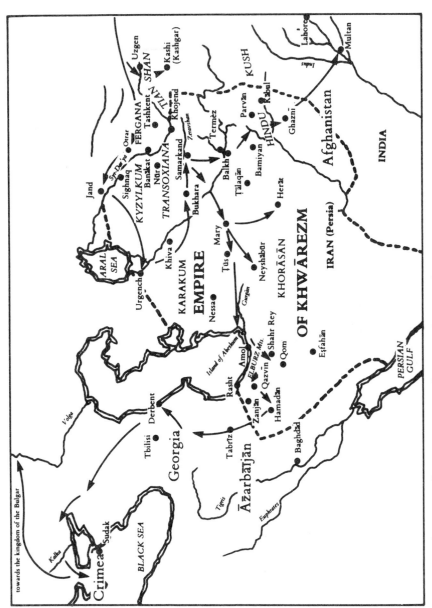

Map 7.   The Mongol Campaigns in the West (1219–25)

239

**Death of the Cities**

Genghis Khan stayed until the autumn of 1220 in the oasis of Nasaf. Then the cattle were herded together, the camels and small livestock which were grazing all around were rounded up and the carts with their felt tilts were loaded. The army was taking up the campaign again. Its first objective, identified by patrols, was about 200 kilometres away to the southeast.

Built at the confluence of the Amudar'ya and the Surkhandar'ya, Termèz today falls within the borders of the Soviet Union, near the Afghan frontier. Since the city refused to surrender, an assault was launched on it. After a siege lasting eleven days, the Mongols gained entry to the city and the usual massacre followed. Some Mongols are said to have disembowelled men suspected of having swallowed pearls or precious stones rather than surrender them.

Leaving Termèz, the khan's army went into Bactria, in northern Afghanistan, in the region of Balkh. The city has been well known for over 3,000 years and was once a centre of Zoroastrianism. Cyrus the Great occupied it in the sixth century BC. Two centuries later, Alexander, in his turn, occupied it and it was there that he married the princess Roxane. The city had been governed by the Sasanian empire, which leaned towards Buddhism, imported via the Silk Route, and secure within its walls were many sumptuous monuments of primitive Islam. Then the Ghaznavid rulers took control of it. By the beginning of the thirteenth century, Balkh was a place of flourishing craftsmanship and agricultural prosperity. When Jebe arrived there while pursuing Mohammed, the Balkh authorities chose to recognize the sovereignty of the Mongol occupiers and declared Balkh an open city. This offered it protection from the ravages which would otherwise have been its lot.

Ibn al-Athir writes that Balkh surrendered to Genghis Khan and was therefore spared. The Persian chronicler Juwaynī, however, says that, although the surrender was accepted by the khan, he later went back on his word and that, true to form, the civilian population was 'divided into hundreds and into thousands and then put to the sword'. In autumn 1222, when he passed through Balkh again, the khan had the survivors massacred. 'And wherever there was a wall still standing,' notes Juwaynī, 'the Mongols tore it down, and for the second time swept away all traces of civilization from this region.' The Chinese Taoist monk Chang Chun, who crossed the region in the autumn of the same year, seems to confirm Juwaynī's version: 'We passed through the great city of Balkh. Its inhabitants had recently rebelled against the khan and been deported; but we could still hear dogs barking in the streets.' According to Chang Chun, Balkh had become a ghost town. The most likely interpretation is that Balkh was indeed declared an open city, but that some incident occurred which led to the massacre and deportation.

The cities of Khwārezm which surrendered to the invaders seem, by and large, to have been spared, but those that refused to submit or that shut their gates as a sign of hostile neutrality were subjected to the most violent penalties. One of the highest costs they had to pay was the destruction of the *qanāt* — irrigation channels — so important to oasis towns. Reservoirs, floodgates, dykes and dams painstakingly constructed by generations of horticulturalists were damaged or destroyed. Fields and gardens were flooded and the canals soon became silted up. In those of Khorāsān, as in all oasis cities, water and water alone is the lifeblood of existence.

Nessa fell prey to Genghis Khan's son-in-law, Toguchar, who had at last been pardoned for having taken part in unauthorized pillage and reinstated in his former position of command. Toguchar apparently had twenty catapults at his disposal. He moved them up to the fortifications of Nessa and sent volleys of large hewn stones over the town's defences, where they caused terror and death; meanwhile, sappers, under the protection of wheeled engines, advanced towards the walls of sun-dried bricks. This type of operation could last for weeks, even months, if the assailants were unable to count on the collaboration of people within the besieged city, or if they failed by some trick to find a way of getting into the enclosure. Those who were defending Nessa filled in the breaches in the town's walls by piling up stones, rubble, thick planks and carts behind the gaps. After about a fortnight, some Mongols managed to penetrate the city, and thus began its martyrdom. History records that the besiegers forced the citizens to tie themselves to each other and to gather in their thousands outside the ramparts, where archers shot arrows at them with the coolness and application of marksmen at target practice. Those who were only wounded were mercilessly cut down with sabres. According to Persian chroniclers, the death toll was 70,000.

In November 1220 it was Neyshābūr's turn to suffer the wrath of Toguchar. The town was famed for its ninth-century monuments and its ceramics with geometric or animal designs, partly Chinese in inspiration. Toguchar ordered his men into the assault, but was struck by an arrow let fly from an embrasure of the battlement and mortally wounded. His troops called a temporary halt to the operation and lifted the siege, turning for revenge instead to the outlying villages, which they devastated.

A few months later, in February 1221, Genghis Khan's fourth son, Tolui, at the head of 70,000 horsemen — mostly mustered from neighbouring colonies — advanced on Merv, now called Mary and located in the Soviet Republic of Turkmeniya. The town had been the capital of Margiana and had later belonged to the Sasanian empire, before falling under Arab control. Under the Seljuk Turks it had experienced a great upturn in its economic fortunes and cultural life: one notable reminder of this was the dome covered with turquoise-coloured ceramics that had been built above the tomb of the sultan Sanjar. Merv's defenders had few doubts about the security of the ramparts even when Tolui's Mongol troops arrived at the gates of the city on 25 February 1221. Tolui, who had 500 horsemen with him, spent six whole days inspecting the fortifications before mounting his assault. Twice men tried to break out of the beleaguered city, but both times they were forced back. The governor then announced that the city would surrender, having received an assurance that the nomads would not commit any violence.

Tolui did not keep his promise: throughout four days and nights a steady stream of inhabitants were forced to evacuate the city. From among their number the Mongols chose 400 craftsmen and some children whom they were to enslave. The others were put to the sword: for this, they were divided among all the army units and each attacker had single-handedly to execute between 300 and 400 persons! Juwaynī reports that those who responded with the greatest ferocity and enthusiasm to this macabre task were the peasants from neighbouring villages who detested the inhabitants of Merv. In the surrounding area, scores of thousands of peasants hid deep within caves in an attempt to escape the Mongols' mass slaughter. Ibn al-Athir speaks of 700,000 dead, while Juwaynī goes one better in this gruesome census and says that one 'Izz al-Dīn Nassaba, 'accompanied by several others, spent thirteen days and nights counting the bodies of the dead in the town. Counting only those who were actually found, and discounting those who had been killed in caves and hollows or in the villages and in the desert, one arrives at a figure of more than 1.3 million dead.'

From Merv the Mongol prince moved on to Neyshābūr, scene of the death of the great khan's son-in-law Toguchar. Here again the Mongols demonstrated their military superiority. This time the city was smashed by a deluge of stones and naphtha-filled incendiary devices. The besieged inhabitants seem to have had some countersiege engines; Persian chronicles speak of several thousand of these, but this is undoubtedly one of their wild exaggerations. It is, however, known that Tolui abruptly terminated negotiations for surrender. A full-scale assault was launched on 7 April 1221: two days later the walls were demolished; the next day the town fell. As at Merv, the Mongols made the inhabitants leave the city and then, to avenge Toguchar's death, ordered 'that the town be razed to the ground so that a cart could pass unhindered right through the streets; and that, to complete their revenge, not even a single cat or dog be left alive' (Juwaynī).

Toguchar's widow and her entourage are supposed to have taken part in the massacre. There once more, 400 craftsmen were taken prisoner and deported to Mongolia. The rest of the population of Neyshābūr were put to death in the usual fashion. As at Termèz, inhabitants suspected of swallowing precious stones or pearls in order to conceal them from the invaders were, so the story goes, disembowelled. It was further reported that several great heaps of heads were made: some contained men's heads; others, women's and children's.

'The last town to suffer was Herāt', wrote Juwaynī, although he did not describe the assault on that town. On this occasion, Tolui spared the civilians. The historians Barthold and d'Ohsson seem to concur on this point. Juwaynī, a Persian, who took part in the war against the Mongols not far from Herāt, gives an account of a siege lasting eight months and the massacre of the entire population. The source of this confusion may be that Herāt was the scene of two separate sieges. In *Tārīkh-Nāma-i-Harāt (History of Herāt)*, Sayfī, who was born in the city in 1282, says that Tolui laid siege to the town for eight days, had all the mercenaries killed, but liberated the inhabitants before setting off to wage war on Ṭālaqān, in Khorāsān. Now a little while later Herāt was racked by a revolt which cost the lives of the *malik* (governor), a Mongol appointee, and the *shaḥna*, the khan's resident minister. The result of this double assassination was that the Mongol general Eljigidei was given the mission of destroying the city. It was during this second siege that Herāt's inhabitants were executed. Sayfī speaks of 1.6 million dead, a modest estimate compared with Juwaynī's figure of 2.4 million! The worst ravages certainly occurred in the town of Herāt itself, where, it is claimed, there soon remained 'not a man, not an ear of wheat; no scrap of food, no item of clothing'.

Bamiyan, situated at an altitude of 2,500 metres, was a stop on the Silk Route between the Buddhist centre of Kapisa and the Zoroastrian town of Balkh. It was a halting-place for caravaneers, an emporium for luxury commodities and an unparalleled focus of culture. In the area round about, monasteries had been hewn out of rock faces since the fourth century. Carved out of the cliffs and painted in bright colours were statues of Buddha 35 to 53 metres high, and pilgrims came to worship them. These giant Buddhas, the most famous jewels of the Khwārezmian empire, are still to be seen today at the amazing site of Shahr-e Gholghola (the City of Rumours). All around the little valleys of Kakrak or Ajar, peasants, craftsmen and others had created a centre of great activity. And it was this town of Bamiyan that Genghis Khan was to wipe out for three whole centuries. Today some nearby sites still bear names that recall the terror that was the Mongol onslaught: Dasht-e Chingiz (Desert of Genghis), Takht-e Tatar (Stone of the Tatar).

In the course of the war against Bamiyan, Mütügen, Chagatai's son, was killed by an arrow. The loss of his grandson unleashed such rage in Genghis Khan that he reportedly fell upon the enemy, sword in hand, without even troubling to put on a helmet. The young warrior's death resulted in a massacre as tragic as it was monotonously inevitable. There is an apparently apocryphal story connected with this event: since Mütügen's death occurred when Chagatai was away on other military operations, Genghis Khan decided to conceal news of the death from his son. But a few days later the khan made a pretence of reproaching his sons for disobedience. Chagatai was the one who seemed most anxious to justify himself, so his father coldly asked him whether he thought he would readily obey an order of his father's, whatever it may be. When Chagatai said yes, the khan said, bluntly: 'Well, your son Mütügen has been killed, and I forbid you to lament!'

An Afghan legend has it that the town of Bamiyan fell into the hands of the Mongols by virtue of the princess Lala Qatun's treachery. The princess was of a very independent nature, cruel and immensely haughty, and she wished to take revenge on her father who was determined to marry her off against her will. She had been pondering how to avenge herself for some time when she heard that the Mongols were on their way. She sent out a message attached to an arrow, in which she told them how to cut off the water supplies to the citadel that stood guard over the valley. The khan had the young woman stoned to death soon after, thus giving the lie to the Afghan proverb that 'a tender neck does not deserve the sword'.

## At the Gates of India

After the death of Shah Mohammed, power passed to his son, prince Jalāl al-Dīn. More vigorous than his father, the son was a brave and intrepid man who was very anxious to take an active role in leading resistance against his country's invaders. He concentrated his troops — about 60,000 men conscripted on the spot and some Turkish mercenaries in addition — and deployed them around the town of Ghaznī, 150 kilometres southwest of Kābul.

The Mongols were daring enough to attack the fortress, but had to retreat after losing more than 1,000 men. Genghis Khan then commanded his adoptive brother Shigi-Qutuqu to march on Ghaznī. Since he did not have sufficient horsemen to risk a sudden strike against their adversaries, who were so well dug in, Shigi-Qutuqu devised a ruse, which he put into operation outside Parvān. He had hundreds of dummy men made, 'mounted' them on horses and then sent this straw army off to one side of the town: from a distance, Jalāl al-Dīn's men thought that what they were seeing were enemy relief forces, and some of the officers ventured to say that the time had come to make a getaway. But the prince stood firm; he decided to fight. It was lucky for him that he did. Shigi-Qutuqu's troops advanced but soon fell back again, riddled with deadly arrows. Moslem regiments pursued, hard on their heels. For the first time in Moslem territory, the Mongols suffered a defeat. Moslem soldiers surpassed even the nomads in savagery; they are supposed to have driven nails into the ears of all their prisoners.

When Genghis Khan heard of the disaster that had befallen Shigi-Qutuqu at Parvān, his reaction was instantaneous. He leapt into the saddle and, followed by fresh troops, galloped towards Ghaznī. Two days and two nights the men are supposed to have been continuously mounted on their horses. They had no time to cook meals, so whenever they felt hungry or weary they made an incision in a horse's neck and sucked off a little of the blood for nourishment. Genghis Khan was full of bitter reproaches for his adoptive brother who, he insisted, had committed errors of strategy. Then, assembling all available forces, the khan marched on the still inviolate city of Ghaznī. However, trouble had broken out in the city between the Turkish mercenaries and the native troops. Prince Jalāl al-Dīn was obliged to retreat westwards at the end of the year 1221. His plan was to cross the Indus and penetrate the Punjab, in what is now Pakistan.

On 24 November, when he was at the river bank, Jalāl al-Dīn saw approaching him the first of the Mongol units that had been tailing him. His route was cut off by the Indus and so he resigned himself to meeting the enemy face to face. But his troops had diminished in number and his possibilities for manoeuvre were limited. Soon his 700 or 800 warriors formed a protective square around him and he came out fighting, shielded by this wall of steel. Gradually Mongol squadrons thinned out the ranks of the prince's men. With the Mongols in their fury now bearing down hard on him, the prince looked for an opening through which he could make an escape and boldly made a dash for it. The enemy saw him running away and the khan ordered that he be taken alive. Jalāl al-Dīn took advantage of a short delay in their pursuit to make for a promontory. He made an amazing leap — the chronicles mention a distance of 20 feet (about 7 metres) — and plunged into the water, to disappear from his enemies' eyes forever. He soon found refuge with the sultan of Delhi.

Genghis Khan, seeing the fugitive leap on horseback into the river, immediately called off the chase. Pointing to the man who was being carried out of view by the current, he held the prince up as an example of valour, a man who made skilful and unsentimental use of his soldiers and allowed them to protect his life even if it meant giving up their own. No doubt he admired, with an expert's eye, Jalāl al-Dīn's horsemanship and the panache with which he had got out of trouble. Some of the Moslems who had followed the prince's lead had also taken to the water to escape from the enemy, but the khan had them riddled with arrows. His clemency was not limitless.

The great khan then crossed Afghanistan again from east to west. Why did he not push his victorious advance further in the direction of the Indian subcontinent? Did he, perhaps, lack boatmen and craft to ferry his troops to the other side of the Indus? On this upper section of the river, the water could have been crossed using leather floats. Did he have another project in mind? Like Alexander in 326 BC and like Tamerlane at the end of the fourteenth century, Genghis Khan made only brief incursions into Indian territory. Perhaps the difficult climatic conditions accounted for this. Like Alexander, Genghis Khan had mounted his raids at the height of summer. In the Punjab the monsoon rains normally fall between June and September, and at this time the waters of the Indus and its major tributaries are still swollen from the melting snows and carry a much increased volume of water. We know that a Mongol raid on Multan was thwarted by the onset of the dog days in 1222: this expedition, led by Bala-Noyan, penetrated what is today Pakistan and laid waste several villages around Lahore, not far from the modern border with India.

By the spring of 1222, Ögödei had finally brought Ghaznī to its knees. As usual, its inhabitants were killed or deported and the city's defences dismantled. Then it was the turn of Herāt, but here it was believed that a decisive defeat could be inflicted on the Mongols in the wake of Shigi-Qutuqu's unfortunate experience with Jalāl al-Dīn. Despite disagreements within the town's command over the wisdom of such a course, an open attack was launched on the Mongols. In June 1222, one of Genghis Khan's lieutenants had a large part of the population massacred, then withdrew to a distance of some kilometres, taking care to conceal his forces. By this ruse he was able to surprise Herāt, where many of the inhabitants had emerged from the rubble or from nearby caves and gone home once the enemy had left. The Mongol hordes now fell on the ill-fated city again and this time destroyed everything that was still standing.

This tragic episode shows, paradoxically, that the massacres and the destruction were perhaps not as systematic as the Persian chronicles claim. Thus we know that when the city of Merv learned — as had Herāt a little while previously — of the defeat of the Mongols at Parvān, the citizens were very quick and vociferous in their response. People spewed out into the main streets of the city, howling down the new governor whom the Mongols had set up at the head of the ruling council, accusing him of collaboration with the occupiers. Some former officers, loyal to prince Jalāl al-Dīn, burst into the governor's palace and killed him. The people of Merv repaired their damaged homes and buildings, reconstructed the town fortifications, and then set about dredging the silt out of the irrigation trenches and rebuilding dams so that the market gardens and orchards which ringed the city could be brought back under cultivation. Apparently there were people left in and drawn back to the town of Balkh also, so that it was partly repopulated after the departure of the invaders. Here too the threads of everyday life were picked up again. But at Merv, as at Balkh, the Mongols despatched new contingents to wipe out all those who had joined the exodus into the countryside or the caves of the region, and who had turned themselves into 'colonists' on their own ransacked lands.

The Mongols appointed prominent people to serve in their pay on the governing council of Merv for the very reason that the town had not lost all its inhabitants. The search for collaborators within this circle of prominent people makes sense only if Merv could have supplied the Mongols with provisions and perhaps even with temporary protection. Besides, popular uprisings motivated by hatred for the invaders, such as occurred in Merv, could not have arisen out of a desert; this leads one to think that resistance movements, however sporadic, must have sprung up in several regions of the Khwārezmian empire. But is there an invader who has not left more or less permanent scars on the country he has oppressed?

In his *Perfect History*, Ibn al-Athir, recalling the passage of the Mongol armies through the Islamic world, uses these words that are full of pathos and of bitterness at the same time:

The events I am about to relate are so horrible that for years I have avoided referring to them. To announce that Islam and the Moslems have been struck their death blow is not an easy thing to do. Ah! how I have sometimes wished that my mother had never brought me into the world, or that I might have died without witnessing these misfortunes. If you should hear that the earth has never, since God created Adam, known such calamity, I urge you to believe it, for it is the absolute truth... No, indeed, I do not believe that between now and the end of time we shall ever again see a catastrophe of such proportions.

The terrible storm that swept over the Islamic world from the east added to the sufferings of the Middle East, which had been buffeted by the winds of ill fortune since the Crusaders had seized Jerusalem in 1099. The invasion of Genghis Khan was the first wave in a tide which was to submerge Baghdad and Dimashq (Damascus) 25 years later. 'The Moslems, attacked by the Mongols in the east and by the Franks [Crusaders] in the west, have never been placed in such a critical situation. God alone can bring succour to them,' wrote Ibn al-Athir at the time when the European invaders were entering into alliance with the Mongols to inflict yet greater torments on the Moslem world.

**Days of Atonement**
Towards the end of 1222, Genghis Khan turned his back on Khorāsān, crossed the Amudar'ya and re-entered Transoxiana, where he set up his encampment between Bukhara and Samarkand. For the first time since he had ravaged the city of Bukhara two years earlier, he now made contact

with some of the people who had fallen within his sphere of conquest. What was it that interested him, that was, in his view, worth getting off his horse to go and look at? A ceramic with a delicate motif, perhaps, or the interior of a mosque? Who knows? What is beyond doubt is that at this time he began to seek to understand this Arab–Persian civilization which he had previously overturned with the point of his sword. As a warrior, he perceived the architecture of the oriental cities as nothing more than a collection of posterns, merlons and loopholes. As a conqueror, among the orchards and the fields of buckwheat, all he could see were sites for his camps and pasture for his horses.

The khan must have found echoes of the Khwārezmian civilization among the people of his own entourage. Among the officers, scribes and interpreters who formed his travelling chancery, and within the ranks of notables who had become collaborators, there were many Moslems — Turks and Persians — who would have given him insights into the culture of these eastern countries: exotic customs, peculiarities of dress or cuisine, craft techniques or religious practices, and no doubt the details he was given would have aroused his curiosity to know more.

Accordingly, while he was in Samarkand, Genghis Khan demanded that he be allowed to attend a prayer service in a mosque. Since he expressed a wish to have the rudiments of the Moslem religion explained to him, some ecclesiastical dignitaries were presented to him. Perhaps they cherished a timid hope of converting this monarch of the nomads and their erstwhile enemy to their own belief. It is hardly likely. Nevertheless, the *khaṭīb* or imams who were responsible for instructing him were treated with respect by the khan, and he accepted the principal Koranic precepts. The profession of faith (*shahāda*) that proclaimed the oneness of their god was very much in keeping with his own faith in Tenggeri, the Heavenly Being of the Turco-Mongol nomads. However, the idea of a pilgrimage to Mecca (today called Makkah) surprised him, according to René Grousset: 'since Tenggeri is everywhere', he could not understand how there could be a fixed holy place. Genghis Khan seems fairly readily to have accepted Islam, or rather the notion he constructed of it in his own mind. This newly discovered Moslem faith probably seemed to him but another facet of the vast and varied array of religions that had come into being after the Buddhism and Nestorianism which prevailed among the Kereyid and the Naiman.

While Genghis Khan and his line have always been condemned for the brutality of their rule, attention has also often been drawn to their great tolerance in religious matters. This tolerance was not a function of Genghis Khan's individual character but was inherent in the Mongol people; unlike the great Christian, Byzantine and Moslem empires, which were based on a state religion, the Mongol empire had no such foundation. Genghis Khan may have been convinced that he had a celestial mandate from Tenggeri to rule the world, but he was quite innocent of any parallel conviction that he himself represented the entire religious faith of his people. On the other hand, with his boundless ambition he was surely eager to supplant the shah, 'prince of believers', now driven from his throne in Khwārezm.

In the city of Bukhara, the khan met two Turks who had occupied government posts at Urgench, the capital of Khwārezm. One was called Maḥmūd Yalavach; the other, his son, was called Mas'ūd. These two high officials of the empire were at great pains to persuade their guest of the merits of good administration, citing the advantages of agricultural prosperity, the maintenance of grain stores, permanent commercial trade and regular fiscal payments into the coffers of the *ṣāḥib-dīwān*, the minister of finances. These were the cardinal principles on which every sedentary society was based. The Khitan Yelü Chucai had put the very same arguments to the khan after his return from the war in China. Surprisingly, Genghis Khan accepted the two men's reasoning and installed them alongside the *darughachi*, the provincial governors. Their skills were therefore placed at the service of the governors of Bukhara, Samarkand, Hotan and Kashgar (Kashi), who acted rather like satraps of the great cities of Khwārezm.

Coming hard on the heels of the massive destruction he had ordered — notably in Bukhara and Samarkand, where he himself went in with his troops — the khan's decision is astounding, to say the least. What was it that accounted for this sudden and total reversal? He had heard arguments in plenty of favour of moderation and generosity from the lips of the Khitan functionary who was in his service: he seems not to have taken any notice of them when he was occupied with the conquest of the Khwārezm empire. And yet Genghis Khan had been amenable to the reasoning of Yelü Chucai.

Two suppositions underlie the notion that the khan's sudden volte-face was an attempt on his part to redeem all the blood he had spilled. The first involves putting aside much of the very weighty evidence that has been accumulated of the khan's savagery and mentally wiping the slate clean. Historians such as René Grousset and the Russian Vladimirtsov acknowledge that the khan had blood on his hands, but assert that he never committed gratuitous violence, doing only what the requirements of war demanded. Chroniclers — some Chinese, but especially Arabs, Persians and Russians — may all have exaggerated the extent of Mongol atrocities. If this premise is accepted, it becomes quite easy to believe that the man possessed good sense and balance.

The second supposition does not altogether exclude the first: men in Genghis Khan's entourage may have gradually encouraged him to mend his ways and repent. Through some of his collaborators — Chinese or Khitan such as Yelü Chucai, Uighur and even Persians or simply Mongols — the khan would have come to know of the existence of principles of government other than his own. There must have been times when he was neutral or even resistant to new ideas, but these men's wise counsels must have gradually penetrated his thinking: the 'Bukhara conversations' thus gave the khan the opportunity to introduce a 'pacifist' policy. This was no devil suddenly transformed into the Good Lord in an attempt to wipe up spilled blood. The change in him can only have been the result of a long process which came to maturation towards the end of the conqueror's life.

### The Mongol Whirlwind

What impact did the Mongol conquest have on the Moslem countries of the Middle East? True, the information we have from Moslem chroniclers is, in both senses of the word, partial, and the figures they put forward quite frightful. Since there had been no censuses of the local population, we do not know how populous the Middle Eastern cities were before the Mongol conquest. Archaeological excavations at the relevant sites do not bear out the chroniclers' very high estimates of the numbers of people within the devastated towns in the thirteenth century, even if one allows for the fact that some of those killed by the Mongols may have been from rural areas, come to the towns temporarily to seek refuge. Thus, although these cities underwent periodic reconstruction because of the frequent earthquakes in this part of Iran, examination of the foundations and the ruins of ramparts and those of houses confirms that the cities of Samarkand, Balkh or Herāt and the neighbouring towns were not capable of supporting very large populations.

In the last analysis, we do not know much about these massacres, be they real, alleged, or exaggerated. All we can say is that, in Iran, the first wave of destruction by the Mongols, who descended like a plague of

---

locusts for nearly a dozen years on various regions of Transoxiana, Fergana, Khorāsān and Tukharistan, left a deep scar and also brought in its wake another trauma, slower in coming but more profoundly damaging: a sharp drop in agricultural production. On the high ground of Iran and Afghanistan, where there is very little river water, agriculture depends essentially on artificial irrigation, based on a network of canals, some of them underground: the *qanāt*. The flight of the peasants before the advancing Mongol troops and the massacres which followed the sieges of the towns meant that the *qanāt* were partly or, according to the region, totally abandoned, and therefore that the land returned to its former state of aridity and sterility. Without irrigation, the market gardens and grain fields could not produce food for the towns.

A contemporary historian, Lewis, claims that, although the Mongol conquest wreaked havoc in Transoxiana and Khorāsān, its impact was less marked in other regions subjected to Mongol invasion because the local authorities decided it was better to surrender with the minimum of delay, and because the general aridity of the Middle East — and thus the absence of extensive pasture lands — were a discouragement to the nomads. It is of course possible that the destruction was severe in some regions and much less widespread in others. Marco Polo and the Arab Ibn Battuta, at the ends of the thirteenth and fourteenth centuries respectively, noted that certain cities had not risen again from the ruins to which the Mongols had reduced them, while others were flourishing. In Iran the invasion of the Mongols pushed back the frontiers of sedentary existence in favour of nomadic life. Whole villages of agricultural workers were displaced by nomads of Turkish stock. Arab geographers and historians indicate that Turkish nomads began to erect their black tents in Iran from the beginning of the twelfth century onwards. The Mongol conquest hastened this process and, in some cases, Iranians who had adopted a sedentary way of life, such as those in the Bakhtiari country in the Zagros mountains, actually returned to nomadism.

Until approximately the year 1000, Turks had been the predominant ethnic group in much of Mongolia. Xiongnu, Tujue, Kirghiz or Ruanruan with established homes in high Asia had cast covetous glances towards both China and the Middle East. But in the thirteenth century the Turkish tribes withdrew to the periphery of Mongolia proper in the face of the growing power of the Mongols. Some went towards Siberia, north of Lake Baikal; others migrated westwards. Gradually, Khwārezm, Transoxiana and Iranian, Iraqi and even Egyptian lands were to experience influxes of Turkish people. Just after the empire of Jalāl al-Dīn, the Khwārezmian sovereign, had been torn apart and he himself had fled in 1221, remnants of his army fell back towards Syria, which at that time was ruled by the Ayyubid dynasty. In 1244, the Khwārezmian Turks felt strong enough to go on the offensive against Damascus and, in July of the same year, to wrest Jerusalem from the Crusaders. This westward tendency of the Turkish population was accompanied by general Islamization. This process came to fruition under the followers of Tamerlane (1336–1405), Genghis Khan's descendant, who had made up his mind to stamp Turkish and Islamic influence on the Mongols.

Finally, it is interesting to note here the first signs of pragmatism among the conquering nomads. They were never slow to take advantage either of individuals or of the administrative structures of vanquished territories. Once the lightning military campaigns were over, the Mongols who had taken part in the first stages of the conquest apparently did not pursue systematic territorial occupation. Their invading army, organized to deliver offensive strikes, was not large enough to be split up into garrisons and scattered widely over vast areas. All the same, from the time of Genghis Khan onwards, the nomad invaders recruited collaborators among both military and civilian populations. The former were, willingly or by force, drafted in as quasi-mercenaries to serve with the Mongol troops; the latter agreed, under pressure or out of political opportunism, to enter the service of the enemy, where they acted as chancery secretaries, scribes or interpreters. The Khitan, who had been conquered by the Ruzhen, were among the keenest to collaborate with the new conquerors; the Persian historian Juwaynī mentions that there were Khitan who had become *basqaq* (provincial governors) as far away as Bukhara.

From the time of their conquest of Turkestan, the Mongols began to bring in their own people as *darugha* (or *darughachi*), who were like prefects or chief officials and were assigned the task of administration and of requisitioning provisions and pack animals on behalf of the occupying power. According to the modern historian, Buell, the function of the *darugha* was borrowed from the Khitan, who assisted the Mongols in the administration of their infant empire. Equally, there were Moslem collaborators associated with the Mongol prefects in Samarkand, Bukhara and Hotan. After the death of Genghis Khan, sons of the Persian chronicler Rashīd al-Dīn served the new rulers in elevated posts within the governing bodies. It appears that it was only during the reign of

Genghis's son Ögödei that a true system of taxes was introduced to levy funds from the populace. And it was not until 1279, when the dynasty of Genghis Khan, in the person of Kublai Khan, finally conquered China, that a systematic policy was adopted: outside the Beijing area, which was the seat of the imperial government and was under direct Mongol administration, the conquerors merely sanctioned the pre-existing system, only bringing in at the top certain senior officials, usually Mongol but sometimes Khitan or Turkish instead.

# 13
# The Russian Campaign

[God] *then sent against us a merciless people, a savage people, a
people who did not spare beauty or youth, nor the frailty of old
age or infancy. We called for the wrath of our God.*

**Serapion, bishop of Vladimir
(sermon given in 1240)**

### At the Foot of the 'Mountain of Nations'

Throughout the winter of 1220–1221, Sübetei and Jebe had been hard on
the heels of Shah Mohammed of the Khwārezm empire; when the chase
was over, they continued their rampaging ride. Heading some 20,000
horsemen, they arrived at the holy city of Qom, which was already a
centre for the most fervently committed Shiite Moslems. Two hundred
kilometres west of the present-day capital of Iran, the city boasted the
famous tomb of Fatima, sister of the imam Reza, and was a magnet for
Shiite pilgrims. Now the orthodox Sunni Moslems apparently appealed
to the Mongol generals to rid them of this dissident rival town. Moreover,
the fragmentation of Khwārezm facilitated such acts and the Mongols
were keen to take advantage of the opportunities. The khan's two
captains did not require much persuasion to launch an attack on Qom.

Zanjān was next in line. The nomads spared Hamadān, which had
agreed to pay a tribute. Then they marched on Tabrīz, between Lake
Urmia and the Caspian Sea, in Āzarbāījān, but there too the city governor
decided it was best to parley and pay the price demanded to guarantee the
city's safety: the transaction undoubtedly redounded to the good of
Tabrīz, which was not only spared destruction but also later became a

capital city under the dynasty of Genghis. For several weeks, the nomad horsemen installed themselves on the southern shores of the Caspian, not far from the mouth of the Kura, where they found fodder for their horses on the coastal steppes. But soon, in the very middle of winter, the invaders jumped back into the saddle and, first hugging the western shore of the Caspian, followed the Kura to its upper reaches and to the foot of the Caucasus mountains.

Wedged between the Caspian in the east and the Black Sea in the west, the Caucasus separates southern Russia from Asia Minor. This part of the world is the location of Mount Ararat, where Noah's Ark was supposed to have rested at the end of the Flood and which is thus said to be the cradle of humanity. Even today this region, which is sometimes called the 'Mountain of Nations', has an astonishing diversity of peoples: between the mouth of the Volga and the Turkish–Iranian border, Mongol, Semitic, Turkish, Indo-European and Caucasian languages are spoken.

At the time of Genghis Khan, most of the Caucasians were agriculturalists living spread out in narrow valleys ruled over by feudal princelings who were jealous of their independence and often bellicose. Georgia, one of the most important states of the region, was born out of the unification of two very old principalities, Colchis and Iberia. Situated between the mountains of Armenia in the south and the Terek river in the north, this state probably arose out of a confederation of tribes, with an admixture of Hittites. Strabo, Herodotus, Xenophon, and Plutarch all say that, from the first millennium BC, this mountainous country was quite densely populated and that its prosperous towns minted their own money. Ancient Georgia was occupied by the Romans under Pompey, in the first century BC, and then by the Persians in AD 368. A Georgian monarch, Vakhtang Gorgasal, chased the latter out and founded the town of Tbilisi (Tiflis), which replaced the old capital of Iberia. In 337, under King Mirian, Christianity became the state religion, and the Georgian clergy promptly appropriated a good deal of power for themselves; their churches and monasteries displayed great opulence and maintained links with other communities as far afield as Greece and Palestine. Under the Bagratid dynasty, Georgia gained ground, profiting from the Byzantine decline and the weakness of the Arab caliphate. The Turks occupied Tbilisi in 1088, but the Crusades were what brought the kingdom its splendour. Under King Giorgi III (1156–84) and more particularly during the reign of his daughter Tamar (1184–1213), Georgia extended its conquests and at the same time experienced a burgeoning, very sophisticated culture on the Byzantine model. It was this remarkable civilization that was to be suddenly confronted with the brutality of the Mongol invasion.

From what the medieval chroniclers say, it seems that the Georgian cavalry represented one of the mightiest forces in the region. Nevertheless, it was decimated in February 1221, beside the rushing waters of the Kura near Tbilisi. Then Genghis Khan's troops suddenly changed direction and headed south again towards Āžarbāïjān, where they raided a number of towns. With the approach of spring, it looked as though they would soon swoop down on the Middle East and lay siege to Baghdad: they advanced towards the Tigris, but did not go beyond the town of Hamadān, which refused to pay a second tribute to the invaders, closed its gates and barricaded itself behind its defences. Sübetei and Jebe therefore took the town by force, sacked it, and finally set fire to it.

At that time the Near East was riven by internal dissension and by invasions by the Europeans all along the western shore of the Mediterranean: Palestine was in European hands and, from 1218 to 1221, the Crusaders who had disembarked at Damietta (now Dumyât) were threatening Cairo (El Qâhira). The Abbasid were under fire from both sides; the sparse lines of troops left to defend Baghdad were incapable of holding back the conquering Mongols at this critical time, while the Arabs were hard put to resist the onslaughts of the Crusaders. Evidently, however, the Mongols' intelligence system had failed to discover just how weak the Arab forces were; it is hard to believe that they would otherwise have resisted the temptation to deal a sudden blow to the caliph's capital.

Jebe and his companion-in-arms thus went north once more towards the range of the Caucasus and on the way met some Georgian feudal lords who had meanwhile managed to muster quite a considerable force behind them. In this fairly familiar situation, Genghis Khan's two captains had recourse to a strategy that had often worked for them before: Sübetei and his riders closed on the Georgian cavalry, then, faking a headlong retreat, fell back in apparent disorder. Screaming cries of victory, the Georgians gave chase. They fell into an ambush set up by Jebe and, when Sübetei rejoined him with reinforcements, they were decimated. The countryside all around was subjected to raids but Tbilisi escaped destruction. For years afterwards Georgian poets continued to lament the ruin wrought by the enemy, and today there are still to be heard many folk songs which recall the dark days of the Mongol avalanche at the foot of the Caucasus.

Following the Mongol conquests in the trans-Caucasian countries, the kingdom of Georgia underwent a slow decline until the Ilkhanid, a dynasty descended from Genghis Khan, settled in what remained of the Caucasian principalities that formed part of the empire founded by Hülegü in 1256.

## Horsemen of the Volga

After their victory over the lands of the Christian kingdom of Georgia, the Mongol nomads, led by Sübetei and his companion-in-arms Jebe, crossed the spurs of the Caucasus range. Then they penetrated the steppes of southern Russia, between the two rivers Terek and Kuma, which both flow into the Caspian. Genghis Khan's nomads were now more than 5,000 kilometres as the crow flies from the sources of the Onon Gol, in eastern Mongolia. They must, in fact, have covered nearly 8,000 kilometres! They had gone this incredible distance on horseback, across regions where, more often than not, there were no real roads, without maps or compasses for orientation, simply by sending out reconnaissance patrols and interrogating interpreters: a ride of enormous proportions which, in the words of the historian Gibbon, 'had never before been attempted and has never since been repeated'.

Living on the other side of the Caucasus, where the steppes spread out in the direction of the Volga, were sedentary people such as the Alans. They were descended from the ancient Sarmatians and had experienced vicissitudes of many kinds: some of them had been scattered by Attila's Huns around 375 and certain tribes, mingling with the Sueves and the Visigoths, had swelled the flood of the great barbarian invasions. Some of the Alans had gone no further than the Rhineland, in the Holy Roman Empire; others had continued into Gaul; and still others as far as North Africa (fourth and fifth centuries AD). A large number of Alans had, however, remained between the Caspian Sea and the Sea of Azov, at the northern limit of the slopes of the Caucasus. In the tenth century, on coming into contact with the Byzantine empire, they converted to Christianity. They maintained relations with other Christian peoples (Slav, Georgian). William of Rubrouck met Alans during his journey to the Mongol empire: they had been subject to so many foreign influences that they had forgotten the Christian rituals:

They asked — and many other Christians posed the same question, Ruthenians and Magyars — if they could yet be saved, when they had to drink [*koumiss*] and eat the flesh of animals that were dead or had been killed by Saracens and other infidels . . . and when they did not know when the periods of fasting should occur and were in any case unable to observe them even if they did know.

Before the Asiatic nomads burst upon the scene, the Alans — one of the tribes of which were the ancestors of the inhabitants of present-day Ossetia — were the allies of Caucasian mountain peoples, the Lezgians and the Circassians. The people of the Caucasus were stupefied by the sudden appearance of the nomad invaders. Kirakos of Ganjak, an Armenian historian captured by the Mongols and obliged to enter their service as a secretary, commented on the terror aroused by the riders from the steppes:

They were hideous and terrifying to look at, beardless, although some of them had a few hairs growing on their chins or their upper lips. Their eyes were narrow and keen, their voices shrill and piercing; their life was a hard one and they were intrepid. When they had the opportunity they ate constantly and drank greedily; when there was no such opportunity they were abstinent. They ate all living things, whether cleaned or not, and what they liked best was horse meat, of which they would cut off one chunk after another and boil it or roast it without salt . . . Some of them ate kneeling, like camels, others sitting down . . . And if someone brought them something to eat or drink they first forced the person offering it to eat or drink some of it himself, as if they were afraid they were being given some fatal poison.

Soon some Kipchak Turks came to range themselves alongside the Alans and other mountain people of the Caucasus: the Kipchaks are sometimes known as the Comani or Kuman and the Russians called them Polovtsy. They lived as nomads in the steppes to the south of the Volga. The coalition between these two peoples formed quite a barrier to the advance of the Mongol cavalry. Genghis Khan's men seem to have been remarkably well informed, because they were aware that their first task must be to break up this ill-assorted mass. They sent emissaries to the Kipchaks and these came leading carts filled with merchandise. It was hoped that they could thus bribe the Kipchaks into betraying their allies. The Kipchaks did indeed defect and the ensuing fragmentation of the Alans and their Caucasian allies caused their defeat. Shortly afterwards,

Sübetei and Jebe's men rode off to attack the Kipchak encampments, and devastated them in turn. Naturally they also recovered the booty which they had sent the Kipchaks to buy their desertion.

Some of the Kipchaks were becoming Christianized, and certain tribes maintained relations with the Slav populations of southern Russia: one of the Kipchak chiefs, Kotian by name, had given one of his daughters in marriage to the prince of Galich, Mstislav. After their defeat, the Kipchaks cast around for sources of assistance and managed, by virtue of the family union, to obtain a political treaty with the Russians. The consequence was that the Mongols left trans-Caucasia bound for the lower Don basin.

**The Battle of the Kalka**
Thirteenth-century Russia — sometimes called Kiev Russia, from the name of one of its principalities whose capital was Kiev — was as fragmented as a jigsaw puzzle. Bounded in the north by the Baltic Sea and in the south by the middle or upper reaches of the rivers Bug, Dnepr, Donets and Don, it shared a border on the western front with the Polish and Lithuanian principalities. In the southwest the Russians were contained by the Hungarians and the Wallachians, while the great desert or semidesert steppes of the southern Ukraine and the lands of the lower Volga were in the hands of Polovtsian and Pecheneg nomads, and the huge open spaces of the northeast in those of Finnish–Hungarian tribes.

The territory was thus confined to just a part of European Russia, and was divided into a multiplicity of principalities which rivalled one another to varying degrees: Kiev, Vladimir, Suzdal, Ryazan, Pereyaslavl, Smolensk, Novgorod, Polotsk, Galich, Chernigov, etc. Each of the princes (*knyaz'*) came to the throne by a system of collateral succession (from older brother to younger; from uncle to nephew) in such a way that no principality ever quite came to the end of a line, since, through marriages and deaths, younger members of a family succeeded to vacant seats, obtaining a kind of advancement up the 'genealogical ladder'. This complicated system did not permit the principalities to maintain real political relationships which could be followed with any continuity, and it was not until 1722 (in the reign of Peter the Great) that the right of the sovereign to designate his successor came to be accepted. Russia had come under Christian influence from the end of the tenth century onwards and the Church had helped to regulate the various social classes: nobles, free men, semifree peasants and slaves. The social hierarchy was not quite as firmly set and sealed as in western Europe, and people had the freedom and flexibility to wander along the rivers and in the forests and colonize virgin land when they found it.

The virgin steppe lands led, by way of a no-man's-land, to another world, that of the nomads. This world spelt peril. For centuries the southern Slavs had had to contend with numerous incursions by Asiatic nomads. Between 1068 and 1210, the Polovtsians launched almost fifty armed raids, penetrating as far as the walls of Kiev in 1096. Though there were peace treaties, links by marriage and agreements to pay tributes, the nomad hordes continued to sweep in almost without a pause. The Mongols were better organized, better led, and more daring, and were thus able to administer the *coup de grâce* to the Kiev civilization, which was already undermined by gaps in its institutional structure and by jealous rivalry among its princes.

Having received an appeal for help from the Kipchaks, the prince of Galich had succeeded in persuading the princes of Smolensk, Chernigov and Kiev to join forces to intervene. Jebe and Sübetei sent the princes envoys bearing proposals that an alliance be formed against Kotian's Kipchaks. It is remarkable how well informed the Mongols were. They adduced two arguments: the Kipchaks had always been enemies of the Russians and now here was an opportunity to attack them from both sides; and the Kipchaks were idolaters, unlike the Mongols who worshipped Tenggeri, the Cerulean Sky. But the Russians rejected their offer and, at a stroke, the initiative passed out of the hands of diplomats and into those of military commanders.

Prince Mstislav, having mobilized his army in Galich, his principality, advanced along the Dnestr towards the steppes that dominated the Crimea. The other princes descended the Dnepr towards the Black Sea. The various army corps — which totalled as many as 80,000 men — met along the upper reaches of the Dnepr, in the vicinity of Khortitsa, near Aleksandrov. Confronted with such numbers of Russian troops, the Mongols at first apparently fell back: they drifted back in some disorder, though they remained close by. The Russian princes, along with some Kipchak corps, decided to pursue them to force them to give battle. Numbering only 20,000 men, the Mongols lay low for nine days; squadrons now and then made small forays but then retreated again to a safe distance. The Russians were within sight of the Kalka, a river that flows into the Sea of Azov, when they caught up with the nomads led by Jebe and Sübetei, in the area of the modern town of Donetsk.

Genghis Khan

Mstislav's troops and the Kipchak men were ready for the fray, but the other princes were still some way behind. Without waiting for the other troops to join them, Mstislav and his forces went ahead and attacked the Mongols in May 1223. The result was a defeat. The Mongols had chosen a site that favoured themselves and there waited patiently for the enemy to appear; here it was that many Russians and Kipchaks fought and died. The prince of Galich is said to have barricaded himself inside his camp with his followers and to have fought bravely for three days before giving himself up. The Mongols had him executed in revenge for their emissaries whom the Russian princes had had stabbed to death. The wretched Mstislav was wrapped up in carpets and suffocated, an honourable means of execution among the nomads since it avoided the spilling of blood and was thus a way of demonstrating the respect in which the victim was held.

The battle of Kalka — an epic battle by any standards — left a deep impression on the Russians and ultimately spelt the beginning of the nomad invasion and occupation — the *tatarchina*.

Seeing the defeat of the prince of Galich and his Kipchak allies drained the courage from the Russian princes of Chernigov, Smolensk, and Kiev and they abandoned their plans to pursue the Asiatic invaders. Survivors described to them the horror of the disaster, the first the Russians had suffered at the hands of the Mongols. This defeat was the source and inspiration of many narratives and chronicles, of which the best known are *Slovo o Pogibeli Russkoy Zemli* (*The Story of the Ruin of the Russian Land*), *Ipatevskaya Letopis* (*Hypathean Chronicle*) and *Nikonovskaya Letopis* (*Chronicle of Nikon*). All of them conjure up dreadful images of the Russian people's sufferings under the lash of the Mongol whip.

The Russians had some horsemen, but for the most part their troops were infantrymen. Almost all the warriors wore helmets, and some had coats of mail, but only the noblemen and the rich possessed full armour. The Russian knights, sheathed in iron and bearing aloft lances with streaming banners, were an impressive sight. From a distance their steel rampart looked impenetrable. Behind each shield every fighting man concealed a heavy axe, a sharp sword and a spear tapering to a deadly point. To the Mongols, who had the chance to observe them over several days, these warriors looked like dogs with yellowish fur, leaping up to attack the ruddy-faced intruders. The nomads, who had so far won every battle where troops had been mustered against them, now weighed up the strength of the Russians' effective forces, but they knew that these warriors lacked mobility in hand-to-hand fighting as well as in large-scale tactical movement. They were slower than themselves and less well organized.

At a given signal, immediately transmitted by means of small flags which were dispersed among the ranks of their mounted squadrons, the Mongol riders seemed to tremble on their mounts. There were some shouted orders, then silence fell on the huge battlefield lit by the late spring sunshine. And suddenly there came the commands each man had been waiting for for days. The nomad cavalry launched its troops into the assault. The Russians were amazed suddenly to see these small horses galloping towards them. Little enough time to register their surprise before they had to deal with the riders — brown-skinned men wearing odd garments, who swarmed around the camps, twisting and turning this way and that. The very earth shook under the impact of thousands of hooves. The nimble little horses stirred up a cloud of dust that drowned men and animals. The charge of the cavalry was like a tidal wave.

Now the Mongols were 100 metres away, now barely 50. All at once a volley of arrows fell on the Russians, cutting swaths through their lines. The Russians had too few bows and could not retaliate. Then, in an instant, the tumultuous band of archers melted away, leaving the place empty. Men took stock of their dead, collected the arrows that had fallen to the ground and, in a gesture of rage, snapped them in two before throwing them away. Where were the enemy now? Obviously, they must still be quite near. On the battlefield itself chaos and panic reigned. Then the horsemen appeared out of nowhere and charged again. Showers of arrows caused more terror and further deaths and injuries. Along the battle-lines the air rang with cries and oaths. The nomads began to bring extra pressure to bear on one wing. The Russians stood waiting for minutes on end for orders that did not come, while at the same time more Mongol marksmen surged forward and let fly some arrows before withdrawing again.

The men on the little black-and-grey horses relentlessly kept up their harassment. There were brief commands and shouts hurled out against a background of ceaseless uproar and turmoil. The second rank of Russians gave way under a frontal assault. At last their orders came and were heard above the noise, but they were incomprehensible. The lead fighters fell back before the enemy and everyone else followed. Mongol horsemen were everywhere, brandishing their swords, thrusting their spears forward, slashing at the wounded and seeking out in the mêlée anyone who, having thrown any last hope to the winds, was simply running away.

As far as the Russian cavalry was concerned, the battle was even more desperate than for the infantrymen. The horsemen put up strong resistance to the sudden charges and swirling movements of the attacking nomads, striking out at random and working themselves up into a frenzy by uttering shrill cries and roaring at the top of their voices. Amid the confusion, the Russians nevertheless tried to marshal their strength again and come back into the charge with bold resolution. These great medieval battles always consisted of a great many individual encounters when every action automatically triggered a reaction geared towards survival and defence. It was a terrible game in which the score was the mounting death toll; a kind of street carnival in which all the dancers doubled as killers. In a soldier's hands every piece of metal became an instrument of death: swords to hack off legs, axes to stave in skulls, lances to burrow into bellies and rip out entrails, bits of which would be carried off trailing from the edge of a blade; even a broken shield, wielded with enough fury, could smash a face.

And then suddenly the swarms of riders withdrew. It was the last day of May 1223. Here and there men from both sides of the battle dragged themselves along the ground, as though waiting for the fatal blow that would deliver them from their agony, but no one had time to care for the wounded. Within a few days there was no longer even anyone left who would trouble with the dead, such was the fear that pervaded the whole area of the battlefield of Kalka. Only the wild animals wandering on the steppe or the wooded slopes dared to come near the deserted site. And the ultimate quarry belonged to the wolves and crows alone.

Sübetei and Jebe's men rested for a short time, and then headed westwards and down into the Crimea, where they soon reached the port of Soldaia (Sudak). Like many of the sites scattered around the shores of the Black Sea, the town was an ancient Greek colony. The Genoese had used it as a commercial clearing house, where they obtained furs and slaves to resell in various Mediterranean ports. The Mongol nomads plundered the warehouses of Soldaia, but on this occasion they did not venture beyond into the European world.

At the end of 1223, the invaders went northwards again, following the course of the Volga, foraging for food wherever they could. They arrived thus at the upper section of the great river, where the Vyatka and the Kama flow into it. Here lived the Bulgars, a Turkish people, who had founded a kingdom that prospered through trade in forest and fishing products. In the twelfth century the Bulgars had turned towards Islam and Baghdad had sent them scholars of Koranic law and architects. Suvar and Bolgar, which were both on the caravan routes, were fine cities with ornate mosques and a number of notable buildings. The Bulgar kingdom struck its own coins and traded in precious goods such as amber and walrus ivory, no doubt purchased from the Finns somewhere in the east (Khwārezm). The Bulgars, who also sold sable furs, boasted some fine skilled furriers. Their prosperity stirred rivalry among certain Russian principalities, where covetous eyes were cast at the game-rich lands of the upper Volga.

This was the situation in the Bulgar kingdom when the Mongols burst upon the scene. The Mongol armies routed their adversaries with ease and emptied their towns of all their riches. Then, loaded with valuable booty, the nomads went down the Volga again, crossed over to the eastern side and, skirting round the southern edge of the Urals, entered the territory of another Turkish people, the Qanglin, who were settled in the very north of Kazakhstan, in the region of modern Ural'sk. These people, too, succumbed to the Mongols. The nomads then travelled in stages to rejoin the great army of Genghis Khan, which was camped a little way north of the Syr-Dar'ya, and from there they all set off again, bound for central Asia.

In 1237, ten years after the death of Genghis Khan, the Mongols returned to Russia, which they then occupied for the next two and a half centuries. In the lands to the west of the Irtysh, Batu, Genghis's grandson, was to found the Kipchak khanate — better known as the Golden Horde. The khanate comprised the kingdom of the Bulgars on the Volga, southern Russia and the Crimea, and the more it came under Turkish influence the more it became Islamized. Batu was at variance with his brother Orda and his White Horde, a discord which developed into a rivalry between them, and in due course the Golden Horde fell under the impact of the Crimean khanate in 1502.

To lament the misfortune that had befallen their homeland, the Russians simply did not have enough words, tears or blood. For generations, popular narratives, chronicles and poems went on recalling the *tatarchina*:

They devastated the churches of God and before the consecrated altars they spilled quantities of blood. And none was spared, all perished equally and drank the cup of death to the lees. No one remained to sob or weep for the dead — neither father or mother for their children, nor children for their father and mother, neither brother for brother, nor cousin for cousin — for all without exception lay lifeless. And this happened in requital of our sins (*The Story of the Destruction of Ryazan*, by Batu).

# 14
# Return to the Steppes

*I have committed many acts of cruelty and had an incalculable
number of men killed, never knowing whether what I did was
right. But I am indifferent to what people may think of me.*

**Words attributed to Genghis Khan**

Genghis Khan had left the Russian campaign in the hands of his captains
and had not himself taken part. He had stayed behind in Khwārezm. Now
aged about 65, he was no longer the warrior in the prime of life who had
set off on expeditions against the Merkid or the Naiman. He had entered
the autumn of his years.

For a long time Genghis Khan had been listening with interest to
rumours that were then current in northern China about a monk,
Qiuchuji, a disciple of Wangzhi and an alumnus of the Quanzhen school,
who was supposed to possess supernatural powers, not the least of which
was the ability to achieve immortality. He was also known by his
descriptive name of Chang Chun — Eternal Spring — and had become a
monk in 1166. After his studies in the province of Shandong, where
Confucius had been born five centuries before Christ, Chang Chun had
followed the teachings of Wangzhi, founder of a Taoist sect, the Absolute
Sublimation, which was known for its asceticism. Little is known of
Chang Chun, except that he forbade the consumption of fruit and of tea,
and that it was his moral authority that had taken root in a large part of
northern China. In 1188 he had even been received at the court of Beijing,
where he had been asked to stay on as adviser to the sovereign. But the

monk chose to be out of the limelight and returned to live near Ninghai, in Shandong, in 1191.

Chang Chun's brand of Taoism had been founded by Laozi, the Old Master, who lived in the sixth century BC. Taoism was a shoot that had sprung up out of the earth of Confucianism; it was an 'atheistic religion', originally in use among the mandarins, but it soon spread and took hold among all classes of Chinese society. The Taoist school emerged out of a religious crisis which, between the fifth and third century BC, caused much disturbance in Chinese intellectual circles. Opposed to the official religion and its concepts regarding the relationships between men and gods, many intellectuals were beginning seriously to question the notion of sacrificial practices, which reduced the cult to a form of negotiation between human beings and their gods, who were devoid of any conscience and acted only in response to occult forces. Weary of an official religion whose sole purpose was to ensure material and political stability, they were now seeking one which took into account individual conscience, the inner life and spiritual happiness. From this need arose the idea of a communion between the microcosm, which is the human being, and his respondent, the macrocosm of the universe: the interaction opens the doors that lead to Tao, the 'Heavenly Way'. The Taoists firmly believe in the permanent transformation of the external principles of this Way (*dao* or *tao*), the *yin* and the *yang*, a belief which implies rigorous conformity with the natural order of things. Where Confucian law and morality constrain, Taoism liberates, offering an ideal life in which the individual discovers perfect simplicity in conforming with the rhythm of the universe.

According to the Taoist canonical works — the *Daode Jing* (*The Book of the Way and its Power*), attributed to Laozi, the *Liezi* (*The* [Book of] *Master Lie*) and the *Zhuangzi* (*The* [Book of] *Master Zhuang*) — there are different states which souls may enter after death: life within the burial chamber, existence at the heart of the Nine Obscurities of the Yellow Sources, and happiness in the presence of the Lord On High. Taoism generates a whole pantheon: naiads in the springs, genii in the mountains, immortal and blessed. This doctrine was probably elaborated by librarians and archivists working in manorial houses, a company of people who were fiercely possessive and protective of their knowledge as well as of other sciences and technical matters to which at that time only a select few were privy: medicine, pharmacology, dietetics, astrology, magic and fortune-telling. Clearly, it was this aspect, overlaid on a naturalistic and monistic base, that attracted new adherents to Taoism, at the expense of Confucianism, the religion of the establishment and almost the religion of state.

From the seventh century onwards, Taoism had a clerical hierarchy and numerous temples. Certain members of the upper classes in search of religious revival were quick to embrace it. Its complex rituals, its large body of liturgy, and its ascetic practices inevitably appealed to princes, rulers and intellectuals who had the ability to apply themselves to its study. Added to this was the fact that there were claimed to be Taoist practices that would transform impure water into drinking water, achieve communication with heavenly divinities and hypostases of the supreme Unity, or provide recipes for potions that would ensure immortality. A number of Taoists were therefore very famous, notably those from the provinces of Sichuan or Shandong, where the religion had initially been developed. And it was from Shandong that Chang Chun came too. The man was not merely an alchemist doubling as an astrologer; he was also a thinker of great intellectual rigour.

Genghis Khan thus sent to China for the holy man whose fame had spread as far as the Mongolian steppes. He who had, in Juwaynī's words, become 'master of the world' now apparently wanted to conquer other domains than those that could be won by the sword.

## Chang Chun's Journey

The Chinese monk was aged 72 when he received the message from the khan. Despite his age, he decided to undertake the long voyage which would lead him to the Mongol monarch's travelling court. That he did so was rather surprising, since he would be brought face to face with the conqueror of his own country, the man who, only a few years earlier, had been responsible for such large-scale destruction. When the khan's envoys proposed that he make the journey in a cart, travelling beside other vehicles bringing women of pleasure bound for the nomads' court, Chang Chun is supposed to have objected violently. Probably there was some lingering trace of Confucian philosophy in him that made him publicly reject the suggestion that a scholar should be put on the same footing as women!

In March 1221, before the last squalls of winter had died away, Chang Chun thus left the region of Beijing and set off along the tracks that led into ever more arid countryside. The Taoist monk was accompanied by one of his disciples who carefully noted down all the events, large and small, that punctuated their long journeys through high Asia. It was not the first time that Chinese explorers had covered this area. In the year 138, Zhang Qian had already met the Yuezhi 'barbarians' in the course of a journey that took him to Sogdiana and Fergana. Buddhist monks had gone as far as India between the fourth and the eleventh century, and we still have the accounts of the travels of Faxian (around 414) and of Xuanzang (*Papers on the Occidental Countries*), written in the middle of the seventh century. Then, under the Tang dynasty, Xu Kangzu and Song Huan, two imperial commissioners, wrote reports on Dzungaria and Turkestan, and on the Ruzhen and Khitan peoples.

Chang Chun's narrative (*Chang Chun Zhenren Xiyulu* [*The Pilgrimage to the West of the Adept Chang Chun*]), edited by his disciple Li Zhichang, is an exact account of his voyage which in many respects tallies with the descriptions left by Europeans such as William of Rubrouck and Saint-Quentin. The story retraces, *li* by *li*, the astonished reactions of an intellectual who was leaving Beijing to go to meet the greatest 'barbarian' sovereign in the inhabited world.

At the end of April 1221, when winter was drawing to an end, Chang Chun arrived at the banks of the river Kalka, where the camp of Temüge, the khan's younger brother, had been set up:

The ice was beginning to melt and the new grass was beginning to spring up in the soil. A wedding was being celebrated and several Mongol chiefs had just arrived with some mares' milk. We saw several hundred dark-coloured carts and felt tents lined up. On the seventh day, the master [Chang Chun] was presented to the prince, who asked him for the means of prolonging life.

Chang Chun was not invited to the wedding which was being held inside the nomads' camp, but Temüge had some hundred horses and cattle sent to the Taoist monk so that he would have both food and transport until his convoy reached the Afghan border where the great khan then was. The traveller had not, incidentally, chosen to take the Silk Road, which was the shortest route from Beijing to the banks of the Amudar'ya. After Luoyang (or Lo-yang, cradle of Chinese culture) the Silk Road split into two different routes: one passed north of the Taklimakan Shamo, the other south, through Khotan and Yarkand (now Hotan and Shache or Yarkant, respectively). Chang Chun steered clear of both these tracks and went a long way to the north, across Mongolia and Dzungaria. This significant detour raises questions about the validity of the Xixias' displays of independence and about the degree of real control the Mongols had in western China: the empire of the Xixia people, Minyak, had been reduced to vassalage by Genghis Khan after many conflicts (from 1205 to 1209), but, in fact, refused to deliver up cavalry contingents to the overlords.

Having followed the Kerulen river along its left bank, Chang Chun then turned westward, bound for the upper reaches of the Orhon Gol. By mid-summer he was at the imperial *ordo*, where the wives and concubines of Genghis Khan were living, awaiting the return of their master. Börte received the Taoist monk, whom she offered some *koumiss* and various 'white foods'. Some of the Chinese and Xixia princesses also had him sent some warm garments (although this was the height of summer) and a variety of gifts. Chang Chun noted that the nomads' camp contained several hundred felt tents, some palanquins and some 'pavilions' of a more or less permanent nature. At the end of July the monk set off again. Along the road he noticed piles of stones: 'The mountain tops are still covered with snow. At their base one often saw *tumuli*. Above us we sometimes saw traces of sacrifices offered to the spirits of the mountains.' Chang Chun passed not far from the ruins of the town of Holuoxiao, before plunging into the sands which were the prelude to the aridity of the Moslem lands.

In the middle of August the traveller arrived at a site called Chinqai-Balγasun, where he encountered colonies of deported captives; these prisoners of war, mainly Chinese, were assigned to various jobs. Here he met again some former concubines from the Jin court, who welcomed him with tears of joy. The governor of the village, Chinqai, arrived a few days later and asked the traveller to move his caravan on at a faster pace, for he had received orders to that effect from the great khan. Chang Chun tried to make haste, but the difficulties of the route slowed his progress: sometimes it was necessary to push the carts along steep hillsides, at other times the vehicles had to be reined back to stop them from hurtling down dangerous slopes. After passing through the valley of Bulgun, Chang Chun noted that the Mongol riders escorting him coated their horses' heads with blood so as to frighten off evil spirits; at the same time, they made it clear that they thought a good Taoist had no need to resort to such superstitious practices. Already the Heavenly Mountains (Tian Shan) were beginning to loom up on the horizon.

It took an entire month for the caravaneers to reach the Uighur village of Beshbaliq, a little over 100 kilometres east of Ürümqi. From there on the journey became easier. There were oases scattered along the way, irrigated land with rows of fruit trees and grain fields surrounding little villages that nestled in the dunes. Here, in this largely Uighur region, Chang Chun was warmly received: he seems to have been very well known, although his disciple's account of his welcome was probably rather flattering. At Jambaliq, Chang Chun was offered wine and melons. From here on they were leaving the area where Buddhist influence prevailed, and entering the Moslem world which took up where the Silk Road left off. Going by Lake Sayrum Hu, near the Talki pass, the monk noticed that Chagatai, the great khan's second son, had built bridges over the rivers.

By this time, nearly a quarter of the way through the thirteenth century, the Mongol conquerors seem to have come to terms with the notion of permanent sites. Contingents of Mongols lived more or less as residents in cities they had taken over and which had from then on been administered by the *darughachi*, chief governors — still often indigenous people — who collected taxes and rents in kind for payment to the occupying power. This was the case in the village of Chinqai-Bal'yasun or the old Uighur capital, Qara Bal'yasun — the Black City — which may have been in ruins at the time of Genghis Khan, but this did not prevent him from setting his tent up there. Within a decade of the great khan's death, Karakorum was to become a proper Mongol city. It had once been a place by the name of Qara-Kuriyen — Black Ramparts — where the carts of the *ordo* had assembled, a kind of camp where there were residential tents for noblemen and officers, and many service tents all around housing servants, food stocks, personal property, and items that had been taken as booty.

'About the city of Karakorum,' noted Rubrouck, 'I must tell you that, apart from the khan's palace, it is not as big as the village of Saint-Denis, and the monastery at Saint-Denis is ten times bigger than the palace. It comprises two sections: one for the Saracens, where the markets are; and where a large number of Tatars gather because of their connection with the court, which is always near this town, and ambassadors too; the other is for the Cathayans [Chinese], who are all artisans. Besides these two sections, there are some large palaces that house court secretaries.' According to the Franciscan, there were still in Karakorum a dozen temples 'of idolaters of various nations', two mosques, and a Christian church. The town was surrounded by a wall of dried mud 3 or 4 kilometres long, with openings at four gates.

In October 1221, Chang Chun reached the town of Almalik, in the middle of the Ili basin, not far from the present-day town of Yining (Gulja). The old man was greeted by an emissary of the great khan, who offered him presents; it was here that he discovered with astonishment that cotton is a plant. Then the caravan train went by boat across the river Talas, which marked the farthest limit of Chinese military conquests in central Asia under the Tang. Beyond lay Transoxiana. The Mongol noblemen escorting the monk warned him that they were approaching the imperial *ordo*. The khan was at the time away in pursuit of Jalāl al-Dīn, the shah of Khwārezm, on the Indian frontier. In December Chang Chun stopped in Samarkand for the winter.

### The Quest for the Elixir of Life

At last, in the spring of 1222, after a journey that had lasted for a year, Chang Chun reached the place where Genghis Khan was. Prior to this, the monk had made the acquaintance of Yelü Chucai — called His Excellency Yi-la by the Chinese. On 16 May, the great khan greeted his guest with these words:

'You have had invitations from other sovereigns, but you have declined their offers. And yet you have travelled ten thousand *li* to be with me. I am grateful to you.'

The holy man was perhaps aware of the regal tone implicit in these words of welcome. His response was, appropriately, highly subtle:

'The mountain recluse [hermit] that I am has come to visit your majesty; it is Heaven's wish.'

Genghis Khan, who believed in the omnipotence of the Blue Heaven, could not, at least in public, contradict this statement. Instead, he came straight to the point. The Chinese Taoist's fame rested on his supposed mastery of certain supernatural forces, on his magical powers and on his knowledge of the secret of the beverage that guaranteed immortality:

'Holy man, what elixir of immortality have you brought me from your distant country?'

'I know some methods for protecting life, but of means to confer immortality I know none,' retorted the Chinese sagely. Genghis Khan seems to have valued his guest's frankness and granted him the signal favour of suggesting he erect his tent east of his own.

We do not know if the great khan was taken in by the old monk's words. Did he really think that there was an elixir of long life? His question suggests that such a thought would not be out of keeping with the beliefs that were current at that time; more to the point, it suggests that the khan was assailed by doubts about his health. In fact, the Mongol conqueror was to die five years later, in the same year as Chang Chun.

Could Chang Chun any longer be of quite such interest to the khan, now that it was clear that he could offer no elixir of immortality? When the great khan set out on a campaign in Khorāsān and present-day Afghanistan, the old monk chose to go to Samarkand instead. The atmosphere of the great city no doubt suited him better than the regimented military life of the camps. We learn from his disciple, Li Zhichang, that the old master took up residence in a palace in the city and was remarkably well treated there. He entered into contact with some of the learned Persian officials known as *dānishmand*, received some Khitan who had entered the Mongols' service, and even met the Chinese doctor of Chagatai, the khan's son. The travel journal of Chang Chun hardly mentions the troubles in Khwārezm. Nevertheless, we know for certain that the Taoist monk was not indifferent to the sufferings of the subjugated civilian population, for he asked a governor for permission to go and comfort citizens whose dwellings had been burned down.

It is clear that the monk, confronted with the war in Khwārezm, had the wisdom to keep his independence of mind, although he refrained from openly making any pronouncements about the events which he may have witnessed. In September 1222, when the conqueror again summoned him into his presence, the old man duly went before the khan, but he reminded him that Chinese custom required that a master of Taoism be excused from kowtowing — going down on one's knees with forehead touching the ground. Magnanimously, the Mongol sovereign acceded to this request and allowed his guest to appear before him standing. A little while later, Chang Chun declined the cup of *koumiss* Genghis Khan offered him, saying that Taoist dietary principles forbade him to accept it. It was not long after this that the old man informed the conqueror that he wished to return home:

'The hermit of the mountains has devoted long years to the study of Tao and loves peace and quiet. Now, when I am with your majesty, I am constantly disturbed by the noise your warriors make and therefore I am unable to concentrate.'

He could hardly have been more explicit. The atmosphere of the camps, the rows between warriors, the brawls between stablemen, the brutal treatment of slaves and prisoners and the drinking songs that rang out whenever there was feasting were hardly the sort of thing that would appeal to an intellectual like Chang Chun. When the interpreter had finished translating the monk's words, the khan agreed to let the monk leave for his native land.

Chang Chun had expressed his disapproval of the destruction, the deportations and the executions that had been perpetrated by the Mongol invaders. Even so, the great khan was anxious to continue discussion with his guest. When the monk began to explain to him the basic tenets of Taoism, Genghis Khan had his wives and his superior officers leave the tent, keeping by him only an interpreter and a few intimates, as though he wished the conversation to remain private. He had a record kept of the exchanges between them. The transcript made by the old master's disciple shows that Chang Chun was indeed willing to shed light on Taoist philosophy for the benefit of his imperial host. Thus, he declared:

This is how things are: all men, from emperors and princes to the most humble, however different their lives may be, have this in common, that they possess a 'natural state'. All the emperors and monarchs are celestial beings who have been driven out of Heaven. If they can prove their virtuousness while they are on earth, they will return to Heaven to occupy a still more eminent place than they held before. Try to sleep alone for a whole month. You will be surprised at the improvement in your spiritual resources and your energy. The Ancients said: 'Taking a remedy for a thousand days is less effective than sleeping alone for a single night.'

We can only guess whether Genghis Khan understood the full depth of meaning in these words. The Mongol conqueror was not by any means the moral defective he is sometimes made out to be. No doubt he did not trouble overmuch with subtleties, but he was possessed of sound good sense and was usually ready to listen to new ideas; so it is quite possible that the warrior saw very well what the monk meant and how his advice could be of benefit to him. Furthermore, it is very likely that Chang Chun's integrity and force of character, and the extreme privations which he endured, struck a strong chord with the khan. Genghis Khan had certainly already displayed an interest in other religions. Was he simply curious, keen to learn about other practices out of attraction to the unknown?

When, in November 1222, the old philosopher expressed his desire to return to China, it was already well into winter. The inclement weather that was sure to come might make the return journey a hazardous one. Genghis Khan suggested that the monk delay his departure. He himself was waiting for his sons to rejoin him so that he could travel back to Mongolia with them. Why not make the journey together? Chang Chun let himself be persuaded. Perhaps he was anxious to meet the khan's sons. Perhaps he enjoyed the conversations with his guest to some extent and nursed some kind of hope that he might still turn the khan onto a path that conformed better with Taoist principles. Or maybe he simply felt it would be wiser to spend the winter in Transoxiana.

Chang Chun thus celebrated the New Year — 2 February 1223 — with his travelling companions, along with the principal doctor, who was also astrologer-in-chief. It was not long afterwards, on 10 March, that the khan had a fall from his horse while on a boar hunt. Some of the chroniclers say that he came face to face with the animal, enraged by a wound, but no doubt they have embroidered the tale somewhat. The sovereign was carried to his tent in a serious condition. He was nearly 70 years of age and it was feared he might have suffered an internal injury. Chang Chun went to visit him and, reflecting the Chinese version of the legend of the Tarpeian Rock in Rome, a place where traitors were executed, said: 'This fall is a warning from Heaven.' And he reprimanded the khan, adding that he was too old to go hunting. Genghis Khan answered that he knew that Chang Chun gave sound advice and that he would try in future to take account of it. But he also said that he simply could not forgo the pleasures that hunting afforded him.

These last exchanges between the sovereign and the Chinese monk reveal how fundamentally opposed were the characters of the two men. On the one hand, there was the barbarian chief, a leader of men and a seeker of pleasure and power. On the other, there was the ascetic intellectual, reserved, imbued with a high ethical sense and stirred by the deep conviction that it was desirable to reform the individual rather than change the world. The old monk felt able to criticize Genghis Khan, if not to go as far as to judge him, even though he could not be sure of influencing the Mongol king in any way. Nevertheless, being a perfect adherent of Tao, he doubtless wanted to try.

In April 1223, Chang Chun finally parted from the great khan. Genghis presented him with various gifts and also handed him a decree bearing the imperial seal which relieved the monk's disciples of all obligation to pay taxes.

## The *Ordo en Route*

In spring 1223, Genghis Khan left the Samarkand area, where he had had his winter quarters, on a journey that would take him, in several stages, to the north bank of the Syr-Dar'ya and the Tashkent region. From Samarkand to Beijing, the great khan was master of a vast empire that stretched over 4,000 kilometres from west to east. His mighty army, comprising Mongol contingents and also foreign corps, took several thousand prisoners along on the journey, including the members of the family of the shah of Khwārezm. All were destined to spend a long time in captivity in Mongolia.

As the spring of that year gave way to summer, Genghis Khan installed his *ordo*, his travelling court, in the valley of Chirchik, northeast of Tashkent. The chroniclers tell us that he sat on a golden throne, surrounded by his peers, and indulged himself in the pleasures of hunting when affairs of state were not pressing on him. He had with him his youngest son Tolui; and it was not long before he was joined by Ögödei and Chagatai, who had wintered with their troops in the Bukhara region. Jochi, who was camped a little further north, organized a gigantic *battue* and drove towards the valley of Qulan-Bashi, at the foot of the Alexander mountains, thousands of animals which were to be the prey of the khan and the princes.

Gradually Genghis's great army made its way northeast towards the desolate steppes of high Asia. It left behind spies and small groups of men charged with the surveillance of the occupied territories. By persuasion, corruption or threats, the Mongols had managed, to a greater or lesser degree, to win collaborators everywhere, and these had been placed in every local administration. The great khan, gorged with conquests, was returning in triumph to his own country. The Minyak empire had been conquered and reduced to vassalage, Jin China had given way under the Mongol onslaught, the empire of Khwārezm had been destroyed, and other principalities had also fallen under the Mongol yoke. From the shores of the Pacific Ocean to the Caspian Sea, a vast part of the world belonged to them.

When he reached the Khrebet Tarbagatay mountains, on the banks of the river Emel', the conqueror was greeted by a delegation from the *ordo* where he had left Börte, his first wife, his other wives, his concubines, and several other members of his family. Among the riders were his grandsons, Kublai and Hülegü, sons of Tolui, both then aged around 12 years. The khan learned that the two boys had each just killed an animal; the first a hare, the second a deer. It was a nomad custom to smear with animal fat the middle finger of a youth who was going hunting for the first time, since this was the finger that held the arrow in place against the taut bowstring. Genghis Khan was keen to be the one to perform this rite of passage which would put the seal on his grandsons' future as warriors. Kublai was, indeed, to become emperor of China, while his younger brother Hülegü would become ruler of Persia.

The khan was in no hurry to move on and spent several months between 1224 and 1225 on the banks of the great Siberian river, the Irtysh. Perhaps he felt the need to recover from his fall. Perhaps, too, he was simply savouring the pleasures that a warrior might experience away from the heat of battle. It was not until the spring of 1225 that he arrived back beside the Tuul Gol after an absence of six years, spent, for the most part, on the battlefield.

Nothing is known of the events that had meanwhile transpired in Mongolia. There is nothing to suggest that the order imposed by the great khan had been in any way disturbed either by internal revolts or external threats. Yet there were rumours, revived only in the seventeenth century by the Mongol chronicler Saγang Sechen, that Börte, the khan's first wife, was eaten up with bitterness and jealousy. When the khan had left to conquer Khwārezm, he had taken with him one of his favourites, the young Qulan, and Börte had duly taken offence: 'One cannot place two saddles on a horse; a faithful minister cannot serve two masters.' Börte is said to have sent her husband a message warning him that rivalries among princes were a threat to his power. Genghis Khan accordingly decided to return to Mongolia sooner. While en route, out of anxiety about the reception his wife might give him, he sent a messenger to her, and Börte, a woman of great wisdom and tolerance, sent him this reply: 'On the lake with the reed-covered shores there are many wild geese and swans. The master may take from them whichever ones he chooses. Among the tribes there are many young girls and young women. The master may choose the fortunate ones as he wishes. He may take a new wife. He may saddle a wild horse.'

This episode, though probably apocryphal, underlines the attachment which Genghis Khan felt towards his first wife and which she reciprocated.

**The Last Campaign**

After his return from the Moslem lands Genghis Khan was able to enjoy barely a year of peace. The colossus that was China was stirring again: despite the destruction and humiliation it had suffered and despite having been partly occupied by the Mongols and their allies, it was now shaken by violent upheaval. Beneath the ashes, revolts were smouldering and, although they were smothered wherever they occurred, still they were constantly rekindled.

Muqali, who had stayed in China as viceroy of Manchuria, had tried to impose law and order, collect taxes and raise corps of auxiliaries. He seems to have had the good sense to listen to the advice given him by some of his Chinese collaborators. A captain from the Jin army who had entered the service of the Mongols pointed out to him that pillaging was bound to provoke rebellion, and Muqali accordingly acted to instil some discipline into his troops. This 'humanization' of the war bore fruit. However, the Mongols did not have the numbers to ensure unaided the imposition of order on the Jin empire they had conquered. It was therefore the Sinicized Ruzhen and Khitan, in conjunction with the Chinese themselves, who provided what the Mongols most needed: a body of infantrymen to occupy the towns and the countryside. Thus imperceptibly did the Mongols begin the process of Sinicizing their troops and civilian auxiliaries.

It was this constant need for extra troops that unleashed a new conflict, in the autumn of 1226, with the vassal Minyak empire which separated Mongolia from Tibet. In 1219, just before setting off to subdue the Moslem east, Genghis Khan had ordered the Xixia sovereign to furnish him with some cavalry contingents. Now the latter was under the thumb of one of his advisers, Asha Gambu by name, who refused to obey Mongol orders and sent him this stinging reply: 'If Genghis Khan does not have enough forces for what he wants to undertake, why does he assume the role of emperor?' The great khan was at that time preoccupied with the progress of the military campaigns in Transoxiana and Fergana. His next move was to go on into the Moslem lands where he was going to 'kill men as one mows grass'.

The defection of the Xixia of the Minyak empire stung Genghis Khan bitterly. He had waged war for six years and throughout that time he had not forgotten the Xixia treachery. On his return he decided to take his revenge, the more so since the Minyak empire, theoretically in vassalage to him, was showing signs of wanting its independence. The nomad clans were therefore mobilized once again. The officers gathered together thousands of horses and pack camels to ride alongside the warriors. Ögödei and Tolui accompanied their father, as did Yesüi, one of his favourite concubines.

In spite of Chang Chun's advice, Genghis Khan continued to enjoy the pleasures of hunting. Once again, he was thrown from his horse. A herd of galloping dziggetai stampeded across the path of his horse, which reared up violently, dragging the rider along the ground. The khan was carried to his tent. He suffered internal pains and his body was racked by fever. It was decided to set up camp where they were and not to move on. Yesüi sent messengers to inform the *ordo* of the accident.

One of the khan's generals, Tolun Sherbi, proposed that they turn back and put off the invasion of the Minyak empire. 'The Xixia,' he explained, 'are a sedentary people, with walled towns and fixed camps, and therefore incapable of making a getaway in the way that nomads can. When we come back, we shall find them still there.' The khan's lieutenants agreed with Tolun Sherbi. The khan himself expressed the only dissenting opinion: 'If we retreat, the Xixia will be bound to claim that we are faint-hearts.' Nevertheless, he agreed to send an ultimatum to the Minyak sovereign, whose own spirit seemed to be weakening in the face of the Mongols' threats. But his adviser Asha Gambu was loath to lose the initiative and sent Genghis Khan an arrogant message in return: 'If the Mongols want to engage in battle now, let them come to the Alashan [Helan Shan] where I have my camp with my tents and my camels with their freight, and we shall see how we measure up to each other. If they need gold, silver, silks or other riches, let them come and find them in our towns, in Eriүaya [Ningxia] and Eriүe'u [Liangzhou].' Stung by Asha Gambu's haughtiness, Genghis Khan immediately gave orders to proceed. Doubled up with pain though he was, he declared that nothing would stop him from reaching the Minyak capital.

In March 1226, Genghis Khan's army entered the Minyak empire by going up the course of the Xi He in the direction of the Tulai Nanshan range. The riders crossed vast low-lying areas of semidesert where nothing grew except clumps of stunted vegetation, until they came to the edge of the inhabited regions, through which ran the famous Silk Road. Here a few small villages prospered by virtue of the regular passage of camels and horses and the presence of caravaneers and garrisons. This was the case with Suzhou and Ganzhou, indispensable staging posts on the way to Dunhuang. These towns had been subject to foreign influence emanating from central Asia but also from Tibet, India and the West through Buddhism and Nestorianism. They fell fairly readily to the conquering Mongols. The troops were able to live largely off the reserves of grain they found there. But soon the heat became stifling and Genghis Khan moved for a while to higher ground overlooking the oases.

It was during the summer that the Mongols launched their main offensive. Asha Gambu, who had established his camp and his troops in' the Helan Shan, was vanquished. The Mongol invaders in Minyak behaved like drunken veterans, and thousands of Xixia took refuge in the mountain grottoes that were dotted around. There was rampant pillaging. Genghis Khan took Asha Gambu's taunt at face value: he seized his treasures, precious silks, and tents, and he distributed his herds of camels among his own men. Then he ordered that all captured Xixia be delivered into the hands of his troops, to do what they liked with them. All the males old enough to be armed were put to the sword. The Xixia empire of Minyak never rose again from the ruins to which Genghis Khan's armies reduced it. Several weeks after the defeat of Asha Gambu, the khan's horsemen seized the town of Liangzhou. Now they were drawing close to the enemy capital, Ningxia. The city, built on the banks of the Huang He, was surrounded by strong fortifications and protected by a very sizable garrison. It would not yield easily and the Mongols would have to be methodical in laying siege to it.

Meanwhile, in the same year, 1226, Ögödei had been despatched to China. Although their position was extremely precarious, the authorities in Kaifeng were still managing to dig into the enormous human reserves of China and recruit willing supporters. Ögödei proceeded along the Wei He, and then, crossing the province of Henan, reached the Jin capital. Panic-stricken, Kaifeng attempted to open negotiations with the Mongols, seemingly in an attempt to gain time. The Jin rulers had not mobilized any troops: they were not to score any successes until two years later, and even then their victories were only the last sparks of a dynasty that already lay almost in ashes.

The siege of Ningxia still lay ahead. Here lived the sovereign of Minyak, Li Yan, together with his court. The capital of the Xixia empire was situated on the left bank of the Huang He, protected on the western side by the Helan Shan mountains. Ningxia was an important trading centre on the edge of the great Gobi desert, where cloth, white camelhair carpets, silk and weapons were traded. Buddhist and Nestorian communities coexisted here and the town boasted three Christian churches which adhered to Nestorian rites.

While a defence was being mounted within the walls, the nomads outside were deploying their troops to prevent anyone from leaving the town. Genghis Khan and part of his cavalry went on the rampage, causing havoc in various regions of the Xixia empire, while his sons led troops of horsemen into the villages and laid them waste. Their orders were strict and unequivocal: massacre was to be total; not even a chicken or a dog should be left alive. The khan himself took command of several regiments. For much of the year 1227, he seems to have moved about in the area between the Huang He and the upper Wei He, not far from the cities of Lanzhou and Longde and the Liupan Shan mountains. The torrid heat drove him to camp on the slopes of the Liupan Shan where it was both cool and restful.

Trapped in his capital, Li Yan, the Minyak sovereign, tried to play for time. Probably he was counting on outside help reaching him, or hoping that the enemy, wearying of a long siege, would eventually withdraw. However, some time in the first fortnight in June, Li Yan decided to surrender his capital city. He sent emissaries into the Mongol camp to warn Genghis Khan that it would be a month before he finally capitulated. A few weeks later, Li Yan emerged from Ningxia to offer his surrender. Behind him came a very sizable escort and servants carrying extremely valuable gifts. There were 'dazzling golden images of Buddha, gold and silver cups and bowls, young boys and girls, and horses and camels, all in multiples of nine', a number the Mongols considered lucky. We do not know whether Li Yan yielded to the besieging force in accordance with the deadline he had set, that is to say in mid-July, or a few weeks later. Li Yan was escorted to a place near the imperial tent, but he was not led into the presence of the khan himself. He was made to pay his respects from a distance, 'from the corner of a doorway'.

Perhaps Genghis Khan was already dead when Li Yan surrendered? Very likely the Xixia chief was offering his submission to an empty throne, but if so he was never to find out, for he was immediately put to death, as the khan had ordered. One wonders whether Li Yan would have capitulated if he had known the khan was dead. By all accounts, the Mongol headquarters command led Li Yan to believe that he was surrendering to a warrior capable in the twinkling of an eye of 'gathering the clouds together'. According to the *Yuan Shi* (*History of the Yuan Dynasty*), the conqueror died on 18 August 1227 — following an internal haemorrhage — not just outside the walls of Ningxia, but 300 kilometres farther south, near the present-day town of Pingliang, in eastern Gansu province, at the southern limit of the autonomous region of Ningxia. The Mongols are supposed then to have transported his remains to Ningxia when they were about to plunder the city. Part of the population was deported to Mongolia and thousands of Xixia were given to Yesüi, who had accompanied Genghis Khan into his last battle, the battle against death.

Tradition has it that the khan was able to state his wishes for the succession in the presence of his two sons, Ögödei and Tolui. Chagatai was several days' ride away, waging war elsewhere. As for the moody, hot-tempered Jochi, he had died in February 1227, six months before his father. It will be recalled that, according to *The Secret History*, Genghis Khan had come into the world clutching a blood clot in his fist, a sign that he would become a warrior. That prediction came true: right up to the time when, at the age of 72, he was on the very threshold of death, he had never ceased to be a man of war, and even when he was dead his orders continued to be carried out. *The Secret History* also relates that in the course of the siege of Ningxia, the khan, learning of certain celestial movements from some astrologers, declared: 'When the five planets are reunited, the moment will have arrived to halt the war.'

To what conjunction of the planets was the Mongol conqueror alluding? We do not know; but we do know that in 1145, about ten years before his birth, Halley's Comet passed over the earth and that in 1222, some five years after the death of Genghis Khan, it reappeared.

# 15
# The Man who Forged an Empire

*My descendants will dress themselves in clothes embroidered with gold; they will feed on exquisite dishes, they will ride superb coursers and hold the most beautiful young women in their arms. And they will have forgotten to whom they owe all that.*
**Attributed to Genghis Khan**

*What a pity that the superhuman glory of his century —
Genghis Khan – bent his bow and took aim only at eagles!*

**Mao Zedong**

When Genghis Khan died, having united all the Mongol peoples under one yoke, a huge part of Eurasia was still reeling under the impact of the nomad invasions. A tidal wave of unmitigated fury had swept across the continent, from the Siberian taiga to the banks of the Indus; from the shores of the Pacific to those of the Caspian Sea. Genghis Khan's tenacity and ambition, his undeniable qualities as a leader of men and a creator of strategy, all combined to make him a political and military genius. Under his authority, grooms had been transformed into a swift and indomitable cavalry, scattered tribes had put aside their rivalries and united under the same banner, and shepherds who had done nothing more than race across the steppes as they followed their herds had been turned into a vast confederation which thenceforth inspired fear and trembling throughout the states of the Far East, the Middle East and the fringes of Europe.

The man who, with single-minded patience, forged this empire, nevertheless remains something of an unknown quantity. Chinese annals and Moslem, Armenian, Georgian, and Russian chronicles are imprecise, not to be depended upon, and even fallacious, when they try to take stock of the man who unleashed the Mongol avalanche. *The Secret History*, as we have seen, very often magnifies the exploits of Genghis Khan and his blind partisans to the point where historical accuracy is clouded over. The scribes were obliged to write panegyrics on the monarch, thus helping, consciously or unconsciously, to produce propaganda or at least a history that was determinedly biased, exaggerating and embroidering the military exploits and political successes of the conqueror. Their writings served to conjure up the pure hero, the proud aristocrat of the steppes who was as capable of displaying physical courage in destroying the enemy on the battlefield as of devising, in the quiet darkness of his tent, a sophisticated plan for foiling the enemy and consolidating his power. Although they have varying shades of opinion, Pian del Carpini, the Armenian Hetoum, and even Joinville, indirectly a witness of the Mongol invasion, all make the point strongly that the Mongol sovereign scrupulously enforced a rigorous system of justice and the establishment of a social and political order.

On the other side, we have the scribes who watched helplessly as the nomad hordes invaded their native lands: they agree that Genghis Khan imposed a reign of terror in the territories he conquered. It is unnecessary here to dwell upon their descriptions of cities besieged and then set ablaze; of prisoners slaughtered by mercenaries or led away to Mongol lands. Several Arab chroniclers refer to Genghis Khan as the personification of the 'Scourge of Allah'. Ibn al-Athir, who lived between 1160 and 1223, could not find words damning enough to describe the excesses of the nomad invaders: 'Among the most famous dramas in history, the one most often cited to represent the pinnacle of horror is the massacre of the sons of Israel by Nebuchadnezzar and the destruction of Jerusalem. But that was as nothing compared with the events that have just unfolded before our eyes. No, never, until the end of time, will we see another catastrophe of such magnitude.' This terrifying image of Genghis Khan and his armies was to remain in the collective memory of people throughout the region for many centuries.

Was the sovereign merely a coarse and uncivilized barbarian, a violent despoiler? An oriental despot devoured by vaulting ambition and obsessed with the desire to carry out a policy of devastation? A statesman of skill, for whom the end justified the means? A wise conqueror, but one determined to offer the Mongol peoples their place in the sun? An opportunist dictator carried along on a wave of imperialism? The portrait of this man who forged an empire can be built up to give an approximate likeness, layer upon layer of paint can be applied, and still one never brings the picture into sharp, accurate focus.

In the twentieth century, historians have often attributed a more serene character to the Mongol monarch, thus considerably modifying the assertions and claims about his ferocity. In spite of the devastated cities, the civilian populations that were deported or put to the sword, they frequently credit him with a sense of justice, with being a man of his word, and with having a real grasp of the importance and means of advancing his people from barbarism towards civilization. Thus in 1935 Fernand Grenard, a biographer of Genghis Khan, wrote:

He would have shared Montaigne's view that 'a man's crowning glory is to live his life fittingly' . . . He gave himself without restraint and with earnest zeal to every endeavour he undertook . . . He loved life for its own sake and did not trouble himself with searching for its meaning; he enjoyed it abundantly, with a tranquil gaiety, without perverse refinements, without inordinate passions . . . Jealous of his welfare and of his rights, but liberal, lavish towards others . . . He was keenly sensible of his glory and his grandeur, but without haughtiness and without vanity.

And then we have the judgement of Vladimirtsov, writing a few years later:

Genghis Khan appears to us as the very embodiment of the steppe warrior with his instinct for the pragmatic and his inclination to plunder and despoil. Only by exceptional will-power did Genghis Khan succeed in reining in his instincts, in mastering them sufficiently to attain higher goals . . . [Genghis] distinguished himself invariably by his generosity, his magnanimity and his hospitality . . . But it is customary to represent Genghis Khan as a cruel despot, deceitful and vicious . . . He abstained from ever committing acts of futile savagery . . . Genghis could not and would not be an assassin pure and simple . . .; this did not prevent him from committing himself body and soul to destruction when the occasion called for it . . . that is, when the exigencies of war so dictated.

René Grousset too has constructed a fairly flattering picture of the Mongol khan. Taking the view that the bloody episodes of Genghis Khan's conquests were the product 'more of the harshness of the environment and the coarseness of the people, who were the dregs of the

Turco-Mongol line, than of natural ferocity', he stresses that the mass killings were part of a 'system of war', that of the nomads against the sedentary peoples. Without calling into question the pillaging and massacres perpetrated by the conqueror, the author of *L'Empire des steppes* depicts him as:

> fair-minded, with sound common sense; remarkably well balanced; a good listener; a steadfast friend, generous and affectionate; despite his sternness, having some fine qualities as an administrator, although by this must be understood the administration of nomadic peoples and not of settled populations, for theirs was an economy of which he had only a rather dim concept . . . Side by side with his terrible and barbarous inclinations, one finds some lofty and noble facets to his nature, which qualify the man whom Moslem writers call 'the Accursed' to be restored to his rightful place among humanity.

Louis Hambis, essentially concurring with Grousset's verdict, added in 1973:

> He [Genghis Khan] never left for a campaign without taking one of his wives with him. He was calm and collected, never allowed himself to be carried to extremes of emotion, exercised great self-control and exerted his authority in such a natural manner that it was only rarely contested. He took an interest in the beliefs of conquered peoples without showing any excessive leaning towards any one of them, believing that all moral rules were good and no one set of rules better than any other . . . These were the reasons for his success and his greatness; never has a man attained such a degree of power and at the same time harboured less pride.

Lastly, the Turcologist Jean-Paul Roux has written in his recent *Histoire des Turcs* that:

> Genghis Khan and his line were guilty of no particular taste for murder, nor of sadism, nor of any highly-developed penchant for cruelty. They were merely exceptionally well-organized barbarians who carried a system to its farthest limits. They waged war because it was their natural state to be either murderers or victims . . . One might compare their actions to those of a power that possesses the atom bomb

and is determined to use it: they were, however, in no fear of reprisals since they had no cities. They were not particularly wicked but merely served their own interests first and foremost.

Can one really share René Grousset's view that Genghis Khan was 'fair-minded' and 'remarkably well balanced', or Vladimirtsov's that the Mongol sovereign 'was in no way exceptional in terms of his bloodlust or cruelty', or claim, like Hambis, that he was 'calm and collected' and 'never allowed himself to be carried to extremes of emotion'? It is extraordinary to see how relatively kindly these observers have looked upon the Mongol khan's conquests, especially when the destruction wrought by the Mongols was on such a massive scale: Vernadsky has recently calculated that in their military operations outside Mongolia the nomads left a toll of several million dead.

## Son of a Clan

From the sources we presently have to hand, the man remains hard to make out, harder still to describe and understand. At every turning in his destiny, we can add a new piece and adjust the pattern of the complex puzzle which is his character.

There is no doubt whatever that he was a self-made man. Though he claimed to belong to an aristocratic clan, it cannot be said that he was of 'royal' descent. His father, Yesügei, was a *bayadur* (valiant one) who had founded his own clan, that of the Borjigin, with his circle of relatives and a small number of close friends, and led them, with some success, in various escapades against the Tatars and the Ruzhen. Temüjin derived little advantage from the prestige of his father, who died when he was scarcely more than a child, and whose demise brought in its train the family's fall from grace in the context of the clan community.

It was Hö'elün, Yesügei's widow, who saved the family unit and became the forceful head of the household. It is worth emphasizing the fundamental role that Hö'elün played in the life of Genghis Khan. She never abdicated her own position, even when her sons, in particular the oldest, had attained power and glory. She never hesitated to reprimand them whenever she saw fit, even in front of an audience of wild warriors. Around 1206, when Genghis Khan suspected his brother Jochi Qasar of plotting against him and had him arrested, Hö'elün intervened. Genghis Khan's words, related in *The Secret History*, are revealing: 'My mother frightens me; in front of her I feel ashamed.' Was it Hö'elün's stern authority that induced this attitude of submission towards her, or the murder of his half-brother Bekter? Whatever the answer, it would seem that Genghis Khan continued to fear her until her death.

It was at the urging of his wife, Börte, that Genghis Khan took the irrevocable decision to break with his childhood friend Jamuγa. It will be remembered that Genghis Khan was worried about the attitude of his *anda* and went to consult his mother, but that Börte intervened and decided to separate her husband from his companion-in-arms. It was perhaps thanks to Börte that the future khan was placed in a position of clear rivalry with Jamuγa and that his life thus received a new impetus. There is another episode, which we have already related, which demonstrates the attention Genghis Khan paid to the judgements of women: just before he set off on the campaign against the Khwārezm empire, Yesüi urged him to settle his succession. And Genghis Khan, killer of Tatars and Kereyid, conqueror of the Jin empire in China, complied with the suggestion of his concubine. Not only did he comply, but he also announced publicly that he valued her advice — advice, he insisted, that his closest friends and followers had never dared offer him!

It has been claimed that Genghis Khan slept with hundreds of women. Various unverifiable accounts suggest, moreover, that Genghis passed away in the arms of a concubine who had offered him a poisoned drink. A very late chronicle — dating from the seventeenth century — implies that it was the queen of the Xixia, Körbeljin, who caused his death. A first version of this chronicle claims that, after sharing his bed with her, the khan was taken ill and died almost immediately afterwards. What illness could this have been? One can only guess. According to a second version, the beautiful Körbeljin 'inserted inside her vagina a small pair of princers and, having injured the sovereign's member, she took flight and threw herself into the Huang He'. But there is little credence to be attached to this story either, and it is an interpretation of a motif — the toothed vagina — that occurs frequently in legends throughout the world, particularly in Siberia. Moreover, despite the numerous concubines he had, the great khan never lost his attachment for Börte.

Genghis Khan also remained strongly bound up with his family clan. Nevertheless, without raking up the story about the assassination of his half-brother, it must be remembered that he clashed with Jochi Qasar, whom he perceived as a rival, and that he was, apparently without any proof, mistrustful of his son Chagatai. However, the fact remains that he relied very heavily on his family circle.

Those who had begun life in the theatre of his acquaintance as mere 'extras' were soon given leading roles and then a major voice in the running of things: Jelme and Muqali had honours and riches heaped upon them. Genghis Khan reciprocated the loyalty of his followers and accorded them a full share in his destiny and his glory. When he was opposed in good faith, he could be supercilious, but he was just as likely to yield and show clemency. However, should someone take it into his head to try to deceive him, he was totally intractable. This pattern of conduct reveals a person who was something of a stubborn and brutal despot, trapped by a dogma which he only rarely called into question: that he alone was always right. Nevertheless, it would be a mistake, from what we know of him, to cast him in the role of some kind of monolithic figure. Authoritarian, violent, jealous of his interests and his rights, and ambitious he certainly was, but also loyal and capable of magnanimity. He was equally likely to pardon the most glaring shortcomings as to mete out the most severe punishment for trifling misdemeanours. He dealt leniently with To'oril, the ageing king of the Kereyid, despite the latter's mercurial behaviour towards him. And yet he would readily sanction the execution of an enemy garrison who were simply doing their duty.

As soon as he became great khan, Genghis surrounded himself with advisers and servants: these, along with his companions-in-arms and his concubines, constituted a veritable travelling court. Uighur and Khitan scribes, many oriental traders, pilgrims, Chinese artillerymen, artists and simple travellers all called on him on countless occasions. Genghis Khan, anxious to see the caravan routes kept open, was always glad to converse with strangers, and would ask them many questions about their customs, their religion and the countries they had passed through. We have already paid tribute to the religious tolerance of the khan and his successors; adherents of all religions were flattered that their proselytizing fell on sympathetic ears. But perhaps this tolerance was only indifference. It would seem, too, that Genghis Khan was keen to inform himself about the territories which he intended to invade. The Mongols made frequent use of scouts, disguised spies, and propagandists, prior to their conquests.

Both in miniatures and in larger paintings, Persian and Chinese artists have portrayed the monarch seated in the lap of luxury, but we have very little reliable evidence about his personal fortune. The only portrait of the khan that is presumed authentic shows him simply dressed, without affectation. He may indeed have worn brocaded garments when he became master of an empire that stretched from the Pacific to the

Caspian, but he still managed to retain the look of a cowboy, of a livestock herder who doubled as a hunter and had been trained and toughened by much activity in the open air. Genghis Khan amassed considerable booty in the course of his raids and it is claimed that when he succeeded to the supreme khanate he sat on a throne of immaculate mare's hide. His tents were supposed to be overflowing with treasure brought back from the far corners of the world. But he seems to have had little fascination with material things. He remained a nomad, for whom the only wealth that mattered was what could be carried with him.

## A Man of Politics

Genghis Khan's aristocratic origins played very little part in winning him his place in the sun and he could never afford to pause in his quest for advancement lest he lose ground. All the time he strove to 'make good', and to regild the family coat-of-arms that a cruel fate had tarnished. Even when he was very young, Temüjin would leap on his horse to go after thieves who had taken his small herd, and so control the reins of his own destiny. Time and again he took advantage of opportunities to force the hand of Providence.

When his family fell from favour and was threatened by a vendetta mounted by the Tayichi'ud tribes, he was the one who found a 'godfather', in the person of To'oril, king of the Kereyid. The offer of a gift to his protector gave him the right to call To'oril *echige* (father). Flattered, To'oril consented to take care of his young protégé from then on. The young Genghis Khan was obliged to serve his master faithfully, but he also received his share in any booty. As the years went by, To'oril gave the future khan some of his power and some of his wealth.

Later, Genghis Khan was to ride side by side with his powerful ally Jamuγa. But when he parted from his friend he took with him a number of his old *anda*'s followers. Then, in 1206, calling to witness law and good faith, the ambitious adventurer had himself proclaimed khan. This 'legalized coup' confirmed his new power but also drew accusations that he was a usurper. For Jamuγa too had had himself elected Gür Qan, or universal khan.

Genghis Khan was clever enough to take advantage of clan and family dissension among the Naiman and thus conquer them. Then he turned his attention to the Merkid, the Tatars, and the Tayichi'ut, and defeated them in their turn, thus carving out a niche of key importance for himself in eastern Mongolia. It was only when he felt his position was sufficiently strong that he advanced against the internal enemies: the Mongol princes who contested the legitimacy of his power. Thus, one by one were eliminated Jamuγa, who commanded too much power; the princes Taichu and Sacha Beki; and Büri the Athlete. Sometimes he used force of arms; sometimes mere guile and trickery; but Genghis Khan always managed to move in time to knock out of action any operation that threatened to undermine his power.

To oust the aristocrats of the steppes, Genghis Khan at first relied on his brothers-in-arms: Bo'urchu, Kishiliγ, Badai, Jebe the Arrow, and others, often of humble origins — some of them, prior to receiving orders from the khan, had been nothing more than simple herders — but on the battlefield they revealed themselves to be redoubtable swordsmen and fighters. Genghis Khan seems to have learned very early that ambition is the best spur to action. He understood that these men, who had started life with nothing, would serve him with a devotion that was reinforced by self-interest.

Genghis Khan took twenty long years to assemble the Mongol tribes under his banner. At the end of this struggle for hegemony he was proclaimed khan, and it was only then that he devoted himself to the administration of the gigantic territory over which he held sway. The man seems to have had a formidable desire to command and to subjugate those around him, but at the same time to organize his people as he had organized his army. To educate and govern his shifting empire, the *ulus*, he decreed the *jasaγ*, the code of law which was to form the backbone of Mongol society and the expression of its nationalism. Based on old Mongol law and custom, the *jasaγ* was also used as a guide in relations with the occupied territories.

The *jasaγ* — which codified what must be done and what must not be done — can be summed up in a single formula: 'It is forbidden to disobey the law and the khan!' It thus sanctioned an unalterable notion of legality. Theoretically at least, it was no longer the law of the strongest that prevailed. Barbarity fixed its own limits. Thus every offence had to be attested to by witnesses, minor breaches of the law were liable only to fines, and there was a scale of punishments that could be handed down to fit various crimes. The *jasaγ* brought into relief some of the cardinal virtues like honesty, hospitality, loyalty, parental duty, and sobriety. Infringements attracted penalties. This code of law, which was established in 1206, imposed a rigid discipline on society.

At the beginning of the thirteenth century, it was the Mongols' discipline and the order prevailing in their society that aroused so much astonishment and admiration among travellers. 'I have said before,' wrote Pian del Carpini somewhat naively,

> that Tatar men are certainly more obedient to their masters, whether religious or secular, than any other men in the world, and revere them more. And they do not readily lie to them. They rarely, if ever, have differences of opinion, on either side; and indeed never contest each other's actions. Wars, quarrels, and murders never occur among them. Likewise, robberies and thefts of any magnitude do not happen. . . . If some animals go astray, someone may find them and renounce any claim to them. Or he may take them back to those men who own them.[1]

This picture is reproduced by a number of travellers; even the Moslem Abū'l-Ghāzī wrote: 'Under the reign of Genghis Khan, all the country between Iran and Turan enjoyed such peace that one could travel from east to west with a golden tray upon one's head without being subjected to the slightest hint of violence from anyone.'

It is therefore quite plain that in elaborating and decreeing the *jasay*, Genghis Khan effectively ushered in a period of new stability among the nomadic peoples of central Asia. In its rigorous application, the *jasay* placed the seal of order and discipline upon Mongol society and ended the profound anarchy which had characterized it before the thirteenth century.

### The Nomadic Tide

Genghis Khan practised a strategy of systematic intimidation and terror. Too few in number to fight on several fronts, and having little stomach for a long-drawn-out guerrilla war, the Mongols often employed methods that were bloody in the highest degree. The wholesale slaughter of an entire garrison and the mass extermination of civilians were designed to nip in the bud the creation of an army of resistance and to conserve lives within the Mongols' effective forces. Was this strategy of pre-emptive terror so very different from that which led to the dropping of atomic bombs on Japanese cities?

Every study of the Mongol conquest raises two questions which have, to this day, not been answered: Why this brutal invasion of a vast part of Eurasia? And how were the Mongols able to seize such enormous tracts of territory in Eurasia, the largest area that has ever been controlled by one power in the history of mankind?

Between nomad territory and the lands of the sedentary peoples there was often a kind of no-man's-land, which could be crossed in the space of several days but in which it was unwise to tarry too long. The vicissitudes of the pastoral way of life, of persistent climatic changes, of progressive demographic growth, and of conflicts between tribes could all cause populations to shift their ground and encourage wandering tribes to move to other land or even onto the territory of settled people. Often the 'domino theory' applied among nomadic populations who drove other people before them — other people who were fewer in number, less powerful, or simply more peace-loving.

It must also be remembered that nomad conquests began in the third millennium before Christ. The Cimmerians had invaded Assyria and Urartu; and the Hittites, who stemmed from Anatolia, spread throughout the Near East. Central Asia experienced, in fact, cyclical influxes of nomads: Tocharians into the Tarim and Chinese Turkestan, Xiongnu and then Huns sweeping through between the Oxus and the Caspian Sea, and Hephthalites into India. Proto-Turc, Proto-Tungus, or Proto-Mongol nomads came time and again to batter down the fortifications of China or the eastern empires. In classical times, too, the known world underwent waves of nomad invasions: Avars, Alans, Visigoths, Vandals, and Slavs in Germany; Germans in Gaul; and Celts in conflict with the Roman empire. In their turn, Saxons, Gauls, Angles, Vikings, and Saracens, invaders of Europe or of Africa, were all designated 'barbarians' by the sedentary peoples who went before them and who believed themselves to be the sole custodians of civilization.

Conquests by nomadic peoples therefore have a very long history. Nomads spilled out of central Asia both towards China and India and towards the West. Now, with very few exceptions, the bulk of China, India, Iran, the Arab Middle East and Europe had, by the thirteenth century, attained overall an advanced level of civilization, based on the exploitation of agricultural land, craftsmanship and trade.

Nevertheless, extending from the Pacific shores, through Manchuria and into the heart of Europe, even into the Hungarian *puszta*, there still remained a long band of land that was unsuitable for cultivation: the steppe. Now this was the land on which lived, as they had done for one or two millennia, various nomadic populations: Turks, Mongols, and Tungus. The life they led then, squarely in the middle of what we usually call the Middle Ages, could be described as archaic. Yet there were enormous differences in stages of development, from the Chinese of the Jin empire to the Mongols of Genghis Khan; from the Persians of the Khwārezm empire to the Kirghiz: on the one hand, there was the inhabitant of Beijing, who lived in a white-walled city with hundreds of roads, heavy traffic, and bustling markets overflowing with wares; on the other, the Mongol shepherd who set up his tent on his yurt and devoted his time to minding the sheep.

The peasants of China or of the oases of the Near East certainly did not lead a soft existence: primitive methods of agriculture, natural plagues and disasters, the imposition of land taxes and imperial requisitions were all burdens they had to bear. But the nomads, accustomed as they were to the wide open spaces of the steppes, were fascinated by the large towns with their encircling ramparts. In Beijing, and equally in Bukhara and Samarkand, what they were, in the main, covetously eyeing was the loot accumulated in the princely palaces, the lords' manors, the warehouses, the shops and the grain stores. Even in the small country villages, grain, fodder, cloth, jewels and women seemed to be laid out, as though in stone coffers, ready and waiting, for the delectation of the predators

In trying to arrive at reasons for the Mongols' invasion, some climatologists have suggested that at the time of Genghis Khan the steppes of Europe and Asia were undergoing a period of diminished rainfall. Suddenly, the nomads, reduced to a lowered standard of living, were driven to seek other means of obtaining a livelihood: hunting and fishing were one source; war was another. Other experts claim that the climate at the beginning of the thirteenth century would have favoured the growth of steppe vegetation. This would have allowed a considerable development in the size of herds and given the Mongols the wherewithal to equip their cavalry for the vast operations necessitated by the drive to conquest.

The Russian historian Vorobev has advanced the theory that the transcontinental trade routes — in an east–west direction, between Europe and Asia — were at that time undergoing a decline, a decline which had deleterious effects on Mongol life, for the nomads in ordinary circumstances benefited from a 'fall-out' in terms of trade from the various Silk Routes. The tributes which the Chinese paid the Mongols (especially following the treaty of 1147) show that what the nomads wanted from China were not, as previously, manufactured goods, but agricultural products and, stranger still, cattle and sheep. This leads one to think that the Mongols must have been experiencing great difficulties in obtaining enough provisions and, consequently, that their invasions were a response to economic need. In the final analysis, theirs was an imperialism of the most classical kind.

Neither should we forget the centuries-old antagonism between nomads and sedentary peoples. For the latter, protected by walls or penned in within their fields, it had always been a matter of containing the 'savages'. But over and above the 'battle for space', there was always, on both sides, a deep, if unconscious, desire to impose a lifestyle on the other. The Mongols were not content just to steal and to kill peasants and citizens; they also obliged them, by force, to 'be like them'. When they occupied a city or a land they had conquered, they separated families, scattered the inhabitants, taking many into their service, took master craftsmen away from their workers, and creamed off musicians and actors to be put to work for their own pleasure — as if they were intent on 'breaking' the structures of an entire society. Deportation and dispersal of settled peoples: this policy was not peculiar to the Mongols, but is found wherever other nomads carried out invasions. But there is no doubt that it magnified the terror inspired by Genghis Khan and his successors.

When settled peoples brought nomads under their yoke, they, in turn, also tried to make them conform to their own pattern of life. Nomad prisoners were bound into service, forced to remain on the land, or confined within city precincts. Besides serving the immediate interests of the captors (cheap labour, slave-trading), this destructuring exercise apparently reflected more deep-seated motives. For, since time immemorial, sedentary people seem to have had an intense aversion for nomads. It applies in the first instance to individuals and small groups — pedlars, mountebanks, vagabonds and wanderers of all descriptions — but extends also to entire foreign populations or to people who have slipped beyond the control of any authority. Thus were the Cossacks of southern Russia rounded up and put to work (*sluzhilie*) in fortified frontier posts by the tsarist authorities; the Banjara nomads of India excluded from owning any landed property; the gypsies of Europe despised and turned into outcasts; and 'wandering' Jews forced to live within ghettos. Moreover, this violent antagonism between the nomad and his sedentary counterpart has not disappeared. We still find many examples of it: Amerindians confined within 'reservations'; modern gypsies made to live on land reserved for short-stay travellers; mountain people of Southeast

Asia forced to live in 'relocation camps'; and Ethiopian herders constrained to become 'settled'.

The deep-rooted hatred between sedentary and nomadic peoples, along with the extreme primitiveness of the customs of the time, may perhaps be sufficient explanation of the enormous mass killings of which the Mongol invaders were guilty. The historians are few who have questioned the magnitude of the massacres reported by Arab and Persian chroniclers. One such is the contemporary historian Bernard Lewis (*Islam in History*), who doubts not so much the scale of slaughter that took place in battles as the apocalyptic destruction perpetrated by the Mongols; he adduces the argument that the West recovered quickly from the damage caused by World War II, even though the warring nations had at their disposal weapons that were far more deadly than those the Mongols possessed. Against this view one may set the notion that world wars primarily affected the industrialized world and had little impact on the countryside, whereas the nomad invasions of the thirteenth century targeted economies that were based on irrigated agriculture — often located in desert regions and therefore fragile — which could not readily be restored to their original state, failing the technological means and reserves of food. One might add that, according to censuses conducted under the auspices of the mandarins of the thirteenth century and estimates by contemporary demographers, it does indeed appear that imperial China experienced a significant fall in population once the Mongols had breached the gates of the Great Wall.

A specialist on central Asia, the late Owen Lattimore, put forward another hypothesis about the origins of the Mongol conquest: once Genghis Khan had been recognized as the supreme overlord of the different Mongol tribes, he refused to take up residence in northern China. For to settle in China on a permanent basis would have been to create a political vacuum in central Asia, where tribes that were under the loosest of control by any authority would very quickly turn rebel as soon as the khan tried to assume power and exert rule from Beijing. The khan's strategy may have been as follows: to construct a tribal confederation of substantial power on the Mongolian steppes, to neutralize the Chinese threat by launching pre-emptive campaigns against the Xixia and the Jin rulers, and, finally, to return to central Asia to rouse to his cause the tribes that still wandered there free of any control. This would have allowed him to ensure that he was never threatened by opposition from the rear before he went on to complete the conquest of the whole of China, which, in fact, he did not have time to do.

Perhaps one may venture one last theory about the causes of the urge to conquest. Genghis Khan had spent more than 20 years uniting the tribes of the steppes under the yoke of his authority. He thus found himself leader of an army of highly trained and supremely well-commanded horsemen. The unity of the Mongol peoples was too recent, too fragile, for the khan to sit back and allow his army of centaur marksmen to remain inactive. Just as a commercial enterprise in the course of expansion has to grow and progress if it does not want to see its productivity slow and its markets dry up, so Genghis Khan's 'striking force' was virtually obliged to serve on new and more distant battlefields. In unifying the nomad tribes, Genghis Khan had absorbed chaos and division. In order to avoid returning to nothingness, he had to externalize that chaos: the war machine which he had forged could not, without causing disunity and tribal fragmentation, do other than embark on conquest, the only way of draining off internal strife.

The imperial designs of Genghis Khan were perhaps not clear at the outset, but the tool which allowed him to forge an empire was in his hands, and he was clever enough to make the ultimate use of it. Though we know what were the territorial limits of the vast fiefdom conquered by Genghis Khan, we know little about the limits of his authority. It is hard to believe that the nomad tribes constituted a properly organized nation encompassing everything and everyone throughout this vast region of Eurasia. Instead of a centralized state, this was more of a tribal confederation that was working towards unification. At the time of Genghis Khan's conquests, the Mongol nation was still only in its gestation period. When they confronted foreign populations, were the Mongols — united under the same khan — really conscious of belonging to a 'nation'? The Mongol entity, which had been latent since the time of Qabul Qan, certainly surfaced again once clan rivalries had been laid to rest and the struggle mounted against foreigners. Mongol 'nationalism' very quickly acquired the character of an 'ethnic chauvinism'. This was something that became clear when China fell into the hands of the Mongol Yuan dynasty. And the imperialism that was nascent under Genghis Khan did not develop fully until the descendants of Genghis themselves adopted a sedentary way of life: 'An empire may be conquered on horseback, but it cannot be governed on horseback,' says a Chinese proverb.

At the time of Genghis Khan's death, the impact of the Mongol conquest in the Far East and in the West was not yet discernible. The Mongol dynasty that mounted the throne in Beijing was to wield power for 90 years (from 1279 to 1368). In central Asia, the khan's descendants soon conceived further plans for conquest in both east and west. The army had received such an injection of spirit from Genghis Khan that it went from strength to strength, spreading out first into the parts of China that had not yet been subjugated and then sweeping westwards to launch attacks on the principalities and kingdoms of Europe. During the reign of Ögödei, Genghis Khan's son, the Mongol armies were to triumph over all their European adversaries. Ryazan, Moscow, Suzdal, Yaroslavl and Tver fell one by one under the Mongol assault. The Ukraine, Podolia, Volhynia, Silesia and Galicia were invaded and plundered. On 9 April 1241, the Polish and German armies suffered a terrible defeat at Legnica (Liegnitz) and, in July of the same year, the advance troops of the Mongols reached the outskirts of Vienna. In 1242, Transylvania and Hungary were ravaged and Mongol horsemen reached the shores of the Adriatic! The tidal wave of the nomads did not stop there: all of China was subdued in 1279 and occupied until 1368. In the Near East, the khan's forces created a vast empire, that of Tamerlane (from 1336 to 1405). It was in Russia that the Mongol tide took longest to subside: not until the reign of Tsar Ivan the Terrible, in the sixteenth century, did the Slavs at last throw off that yoke. And, indeed, the vestiges of Islamized Mongol khanates persisted, in small independent pockets, in southern Russia until the eve of the French Revolution.

From the time of Genghis Khan onwards, the 'Mongol peace' permitted the caravan routes to be reopened and, arising out of this fact, an appreciable increase in commercial exchanges between the Far East and the West: luxury objects, weapons, and animals made their passage in caravans through central Asia. In response to the Mongols' religious tolerance, the first European missionaries arrived, accompanying Italian traders who had gone to buy silk or merchants from the Middle East dealing in cloth and jewels. In addition to William of Rubrouck, Giovanni da Pian del Carpini, Marco Polo and the historian Rashīd al-Dīn, whom we have mentioned before, there were, among others, the Dominican friar Julian of Hungary and the Italian merchant Pogolotti. In 1254, in Karakorum, the Mongolian capital, Rubrouck even met a Parisian goldsmith, Guillaume Boucher, who was making for Möngke, Genghis Khan's grandson, a fountain that would spill out cascades of *koumiss*!

## The Myth of Genghis Khan

Almost immediately, Genghis Khan passed into legend, to be numbered by some among the pantheon of heroes; by others, among the monsters of the infernal regions. He has been seen, by turns, as a strategist of genius and an oriental despot ravenous for power and blood, but also as the tough but fair leader who brought his people out of the darkness of barbarism into the light, or, alternately, as an autocrat who wielded a sword with the breezy freedom with which others might wave a fan. In the West, and especially in Russia, which suffered the *tatarchina* for close on three centuries, the Mongol khan was held to be an evil spirit. While Alexander and Napoleon were covered in glory, Genghis Khan remained a barbarian, indelibly tainted with the blood he had spilled. On the whole, the collective memory has never let go of this vision and even novelists have taken an uncompromisingly severe stance towards the Mongol conqueror: in his famous fantasy novel, Bram Stoker made Count Dracula, the vampire and purveyor of tragic death, a direct descendant of Genghis Khan!

The story of Genghis Khan has left a deep impression on Mongolia and today, eight centuries after his death, its epic quality continues to resound in the hearts and minds of the descendants of the great khan's former subjects. Upon his death, the conqueror was interred with all the honours due to one of his rank. Immediately he came to be thought of as a sort of demi-god, a protector of the Mongol people. From the thirteenth century onwards, near the presumed place of his burial, in 1127, at Ejin Horo Qi in China, in the Ordos region bounded by the Huang He, a Mongol clan, the Darkhat, were charged with the task of guarding the site of the 'Eight White Tents', where a cenotaph had been erected. Here at this sacred site there unfolded, four times a year, a ceremony in honour of Genghis Khan. Some sources say that a vast tent had contained the coffin and ashes of the monarch. Relics were distributed among eight consecrated sites: among them were the stocking and undergarment of Körbeljin, the woman who was supposed to have caused the khan's death! These relics, however, disappeared a little over a century ago at the time of the Moslem revolts of Gansu and Shaanxi (1856–73) against the Manchu Qing dynasty which ruled the Chinese empire.

In 1939, fearing that Japanese troops, which had already invaded parts of China, might gain control of the region, the Nationalist government of Chiang Kai-shek placed certain relics (among them the state tent) in an underground cave for protection. The Japanese, wishing to sow dissension between the Mongols and the Chinese, promised the Mongols that they would have a permanent temple built at Horqin Youyi Qianqi (formerly called Wang-yeh-miao). This plan foundered after the defeat of Japan in 1945. Soon after Mao Zedong's Communists had seized power in 1949, the new revolutionary authorities built at Ejin Horo Qi the 'palace of Genghis Khan', which houses the famous tents. Then, with the blessing of the Communist Party, which was anxious to appease the feelings of the Mongol minority living on Chinese soil, the ceremonies in honour of the great khan were allowed to recommence. In 1962, the 800th anniversary of the birth of the hero of the steppes was celebrated in highly official fashion both in the People's Republic of Mongolia and in Inner Mongolia (within the Chinese People's Republic).

Sino-Soviet ideological differences put a stop to this cult that cut across religious faiths. Under Khrushchev, Moscow declared in plain words that the cult of Genghis Khan had a 'nationalist' and consequently anti-Marxist character. This drove the final nail in the coffin of official veneration of the warrior-king: anxious to maintain its close collaboration with the Soviet capital, Ulan Bator, the Mongolian capital, quickly fell in with the Kremlin's reasoning. In 1965 the Chinese Cultural Revolution also attacked the cult of Genghis Khan, pouring scorn on it, and the mausoleum was converted into a hangar.

Since the late 1980s, the Chinese authorities have rehabilitated Genghis Khan. Beijing has committed itself to the restoration of the great khan's palace: a flight of steps leads up to it; three glazed cupolas symbolize three enormous felt tents; and a fresco done in a style that mixes orientalism with Socialist Realism retraces, on a strip mural, the epic story of the Mongol national hero. Various relics still elicit popular veneration: a saddle supposed to have belonged to Genghis Khan, a harness, a bow and various other objects. This cenotaph, which symbolizes Sino-Mongolian friendship, is one of the more curious tourist attractions in post-Maoist China. Never mind that the official press labels Genghis Khan a 'pillager' who dragged his horsemen along in his wake to 'cause the people profound suffering'. The Commission for National Minority Affairs now holds the view that Genghis Khan was one of a long procession of national heroes who created their history. Be they Tibetan, Mongol or Han (strictly speaking, Chinese), they are all ensconced within the vast multinational crucible which was the source of socialism in the People's Republic. Thus the great khan is today still an object of popular veneration, especially at weddings: on these occasions it is the custom to pour libations and to kneel before his portrait or, sometimes, before that of his son and successor, Ögödei.

On 2 July 1984 a certain Oshir Hukyat died from cancer. He was 84 years old and, having been a first-rate traditional craftsman and at the same time the vice-president of the provincial Assembly of Inner Mongolia, was accorded an official funeral. He was able to trace his descent back 32 generations and thus establish his claim to be the last direct descendant of Genghis Khan. He was buried in the Ordos, near the sacred sites of his glorious ancestor.

Who would have thought that the great conqueror Genghis Khan would one day be idolized by the Chinese Communist Party, while the Mongolian Communist Party, based several hundred kilometres from Beijing, would hold him responsible for 'rapacious wars', label him 'profoundly reactionary' and write him off as a brigand?

# Notes

## Chapter 2

1. Uxores vero habet unusquisque quot potest tenere aliquis centum aliquis quinquaginta aliquis decem. aliquis plures. aliquis pauciores et omnibus parentibus generaliter coniunguntur. excepta matre. filia. et sorore ex eadem matre. sororibus autem ex patre tantum et uxores etiam patris post mortem vel alius de parentela minor ducere tenetur. reliquas mulieres omnes sine ulla differentia ducunt uxores et emunt eas valde pretiose a parentibus suis post mortem maritorum. de facili ad coniugia secunda non migrant. nisi quis velit suam novercam ducere in uxorem. (Giovanni da Pian del Carpini, *Historia Mongalorum*)

## Chapter 3

1. Zoologists adopt this form of the name Przhevalsky.

2. Unum deum credunt quem credunt esse fortiorem omnium visibilium et invisibilium. et credunt ipsum tam bonorum in hoc mundo quam penarum esse datorem non tamen orationibus vel laudibus aut ritu aliquo ipsum colunt. nichilominus habent ydola quedam de filtro ad ymagines hominis facta. et illa ponunt ex utraque parte hostii stationis et subtus illa ponunt quidam de filtro in modum uberum factum et illa credunt esse peccatorum custodes ac eis veneficium lactis ac pullorum praestare. (Giovanni da Pian del Carpini, *Historia Mongalorum*)

3. Cibi eorum sunt omnia que mandi possunt. comedunt enim canes. lupos. vulpes et equos. et in necessitate carnes humanas manducant . . . alluviones que egrediuntur a iumentis cum pullis manducant. Immo eos etiam vidimus pediculos manducare. (Giovanni da Pian del Carpini, *Historia Mongalorum*)

## Chapter 6

1. Nullus audet in aliqua parte morari nisi ubi ipse assignet. ipse autem assignat ubi maneant duces. duces vero assignent millenariis loca. millenarii decanis. centenarii vero de centenariis. (Giovanni da Pian del Carpini, *Historia Mongalorum*)

2. Cum pinguedine carnium polluunt multum manus quando vero comedunt eas ad ocreas suas vel ad gramina vel ad aliquid talium tergunt. solent etiam honestiores habere aliquos panniculos parvos cum quibus

ultimo tergunt manus quando carnes manducant. (Giovanni da Pian del Carpini, *Historia Mongalorum*)

## Chapter 8

1. De ordinatione acierum hoc modo chingis can ordinavit ut decem omnibus preponeretur unus. et ille secundum nos appellatur decanus. decem autem decanis preponeretur unus qui centenarius nominatur. decem vero centenariis preponeretur unus qui millenarius appellatur. decem vero millenariis preponeretur unus et ille numerus vocatur tenebre (c)apud eos. cuncto vero exercitu preponuntur duos duces vel tres ita tamen quod habeant respectum ad unum cum acies sunt in bello si de decem hominibus fugit unus vel duo vel tres vel etiam plures omnes occiduntur. et si omnes decem fugiunt nisi fugiant alii centum homines occiduntur. (Giovanni da Pian del Carpini, *Historia Mongalorum*)

2. Blue Mongols (*Köke Mongol*): this was the term the clan chiefs used to describe themselves; later, it was used also by those of the Genghis Khan dynasty. The colour blue corresponds with the divine blue sky, whose earthly agents the dynasty claimed to be.

3. Quamvis de iusticia facienda vel peccato cavendo nullam habeant legem nichilominus tamen habent aliquas traditiones quas confinxerunt ipsi vel antecessores eorum. unum est figere cutellum in igne vel etiam quocunque modo tangere ignem cutello vel cum cutello extrahere de caldario carnes. iuxta ignem incidere cum securi. credunt enim quod sic auferri debeat capud igni. item appodiare se ad flagellum cum quo percutitur equs. ipsi enim calcaribus non utuntur. item tangere flagello sagittas. item iuvenes aves accipere vel occidere. cum freno equum percutere. item os cum alio osse frangere. item lac vel aliquem potum vel cibum super terram effundere. In statione mingere. sed si voluntarie facit occiditur. (Giovanni da Pian del Carpini, *Historia Mongalorum*)

4. Sed homines occidere aliorum terras invadere res aliorum accipere quocumque iniusto modo fornicari. aliis hominibus iniurari. facere contra prohibitiones et dei precepta nullum peccatum est apud eos. (Giovanni da Pian del Carpini, *Historia Mongalorum*)

5. Mulieres eorum sunt caste nec de impudicitia ipsarum aliquid inter eos auditur. verba tamen quedam ex eis in loco satis habent turpia et impudica. seditiones inter eos raro vel nunquam habere videntur. et quamvis multum inebrientur. inebrietate tamen sua verbis vel factis nunquam contendunt. (Giovanni da Pian del Carpini, *Historia Mongalorum*)

## Chapter 9

1. Arma autem ista ad minus omnes debent habere duos arcus vel tres vel unum bonum ad minus et tres pharetras magnas plenas sagittis. et unam securim. et funes ad machinas trahendas. divites autem habent gladios accutos in fine ex una parte tamen incidentes et aliquantulum curvos. et habent equum armatum crura etiam tecta galeas et loricas quidam loricas et etiam cooperturam equorum habent de corio in hunc modum formatas habent quasdam corrigias de bove vel alio animali ad latitudinem unius manus. et bituminant tres vel quattuor similiter et ligant illas corrigiolis sive cordulis in fine in inferiori ponunt in medio et sic faciunt usque ad finem. Unde quando inclinantur inferiores corrigie superiores ascendunt et sic duplicantur super corpus vel etiam triplicantur. (Giovanni da Pian del Carpini, *Historia Mongalorum*)

## Chapter 11

1. Quando autem ad flumina perveniunt hoc modo transeunt illa etiam si sunt magna maiores unum rotundum et leve corium habent. In cuius summitate per circuitum crebras faciunt hanssas in quibus funem imponunt et strigunt itaque in circuitu faciunt ventrem quem replent vestibus et aliis rebus et fortissime ad invicem comprimunt. post hoc in medio ponunt sellas et alias res duriores. homines etiam in medio sedent et ligant ad caudem equi navem hanc taliter preparatam. unum hominem qui equm regat faciunt pariter cum equo ante natare vel habent aliquando duos remos et cum illis remigant ultra aquam et sic transeunt flumen equos vero pellunt in aqua et unus homo iuxta unum equm quem regit natat. et alii equi omnes illum sequntur. (Giovanni da Pian del Carpini, *Historia Mongalorum*)

## Chapter 15

1. Predicti homines videlicet tartari sunt magis obedientes dominis suis quam aliqui homines qui sunt in mundo sive religiosi sive seculares et magis reverentur eosdem. neque de facili mentiuntur eis. verbis ad invicem raro aut nunquam contendunt. factis vero nunquam. bella. rixe. vulnera homicidia inter eos nunquam contingunt. predones etiam et fures rerum magnarum non inveniuntur ibidem. . . . si alique bestie perduntur quique invenit eas vel dimittit sic eas. vel ducit eas ad homines illos qui positi sunt ad hec. (Giovanni da Pian del Carpini, *Historia Mongalorum*)

# Bibliography

**History of Mongolia, the Mongols, and Central Asia**

Barckausen, J. *L'Empire jaune de Gengis-khan*, Paris, Payot, 1942.

Barthold, W. *Turkestan down to the Mongol Invasion*, London, Gibb, 1928.

Budge, E. A. W. *The Monks of Kûblâi Khân, emperor of China (or the History of the Life and Travels of Rabban Sâwmâ, envoy and plenipotentiary of the Mongol Khâns to the Kings of Europe, and Markôs who as Mâr Yahbh-Allâhâ III became patriarch of the Nestorian Church in Asia)* (trans. from Syriac by the author) London, Religious Tract Society, 1928.

Cahun, L. *Histoire des Turcs et des Mongols*, Paris, A. Colin, 1896.

*La Civilisation iranienne*, Paris, Payot, 'Bibliothèque Historique', 1952.

Commeaux, C. *Chez les Mongols de la conquête (XIIIe siècle)*, Paris, Hachette, 'La vie quotidienne', 1972.

Dars, S. *Mongolie*, Paris, Le Seuil, 'Petite Planète', 1979.

Duby, G. and Mantran, R. *L'Eurasie, XIe–XIIIe siècles*, Paris, Presses Universitaires de France, 1982.

*Les Grands Empires* series, Brussels, ed. by Librairie Encyclopédique (Société Jean Bodin), 1973.

Grenard, F. *Haute-Asie*, Paris, Armand Colin, 1929.

Grousset, R. *Histoire de l'Extrême-Orient*, vol. II, Paris, Paul Geuthner, 1929.

―――――― *L'Empire des steppes*, Paris, Payot, 1965.

―――――― *L'Empire mongol*, Paris, de Boccard, 1941.

Hambis, L. *La Haute-Asie*, Paris, Presses Universitaires de France, 'Que sais-je?', 1953.

Hattori, S. *Genchô Hishi no môgoko wo arawasu su kanji no kenkyû* (A study of Chinese transcription from the Mongol in *The Secret History*), Tokyo, Ryubun Shokyoku, 1946.

Heissig, W. *Les Mongols, un peuple à la recherche de son histoire* (trans. from the German by M.-P. Mathieu) Paris, Lattès, 1982.

Howorth. *History of the Mongols*, London, Longman, 1927.

Huc, R. E. *Souvenirs d'un voyage dans la Tartarie et le Thibet*, Paris, Le Livre de Poche, 'Chrétien', 1962.

Hung, W. 'The Transmission of the Book Known as *The Secret History of the Mongols*', *Harvard Journal of Asiatic Studies*, vol. XIV, nos. 3, 4 (1951).

Kobayashi, T. *Genchô Hishi no Kenkyû* (Recherches sur *l'Histoire secrète*), Tokyo, Nippon Gakujutsu Shinkokai, 1954.

Kwanten, L. *Imperial Nomads: A History of Central Asia, 500–1500*, Leicester, 1979.

Lattimore, O. *Inner Asian Frontiers of China*, London, Oxford University Press, 1962.

Legrand, J. *La Mongolie*, Paris, Presses Universitaires de France, 'Que sais-je?', 1976.

Levine. *La Mongolie historique, géographique et politique*, Paris, Payot, 1937.

Li, W. T. *Yuanchao Bishi Zhu* (Notes on *The Secret History of the Yuan Dynasty*), n.p., n.d.

Lorinc, L. *Histoire de la Mongolie*, Budapest, Horvath, 1984.

Maalouf, A. *The Crusades Through Arab Eyes*, London, Al Saqi Books, 1984.

Mirsky, J. *The Great Chinese Travelers*, Chicago, University of Chicago Press, 1964.

Morgan, D. *The Mongols*, Oxford, Basil Blackwell, 'The Peoples of Europe', 1986; New York, Basil Blackwell, 1987.

Newton, A. P., ed. *Travel and Travellers of the Middle Ages*, London, Kegan Paul, 'History of Civilization', 1926.

Pao, K. Y. *Studies on The Secret History of the Mongols* (Uralic and Altaic Studies), vol. 58, Bloomington, Indiana University Press, 1965.

Paquier, J.-P. *L'Asie centrale à vol d'oiseau*, Paris, Librairie de la Société bibliographique, collection 'Voyages et Découvertes géographiques', 1881.

Pian del Carpini, Giovanni da. *Historia Mongalorum; il viaggio di frate Giovanni da Pian del Carpini ai Tartari* (ed. and with commentary by Giorgio Pullé), Studi Italiani di Filologia Indo-Iranica, Anno IX, vol. IX, Florence, Tipografia G. Carnesecchi e figli, 1913.

Przhevalsky, N. *Mongolia, the Tangut Country and the Solitudes of Northern Tibet* (trans. from the Russian by E. D. Morgan, with introduction and notes by H. Yule), London, 1876; and Farnborough, Hants., Gregg International Publishers, 1968.

Rachewiltz, Igor de. *Monggolun niguča tobčiyan*. Index to *The Secret History of the Mongols* (Uralic and Altaic Studies), Bloomington, Indiana University Press, 1972 (includes transliterated Mongolian text of *The Secret History*).

Rialle, G. de. *Les Peuples de l'Asie et de l'Europe*, Paris, Librairie Germer Baillière et Cie, n. d.

Rubrouck, W. of. *Itinerarium. The Texts and Versions of John de Plano Carpini and Wm. de Rubruquis, etc.* (in Latin and English), 1903.

_____ *Reise zu den Mongolen 1253–1255* (trans. and with commentary by Friedrich Risch), Leipzig, Forschungsinstitut für vergleichende Religionsgeschichte, 1934.

_____ *Voyage dans l'empire mongol* (trans. from the Latin by C. and R. Rappler), Paris, Payot, 1985.

Saint-Quentin, S. de. *Histoire des Tartares*, Paris, Richard, 1965.

Saunders, J. J. *The History of the Mongol Conquests*, London, 1971.

*Secret History of the Mongols, The.* (ed. and trans. by Francis W. Cleaves), Boston, Mass., Harvard University Press, 1983.

Spuler, B. *Les Mongols dans l'Histoire*, Paris, Payot, 1961.

Uemura, S. *Genchô Hishi Shoki* (Notes on *The Secret History of the Mongols*), Tokyo, Tôhô Gaku, no. 10, 1955.

Vernadsky, G. *The Mongols and Russia*, New Haven and London, Yale University Press, 1953.

Vladimirtsov, B. *Le Régime social des Mongols* (trans. from the Russian by Michel Carsow), Paris, Maisonneuve, 1948.

Waley, A. *The Secret History of the Mongols and Other Pieces*, London, George Allen and Unwin, 1967.

Yao, C. W. and Jagshid, S. 'Menggu bishi [*Secret History of the Mongols*]' in *Wenshi Zhexue bao* (Journal des études de littérature, d'histoire et de philosophie), vols. 9, 10, 11, T'ai-pei, National Taiwan University Press, 1960, 1961, 1962.

### Genghis Khan

Adravanti, P. *Gengis-khan*, Paris, Payot, 1987.

Grenard, F. *Gengis-khan.* Paris, A. Colin, 1935.

Grousset, R. *Conqueror of the World*, 1966, reprinted 1972.

_____ *Le Conquérant du Monde* (life of Genghis Khan), Paris, A. Michel, 1944.

Hambis, L. *Gengis-khan*, Paris, Presses Universitaires de France, 'Que sais-je?', 1973.

_____ 'Un épisode mal connu de l'histoire de Gengis-khan', in *Journal des Savants*, Paris, Klincksieck (Jan.–March 1975).

Jagshid, S. 'Gengis Khan's Military Strategy and Art of War', in *Chinese Culture*, vol. V, no. 2 (October 1963), (trans. from the Mongolian by Albert E. Dien).

Liddell Hart, B. *Great Captains Unveiled*, London, Arno, 1928.

Pelliot, P. and Hambis, L. *Histoire des campagnes de Gengis-khan* (incomplete trans. from the Chinese by P. Pelliot), Leyden, 1951.

Percheron, M. *Gengis-khan*, Paris, Le Seuil, collection 'Le Temps qui court', 1962.

—————— *Les Conquérants d'Asie*, Paris, Payot, 'Bibliothèque Historique', 1951.

Polo, M. *The Book of Ser Marco Polo, the Venetian, Concerning the Kingdoms and Marvels of the East* (ed. and trans. by Col. Henry Yule), 2 vols., London, John Murray, 1871.

Prawdin, M. *Tschingis-Chan. Der Sturm aus Asien*, Stuttgart and Berlin, 1934.

Vladimirtsov, B. *The Life of Chingis-Khan* (trans. from the Russian by Prince D. S. Mirsky), London, G. Routledge & Sons, 1930.

**Nomadism**

Bonte, P. 'Les Civilisations nomades', in *La Recherche*, no. 53, n.d.

Constantiniu, F. *Romanians and the Mongols in the XIIIth and XIVth Centuries*, Ulan Bator, Third International Congress of Mongolists, 1979.

Couchaux, D. *Habitats nomades*, Paris, Alternative et Parallèles, collection 'AnArchitectures', 1980.

Digard, J.-P. *Techniques des nomades baxtyâri d'Iran*, Paris, ed. de la Maison des sciences de l'homme, collection 'Production pastorale et Société', 1981.

*Être nomade aujourd'hui*, Neufchâtel, Institut d'ethnologie de l'Université et Musée d'ethnographie de la Ville, editors, 1979.

Khazanov, A. M. *Nomads and the Outside World* (trans. from the Russian by Julia Crookenden), Cambridge, Cambridge University Press, 1986.

—————— 'The Early State Among the Eurasian Nomads', in *The Study of the State*, The Hague, Mouton, 1981.

Krader, L. *Social Organization of the Mongol–Turk Pastoral Nomads*, The Hague, Mouton, 1963.

—————— *Formation of the State*, Englewood Cliffs, New Jersey, Prentice-Hall, 1968.

*Narody Srednei Azii* (Peoples of Central Asia), Moscow, Academy of Sciences.

'Nomadisme: mobilité et flexibilité?', Paris, *Bulletin de l'Orstom*, no. 8 (October 1986).

Roux, J.-P. *Les Traditions des nomades de la Turquie méridionale*, Paris, Maisonneuve, 1970.

Salzman, P. C. *When Nomads Settle: Processes of Sedentarization as Adaptation and Response*, New York, Praeger, 1980.

Shulzhenko. *Zhivotnóvodstvo Mongolskoi Narodnoi Respubliki* (Pastoral stock-rearing in the Mongolian People's Republic), Moscow, ed. Academy of Sciences, 1954.

Schurmann, H. F. 'Mongolian Tributary Practices of the Thirteenth Century', *Harvard Journal of Asiatic Studies* (1956).

Vainshtein, S. *Nomads of South Siberia, the Pastoral Economies of Tuva* (trans. from the Russian by Michael Colenso), Cambridge, Cambridge University Press, 1980.

## Religions

Boyle. 'Turkish and Mongol Shamanism in the Middle Ages', in *Folklore*, no. 84 (1972).

Lot-Falck, E. 'Religions des peuples altaïques de Sibérie', in *Histoire des Religions*, vol. 3, Paris, ed. H. C. Puech, 1976.

—————— 'Le chamanisme en Sibérie', in *Revue internationale* (1946).

Pelliot, P. 'Chrétiens d'Asie centrale et d'Extrême-Orient', in *Toung Pao*, Paris, 1914.

Roux, J.-P. *La Religion des Turcs et des Mongols*, Paris, Payot, 'Bibliothèque Historique', 1984.

Tucci, G. and Heissig, W. *Les Religions du Tibet et de la Mongolie*, Paris, Payot, 'Bibliothèque Historique', 1973.

## China

Eberhard, W. *Histoire de la Chine*, Paris, Payot, 'Bibliothèque Historique', 1952.

Etiemble, R. *L'Europe chinoise de l'Empire romain à Leibniz*, Paris, Gallimard, 'Bibliothèque des Idées', 1988.

Gernet, J. *Le Monde chinois*, Paris, A. Colin, 1980.

—————— *The Cambridge Encyclopaedia of China*, Cambridge, Cambridge University Press, 1982 (collection under the general editorship of Brian Hook).

—————— *La Vie quotidienne en Chine à la veille de l'invasion mongole (1250–1276)*, Paris, Hachette, 'La Vie quotidienne', 1959.

Lattimore, O. and Holgate, E. *The Making of Modern China: A Short History*, London, George Allen & Unwin, 1945.

Lombard, D. *La Chine impériale*, Paris, Presses Universitaires de France, 'Que sais-je?', 1967.

Martin, H. D. *The Rise of Chingis Khan and his Conquest of North China*, T'ai-pei, Rainbow-Bridge Book Co., 1950.
Maspero, H. *Les Religions chinoises*, Paris, Presses Universitaires de France (Publications du Musée Guimet), vol. LVII, 1967.
*Yuan Shi (History of the Yuan Dynasty)*, 1369.

**Russia**
Riasanovsky, N. B. *A History of Russia*, New York, Oxford University Press, 1984.
Vernadsky, G. and Karpovich, M. *A History of Russia*, vol. III: *The Mongols and Russia*, New Haven, Connecticut, Yale University Press, 1953.

**Specific Topics (language, folklore, etc)**
Coyaud, M. *Langues et écritures en Chine et alentour*, 2nd edn. revised and augmented, Paris, UER de linguistique générale et appliquée René-Descartes, 1967.
*Dictionnaire archéologique des techniques*, Paris, éd. de l'Accueil, 1963.
*Études mongoles et sibériennes*, University of Nanterre, booklets 1–14.
Godard, A. *L'Art de l'Iran*, Paris, Arthaud, 1962.
Grousset, R. *The Civilizations of the East, etc.*, London, Hamish Hamilton, 1931–4; New York and London, A. A. Knopf, 1931.
Hackin, R. and Kohzad, A. A. *Légendes et coutumes afghanes*. Paris, Imprimerie Nationale (Publications du Musée Guimet), 1953.
Kara, G. *Chants d'un barde mongol*, Budapest, Akadémiai Kiadó, 1970.
*Mongolia* (bi-monthly magazine), no. 5 (44), 1978; no. 6 (45), 1978; no. 5 (50), 1979, Ulan Bator.
*Mongolian Studies*, Amsterdam, Grüner, 1970 (general editor, Louis Ligeti).
*Zhongguo Wenhua likan* (Chinese Culture), Bloomington, Indiana, Institute for Advanced Chinese Studies (Mongolia Society), no. 1, 1964.

**Works of Fiction**
Bauchau, H. *Gengis-khan*, Lausanne, éd. Mermod, 1960.
Cahun, L. *La Bannière bleue*, Paris, Hachette, 1897.
Eristov Gengis-Khan, M. *L'Empire mouvant*, Paris, Grasset, 1948.
Inoue, Y. *Journey beyond Samarkand* (trans. from the Japanese by G. Furuta and G. Sager), Tokyo, Kodansha International, 1971.
——— *Les Chemins du désert* (trans. from the English by Jean Guiloineau), Paris, Stock, 1982.
Yan, V. *Jenghiz Khan . . . A Tale, etc.*, London, Hutchinson's International Authors, 1945.

# Index